ne Life at a Time

A chronicle of the ancestors of
the author's children as they
arrived in the New World, what
propelled them from Britain,
Ireland and Korea, and what
happened to them and their
descendants once they took root
in America—one life at a time.
This crisp narrative focuses on
the history and development of
New England and its people
while illuminating episodes of
the American experience span-
ning more than three centuries
as lived by ordinary people
forging a New World.

One Life at a Time

A New World
Family Narrative
1630–1960

BY R. THOMAS COLLINS, JR.

Ravensyard Publishing, Ltd.
Fairfax County, Virginia USA

Cover and Book Design by Constance D. Dillman,
Tom Suzuki, Inc. All paper in this book meets the
guidelines for permanence and durability of the
Committee on Production Guidelines for Book
Longevity of the Council on Library Resources.

ISBN 0-9667883-0-3

Library of Congress Catalogue Card Number:
98-092215

Published by

Ravensyard Publishing, Ltd.
P. O. Box 176
Oakton, Virginia 22124
USA

To order:
http://www.ravensyard.com

For
Sun Oak (Kim) Collins
and our children
Lee Kathleen Collins
& Micah Thomas Collins.

Our Ancestors

17th Century: Lockwood, Knapp, White, Levit, Betts, Olmsted,
Newell, Coit, Jenners, Cornwell, Foote, Deming, Mead, Lathrop,
House, Stanley, Scudder, Ferris, Peck, Hale, Peck, Kimberly,
Atwood, Churchill, Shepard, Watts, Hubbard, Moss, Close,
Hibbard, Brown, Potter, Johnson, Reynolds, Beckwith, Parmalee,
Boardman, Strickland, Griswold, Cowle, Benton, Savage,
Dubbin, Ranney, Woodford, DeWolf, Kitchell, Wakefield, Royce,
Sims, Hoit, Cole, Mould, Grannis, Masuer, Smith, Walden,
Butler, Waterbury, Crane, Disbrow, Husted, Brush

19th Century: Collins, Langan, Howard, Welsh, Lunney,
O'Connell, Sheedy, Kearney, MaGee

20th Century: Lee, Kim

Contents

Part Two
Militiamen, Merchants & Pioneers 1728–1818

Part Three
Builders of the New Union 1840–1960

Epilogue

Write the vision, and make it plain.

— *Habakkuk 2:2*

Foreword

It is a rare book of any kind that captures well both the laborious details of genealogy and a spirited sense of historical context. *One Life At A Time—A New World Family Narrative 1630–1960* however succeeds at just that.

R. Thomas Collins, Jr. is a gifted writer with a passion for genealogy and an ability to make the details of each life interesting. In so doing, he sets a standard for genealogical writing that few other writers will be able to match.

Here is why this book works so well: too often we read historical events as the shapers of our lives but ignore the impact each of us has on those very events, assuming somehow that only a few elites actually make history. In fact, all of us all the time make history; and we write history too. Geographical migrants to a strange land or from the field to the factory or social migrants across lines of ethnicity and class, not only respond to the historical forces of change, but they also become agents of that change.

As shown in this volume, people like the Knapps, Whites, Meads and others who left East Anglia and elsewhere in England for New England leaped as if from a moving train as their homeland underwent change. Although they wished to create a new or renewed England, they shaped something altogether quite different. Their descendants and other immigrants remade that New

England, converting it from a land of competent individuals to a land of commercial agriculture on the cusp of an industrial revolution.

The revolution they helped start diffused far and wide, in no small part due to the efforts of their descendants and yet other immigrants. The rise of the modern capitalist economy did not occur without the heroic efforts of people exactly like Irish immigrants Thomas O'Connell, Sinon Collins, and their descendents.

Finally, in the increasingly global world of our times, others, like Yung Ja Lee, brought the impulse to respond to change again to the eastern United States with her arrival from Korea to forge a new life.

Academics like me have terms for these processes. The terms are not important here. The effects of them however are—We do shape the world as it shapes us. Collins has shown exactly how that is done.

Joseph S. Wood, Ph.D.
Professor of Geography &
Vice Provost for
Academic Affairs
George Mason University
Fairfax, Virginia

Introduction

In the spring of 1863, my great-grandfather, James Collins, a 22-year-old blacksmith from the village of Kilrush in County Clare, Ireland, stood on the deck of an Atlantic sailing ship watching as the port of Liverpool disappeared over the horizon. Near him, contemplating the weeks-long ocean crossing, was his father, Sinon, age 50. The father and son were aboard an 181-foot sloop bound for New York, escaping a ruined economy and destined never to return to their home village on the banks of the Shannon River in western Ireland.

The ship on which they would make their journey was not a unique or extraordinary vessel. Made of oak and hackmatack, with iron and cooper fastenings, the vessel had been built in 1851 at a shipyard in Damariscotta, Maine, by Grinnell, Miniturn & Company of New York. At 1,146 tons, the ship had three masts and could hold about 600 passengers on its three decks.

Called the *American Union*, it was one of many ships constructed to handle the increasing trade between the United States and Europe and was part of the Swallowtail Line, which ran passengers and cargo between Liverpool and New York. The *American Union* would operate from 1852 to 1867, when it was taken out of service because of the advent of faster ships powered by steam.

James and his father, Sinon, arrived in New York May 25, 1863. On the ship's passenger list compiled in the Port of New

York, Sinon was listed as passenger number 514, James, as number 520. Both had made the voyage booked on the lower deck and both, despite their trade as blacksmiths, were listed as "labourers."

In the years ahead, they would occasionally look back wondering at the mystery of their journey, contemplating its causes and consequences. In this they were like the others who came before and those who would come after.

More than a century later, I got it in mind to investigate the journey they and my other ancestors had made to America. The idea began simply enough, as an effort to give my two children an understanding of their heritage. As the years of study, reading and writing unfolded, however, the idea evolved. Slowly, as if illuminated by another hand, a world became visible to me, hidden before, but now as real as my own. My past and my people came to life. Now, after studying their lives and their times, their voices whisper in my ear. I hear the songs of the Pagans and the Puritans, the Deacons and the Druids; the lyrics of the ancients emerging in an American harmony.

This chronicle, the result of these labors, begins in the early 17th century and follows the immigration and progress of my children's ancestors from Britain and Ireland and concludes with the arrival of their mother from Korea. The paths taken were similar, with each of the immigrants fleeing an Old World that could not sustain them. In this country, the immigrants and their descendants participated in the formation of the New World, helping forge a new society, which is yet forming. Some led distinguished lives, others common. Some were strong, others less so. Their occupations varied according to era. Yet all were builders. They were farmers, militiamen, laborers, artisans, adventurers, canal builders, railroaders, industrialists, professionals, dreamers and homemakers. Their story is of America, told one life at a time. For me, as I conclude these studies, I find, and my wife's journey confirms, that the *American Union* still sails in waters charted by dreams.

In the newspaper business, where I spent a decade, there was a job called rewrite. An honored task, once practiced around the city desk of every newspaper in the nation, rewrite called on the practitioner to redo words into a set style favored by the editors of the publication, adding facts, quotes, new information and, if necessary, rhetorical flourishes to give body and life to the bare bones of who, what, when, where and why. It is a craft that uses a reporter's own notes from interviews and observation, almanacs, encyclopedia, eyewitness accounts, ideas learned elsewhere, old newspaper stories, wire services—in short, any resource available. The rewriteman's task is to put scattered information together into a readable form. It may not be scholarship up to strict academic standards. It is more storytelling, a way of helping define reality, something we all try to do everyday, with mixed success. One learns the craft of rewrite as one would learn how to shoe a horse, after much practice and usually against a deadline while some creature with a lack of patience waits for results. It is my hope that the reader finds this chronicle well shod.

In struggling to adopt a format for this chronicle, a comment of my grandfather, James Michael Collins, the railroad master mechanic, came to mind: "Put a number on it." He favored bringing an engineer's eye to daily problems, addressing them as one would a problem with a mathematical solution. Such a device would not be appropriate in all things, of course, but it is a way to help measure the dynamics of a problem and decide what might be done. I knew of approaches I did not wish to take, and I knew that unless I adopted some system to deal with the information I was compiling, I would be lost. I followed the advice of my grandfather, the master mechanic, and devised a system using numbers. The numbers are assigned each of my children's ancestors in chronological order as they arrived in the New World as immigrants, and to their subsequent descendants. My grandfather Collins is [#116].

Obadiah Mead Knapp, a brother of my great-grandmother Theodosia Caroline (Knapp) Savage [#109], wrote February 9, 1915:

> "I used to think I'd at some time get to work and make a thorough search to find out all the descendants...Well! It did not take me long to find out that I could not even afford the expense of it. I just can't do such work anymore...I get all mixed up, utterly confused and lost..."

I was more fortunate than Uncle Obe. The number system enabled me to keep straight who was who, and information unavailable to him abounded for me 70 years later. Volumes unwritten in Uncle Obe's time are now carefully preserved in the Connecticut Historical Society and other libraries. Also, Uncle Obe could not know that relatives, close and distant had spent and would spend years gathering information. Many of those family historians never knew others were working on different portraits on the same large canvas. Fortunately much of that work was discovered, collated and saved by Caroline Knapp Savage, sister of my grandfather, Willis Isaac Savage [#115], who, as an historian for the Emma Willard Chapter of the Daughters of the American Revolution in Berlin, Connecticut, kept elaborate records. The rest was in libraries and historical societies. This chronicle, therefore, is a work of journalism with many family collaborators. An historian once said that history is mostly written from the top down, concentrating on the great and noteworthy first. Because of efforts in generations past, I was able to craft a family history that is of America one life at a time. If those in this chronicle would not be of the great and noteworthy to others, at least they were so to me.

I would like to thank Mary Close (Savage) Collins; Robert Thomas Collins; Yung Ja (Lee) Murdock; Paul and Agnes (Howard Savage) Griswold; Charles Wilfred and Ethel (Truss) Savage; Constance Sullivan (Mrs. James Francis Collins) Cain; Rev. Roger and Betsy (Roby) Manners; Alice Rankin (Mrs. Terrence P.) Gromley; Catherine Rankin Darling; Grace (Mrs. Charles) Howard; Richard Alden Howard; Arthur J. Howard; Clifford Earl Howard, and Iva Howard Feldtmose.

Though this chronicle is specifically focused for my children, it also contains as well the heritage of my siblings and cousins, who all provided encouragement. I want to thank my sister, Tara, her husband, David Gordon, and their daughter Samantha; my brother, Bill, Sally Townsend, and their son Townsend Savage and daughter Caroline Sanders; and my cousins: Jim Collins, his wife Nancy (Michel), and their daughters Anna, Elizabeth and Margaret; Tricia Collins, Gino Scarano, and their sons, Dominic and James, and daughter Kathleen; Charles Savage, his wife, Susan (Locke), and their son, Andrew James, and daughters Kimberly and Brittany; Emmy Savage, Mark Borthwick, and their son John Kenyon; Betty Collins; and Mary Collins, and her daughter, Julia Frances.

Also, posthumous thanks to Annette Savage (Mrs. Sheldon) Roby for her faithful and illuminating correspondence; Caroline Knapp Savage, my grandfather's sister, for her family records; and Curtis Morgan, a distant Savage relation, for his handwritten history of Savage Hill and East Berlin. Each greatly assisted in gathering the information used in this chronicle.

In researching this chronicle, I learned what a debt we all

owe to those who maintain books, manuscripts, pictures, maps, orders of battle, regimental histories, diaries and the like in libraries and historical societies.

Historians Will and Ariel Durant wrote:

> "If a man is fortunate, he will before he dies, gather
> up as much as he can of his civilized heritage and
> transmit it to his children. And to his final breath he
> will be grateful for his inexhaustible legacy, knowing
> that is is our nourishing mother and our lasting life."

Obtaining facts about the past and learning from them keeps our culture and heritage alive. Libraries and historical associations are sanctuaries. They help give meaning to the confusion and uncertainty around us, and enable us all to deliver our legacy to our children.

Thanks to the staff, trustees and members of the American Association for State and Local History, the Daughters of the American Revolution, the Connecticut Historical Society, the Stamford (CT) Historical Society, the Crawford County (PA) Historical Society, the Butler County (OH) Historical Society, the Society of the Descendants of the Founders of Hartford, the New Haven Railroad Technical & Historical Association, the Hawaiian Mission Children's Society, the Church of Jesus Christ of Latter Day Saints and the Erie Lackawana Historical Society.

I owe a debt to many authors, but particularly to Albert W. Savage, Jr., for his extraordinary genealogical research, to David M. Roth, whose work, *Connecticut—A Bicentennial History*, helped place the lives of many of my early New England ancestors in context, to Richard I. Melvoin, whose work, *New England Outpost—War and Society in Colonial Deerfield*, helped detail the consequences of war on the frontier for a distant ancestor, and to David Hackett Fischer, author of *Albion's Seed—Four British Folkways in America*, whose work illuminated the subtleties of the complex society that is Britain. Also, thanks to Ellsworth Grant, author, historian and long-time president of the Connecticut Historical Society for his assistance, to Rev. Edith Wolfe of the Women's Board of Missions in Hawaii and to Joe Wood, friend, teacher and geographer, for appreciating this plain vision. Personal thanks as well to Carole Edwards, editor, and to Edward C. Norton, another afflicted with the "brehon's itch," for his encouragement and counsel.

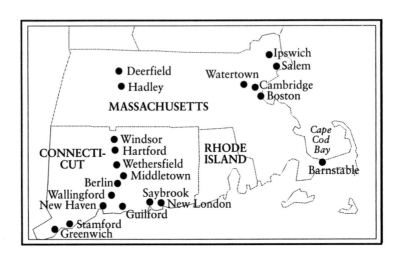

PART ONE

Founders & Settlers 1630–1709

[1] EDMUND LOCKWOOD was born in Combs, Suffolk and came to New England with John Winthrop's fleet, arriving October 18, 1630, with two sons and a daughter.

The Winthrop migration began in 1628, when a group of separatist Puritans obtained a patent (license) from the Earl of Warwick, a proprietor of the New England Company, to form the Massachusetts Bay Company and establish a plantation in New England.

The next year, with other members of the company, leader John Winthrop, a lawyer, signed The Cambridge Agreement, in which members vowed to emigrate if the Massachusetts Bay proprietors themselves could relocate there and take the patent with them. On March 14, 1629, four days after King Charles I dissolved Parliament in the dispute that would eventually lead to civil war, the King agreed to let Winthrop and the Massachusetts Bay Company relocate to New England.

In Massachusetts, Edmund Lockwood was made a freeman May 18, 1631, and lived in Newtowne (today's Cambridge) in

1632. Edmund reportedly moved south to Connecticut with the Rev. Thomas Hooker in 1636.

Edmund's first known ancestor was Rogerus de Lockwood, of Lockwood, Staffordshire. Ancestral histories report that the Lockwood family were long of Combs, Suffolk, though they trace their line to Rogerus of the village of Lockwood in Staffordshire. The French name indicates the Lockwoods were of Norman descent.

Records shows that Rogerus' son Ranulphu de Lockwood, Clericus, married Margeria de Dulverni, a daughter of Radi de Dulverni, Milet. Ranulphu and Margeria had a son Henricus, who married M. Agnes de La Shawe, a daughter of Roberti de La Shawe. Henricus and Agnes had a son, Robertum de Lockwood, who married Johanna Lee, daughter of Richardi Lee. Robertum and Johanna had a son, Thomas de Lockwood, who married Agnes de Bacheton. Their son, Richardus, now of Combs, Suffolk, married Elizabeth Creswell, a daughter of Johannes Creswell. It was Richardus & Elizabeth (Creswell) Lockwood's son, Edmund Lockwood, who arrived in America October 19, 1630.

Emigrating to New England with Edmund were his sons, Edmund and Robert, and, according to tradition, a daughter Elinor [#2] and their families.

[2]

NICHOLAS KNAPP (Knap) was born in 1605 in East Anglia, probably in the village of Bures St. Mary, Suffolk. Nicholas was a weaver, one of a growing number of Puritan weavers and artisans who not only suffered religious persecution but also suffered economically because the long wars in Europe cut off markets for their goods. Early spellings in England were Cnaep, Cnepe, Knepe or Knopp. Nicholas spelled his name Knap, the second "p" not used until the time of the American Revolution. A Saxon name, cnoep meant hilltop, the word knob having the same origin.

Nicholas and his wife, **ELINOR LOCKWOOD**, a daughter of Edmund Lockwood [#1], of Combs, Suffolk, sailed with John Winthrop's fleet of 11 ships in 1630. The Massachusetts Bay Company selected Winthrop governor and established a settlement on the Shawmut Peninsula now called Boston. Nicholas and Elinor Knapp settled in Watertown with the congregation headed by Winthrop's associate, Sir Richard Saltonstall. Their church was established on July 30, 1630.

On March 1, 1631, Nicholas was fined five pounds by the Massachusetts General Court for "taking upon him to cure the scurvy by a water with no worth nor value which he sold at a very dear rate." Unless the fine was paid, the court said, Nicholas was to be whipped and imprisoned. Nicholas' friend, William Pelham and his father- or brother-in-law, Edmund Lockwood, paid three pounds of Nicholas' fine and promised the rest later. When no one who had bought the water complained and some, in fact, said the water helped cure their ailments, the rest of the fine was forgiven.

By 1636, Nicholas owned 30 acres. By 1639, he owned a farm of 117 acres, a home lot of 16 acres, 43 acres of upland, seven acres of meadow, six acres of plowland, two acres in Pine Marsh and one acre in Pond Meadow. On March 6, 1646, Nicholas sold everything and set out for Stamford (Connecticut) spending two years in Wethersfield before reaching his destination in 1648. In Stamford, Nicholas owned a small mill and 16 acres of farmland. Elinor died in 1658. Nicholas later married Unity (Buxton) Brown, the second wife and widow of **PETER BROWN [#24]**. Nicholas, who died in 1670, and Elinor (Lockwood) Knapp had nine children, including a daughter, Ruth [#45], and a son, Joshua [#48].

[3] JOHN WHITE was born about 1602 in Messing, Essex, a son of **ROBERT** and **BRIDGETT (ALLGAR) WHITE**, and grandson of both **WILLIAM** and **MARGARET ALLGAR**, and **ROBERT** and **ALICE WHITE**.

John White's earliest known ancestors, William Allgar, was born about 1536, and wife Margaret, born about 1540, lived in Shalford, Essex. William, who was buried August 2, 1575, and Margaret Allgar had at least five children, including daughter Bridgett, who was born in Shalford and baptized March 11, 1562.

On June 24, 1585, Bridgett married Robert White, a son of Robert and Alice White, who was born in Messing 1562. Robert and Bridgett (Allgar) White resided between Shalford and Messing. Robert White left bequests in his will to both Established and Non-Conformist churches, and was buried at Messing June 17, 1617. Robert and Bridgett (Allgar) had eight children, including son, John.

Among the witnesses to Robert White's will in 1617 was a family friend and Messing neighbor named **WILLIAM LEVETT**. On the day after Christmas in 1622, Robert White's son, John White, married William Levett's daughter, **MARY LEVIT**. Four years later, John White would witness his father-in-law's will. Another White in-law was William Goodwin of Bocking who in

November 7, 1616, had married John White's sister, Elizabeth, who was 11 years older than her brother. By that time, William Goodwin was active in the congregation of nonconformist Rev. Thomas Hooker who preached and taught school at St. Mary's Church in Chelmsford, located near Messing, about 30 miles northeast of London.

William Goodwin lived in Bocking, which like the other Essex communities Braintree and Witham, and Hertford in Hertfordshire, was a prosperous center of weavers' manufacturing. As the persecution of the Puritans by Anglican authorities grew and the sale of weavers' goods declined, talk in the congregation escalated about the formation of "Mr. Hooker's Company" or "The Braintree Company." After Rev. Hooker fled for his life to Holland, then a center of Protestantism, The Braintree Company made plans to immigrate to New England. Hooker was selected company pastor, and Rev. Samuel Stone, born in Hertford, and now a lecturer in Towcester, Northamptonshire, was chosen Hooker's assistant. William Goodwin was chosen Elder.

In 1631 and early 1632, members of The Braintree Company sold their property and relocated to London. On June 22, 1632, John White, his wife Mary (Levit), and their three children joined Elder Goodwin and the others in the Braintree Company and stepped aboard the vessel *Lyon* in London. The *Lyon*'s captain, William Pierce, was under contract to Elder Goodwin to ferry to Boston 123 passengers, including 33 men, 40 women, and 50 children. The *Lyon* arrived in Boston September 16, after a calm crossing lasting 12 weeks. The Braintree Company at first settled at Mount Woolaston (today's Braintree) but were soon ordered by the Massachusetts General Court to relocate to Newtowne (today's Cambridge).

John White settled with his family on a three-quarter acre home lot on Cow Yard Row, near some 30 acres of farmland granted to him as a freeman, which he became March 4, 1633. On August 5, John was granted another three-quarters of an acre near his Cow Yard Row property, to be used, appropriately, for a cow yard. Today the site of John White's property is near Harvard University's Gore Hall.

A month later, on September 4, Rev. Hooker and his assistant, Samuel Stone, arrived in Boston from England. Hooker had slipped back to England from exile in Holland and had stayed undetected in Stone's home while they awaited passage to New England. The Braintree Company congregation now complete in Newtowne, the members began to settle down. In February 1635, the town selected seven "selectmen," among them John White, to "do the whole business of the town."

Soon there was friction between Newtowne and Boston authorities, with Hooker and Winthrop clashing over theology, politics and commerce. In the fall of 1635, Elder Goodwin led an advance party of 60 men, women and children south to a stretch of territory the Indians called Quinnetiquet or "land along the wide river." An English settlement called Windsor had been established there two years before by Lt. William Holmes of the Plymouth Colony. Holmes, in establishing Windsor, had defied Dutch soldiers stationed a few miles to the south at a fort called "The House of Good Hope."

Lt. Holmes had come to Quinnetiquet after Plymouth Gov. Winslow had visited the area at the invitation of two Indian sachems, Wahginnacut and Nattawanut, who were eager for trading partners and friends to help them defend against the Pequots. Since Windsor's establishment, other English from Dorchester and Newtowne had ventured to a place Indians called Pyquag, later called Wethersfield. Through 1635 and 1636, other settlers came in small groups to Windsor and Wethersfield. Elder Goodwin's party selected an area between the two new towns, purchasing land from a local sachem near the Dutch fort.

In Newtowne meanwhile, Hooker's main company, secured the reluctant permission of the Massachusetts General Court to leave and began selling their land, works and tools to a company headed by Rev. Thomas Shepard. Nicholas Danforth of Shepard's company bought John White's house, home lot and most of his outlands October 20. The following May 30, White sold another parcel of meadow and pasture. The deed reads that White was of the new town upon the Quinnetiquet.

In June, Rev. Hooker's main group, some 100 men, women and children, began their journey to their new home. In 1797, historian Benjamin Trumbell wrote:

> "...(Rev Hooker's Company) traveled more than 100
> miles through a hideous and trackless wilderness. They
> had no guide but their compass; made their way over
> mountains, through swamps, thickets and rivers...lodg-
> ings but those which nature afforded them. They drove
> with them 160 cattle, people generally carried their
> packs, arms and some utensils...of this company were
> persons of figure, who had lived in England in honor,
> affluence, and delicacy and were entire strangers to
> fatigue and danger..."

John White was one of the original proprietors of the new settlement, which was named Hartford in honor of Rev. Stone's hometown. White's property allotment included a home lot on

the east side of Cole Street, now called Governor Street, about 10
rods south of the Little River, comprising 40 acres of meadow, 10
acres of swamp, and 150 acres of upland at Hockanum, east of
the Connecticut River. Only 18 of Hartford's original proprietors
were granted more land. His neighbors on Cole Street included
George Wyllys, of Fenny Compton, Warwickshire, who later
became Connecticut Governor. On Wyllys' land stood a giant
oak later known as the Charter Oak, owing to its having been
the hiding place for Connecticut's Fundamental Orders when
Edmund Andros seized the colony in 1688.

In 1642, John White was selected an "orderer" (selectman)
of Hartford, and again in 1646, 1651 and 1656. Prospering as a
farmer, White also served as a juror and arbitrator in the court.

Rev. Hooker died during the flu epidemic in 1647.
Acrimonious divisions broke out in the congregation between
Elder Goodwin and Rev. Stone, Hooker's successor. The dispute
over the future course of the congregation split the town into two
camps, with John White a supporter of Elder Goodwin. The origins of the dispute are lost, though the loss of the charismatic
leadership of Thomas Hooker and the personalities of his successors were surely part of the breach, as well as the nature of the
Puritan faith and the inability of its stricter adherents to accommodate change or compromise.

After more than a decade of dissension, the breach in
Hartford was widely known throughout New England.
Congregations in Connecticut and Massachusetts took sides,
tried to mediate and otherwise occupied themselves with this
acrimonious schism. Finally supporters of Elder Goodwin
decided to establish a new settlement to the north along the
Connecticut River where they believed they could follow Rev.
Hooker's teachings. On April 18, 1659, 60 people from Hartford
and Wethersfield signed an agreement to move to the new town
of Hadley, north of today's Springfield. John White's name was
fifth on that list.

The group selected John White and four other men to go
to Hadley and lay out homelots. These "ingagers" were also to
"order all public occasions that concerns the good of that plantation for the year ensuing." The task was considerable since
Hadley at the time was on the frontier of the English settlement,
with nothing to the west and north except wilderness inhabited
by Indians and adventurers.

John White's investment in the Hadley venture was 150
pounds. His eight-acre homelot was on the east side of Hadley
Street. He was appointed to committees to divide land and lay
highways and other general public enterprises and improvements.
He was chosen selectman for Hadley in 1662, 1663 and 1665. In

1664 and 1669, White was Hadley's Deputy to the General Court in Massachusetts Bay's Boston.

In Hartford, meanwhile, dissent continued at the old Hooker church. On February 12, 1670, the Second Church of Hartford was organized under Rev. John Whiting. Elder Goodwin, now aged and infirm, left Hadley and moved to the Farmington area. John White and his family returned to Hartford on April 9, 1671. On March 28, 1677, he was selected Elder of the Second Church, an office that required that he serve as arbitrator, referee and council in ecclesiastical matters. John served as Elder of Second Church until his death in January 1683. In 1892, Edwin Pond Parker, in a History of the Second Church of Hartford, wrote that the church records shows:

> "...March 28, 1677 the Church having before chosen Mr. John White to the office of Ruling Elder, and he accepted it, he was accordingly this day, ordained to be in that high office, in the presence and with the approbation of the elders and messengers of some neighbor churches. This holy man, having faithfully served the Lord in his place, and that also with good success through grace (he was a good man, and God was with him), fell asleep in Christ, and went to receive his reward January 1683."

John White died in Hartford in January 1683/4. His will was dated December 17, 1683, and inventory on his estate taken January 23, 1684. John and Mary (Levit) White had seven children, including son Nathaniel [#44].

[4]

MARY BETTS was born about 1605 in Claydon, Oxfordshire, in the domain of Lord Saye and Sele. Claydon, a farm parish of some 1,170 acres, was the neighboring village to the market town Banbury, which from 1580 to the English Civil War was a regional center of religious and political dissent.

Claydon was part of "The Banbury Hundred," a tax district. The town of Banbury, located about 22 miles north of Oxford near the intersection of Oxford, Warwick and Northampton counties, began as an early Celtic and later Roman settlement at intersection of Salt Way and Banbury Lane.

Located at a traditional crossing of the River Cherwell, the Saltway was a prehistoric east-west route along a limestone ridge that divided the Thames River Basin from the Midland plain. Banbury took its name from Saxons; Bana is a Saxon personal name, and "burh" means borough or earthen wall.

In the seventh century, the Bishop of Dorchester acquired Oxford, including the area called Banbury Hundred, an area derived under the Tribal Hidage system. Before the manor system, England was divided into districts, each of which was assessed a certain number of animal hides, in multiples of 100, on which the tribute or tax to be paid the king was estimated. Oxfordshire contained 22 "hundreds," of which all but three belonged to the Royals. The Banbury Hundred was one of the three in the hands of the Bishop of Dorchester.

Vikings, called Danes by the Britons, invaded sometime after 913, ravaging northern Oxfordshire, leaving Banbury a burned ruin. But the Danes stayed and, in time, a traditional Norse village grew at the intersection of Saltway and Banbury Lane. After the Norman invasion in 1066, the Bishop moved from Dorchester to Lincoln. Banbury became an administrative center of the Bishop of Lincoln, and thus Banbury began its role as a religious center. Bishop Alexander built a castle in Banbury that became the center of the town and stimulated a prosperous market. By the 13th century, some 1,300 people resided in Banbury.

History records the commercial nature of Banbury with many reports about its cheeses, ales and Banbury cake, as well as the religious fervor of its people. Banbury became the focus of fairs as well as the weekly center for the growing South Midlands wool trade. Wool was first mentioned in Banbury in 1286, ale brewing in 1320 and cheese in 1430. Shakespeare mentions Banbury cheese in "The Merry Wives of Windsor." Banbury cakes were first mentioned in 1586.

The people, residents of a borough paying tribute to a bishop, had a distinct sense of independence from royal interference. Residents resisted paying taxes for the war with France in the 14th century and resented the forced quartering of troops. Banbury also was near a central battle in the War of the Roses, when in July 1469 the forces of York and Lancaster engaged six miles northeast of town at Danesmoor near Trafford Bridge in Northamptonshire. The Lancastrian army led by Robin of Redescales defeated the Yorkist army led by the Earl of Pembroke, who was captured and later taken to Banbury, where he and 10 of his men were beheaded on the church's front porch.

The rule of Banbury changed hands in the wake of the Protestant Reformation in 1547, when the Bishop of Lincoln surrendered the manor and castle of Banbury to the crown. Within a few years, Queen Elizabeth had leased Banbury Castle and Banbury Hundred to the Fiennes family of nearby Broughton Castle. A few years later, Queen Mary granted the town a charter and a Common Council ruled the borough thereafter, encouraging the growth of a town-oriented middle class led by landed lords from a few families who dominated municipal affairs.

Banbury's religious tradition set the community apart during the era that nurtured Puritan dissent and led to the political split causing the English Civil War in the 17th century. By the time of the vocal Puritan divines, Banbury had been home to a weekly market for hundreds of years as well as annual fairs, often celebrating seasonal events with distinctly pagan roots. To the Puritan preachers of the late 16th century, these fairs were nothing more than blasphemy. Maypoles were torn down. Religious icons were also suspect. In 1600, rioting Puritans tore down two crosses in Banbury that were later celebrated in a children's nursery rhyme still heard:

Ride a cock-horse,
To Banbury Cross;
To see a fine lady
Ride on a white horse.
Rings on her fingers,
Bells on her toes,
She shall have music
Wherever she goes.

The sophisticates of Oxford and London mocked the community's religious fervor, helping earn Banbury a reputation as a stuffy community filled with spoil sports. In almanacs of the day, Banbury, once known for its cheese, cakes and ale now became known for its cheese, cakes and zeal. Playwright Ben Jonson in 1614 wrote a play in which "a Banbury Brother" described a particularly loathsome character. In describing Banbury cakes, Jonson noted that one Puritan baker no longer sold his cakes at festivals because they were steeped in pagan traditions. Humorist Richard Braithwait crafted a joke in 1616, with the rhyme:

To Banbury came I,
O prophane one!
Where I saw a Puritane one
Hanging of his cat on Monday
For killing of a mouse on Sunday.

The joke was given wide circulation in the years leading up to the English Civil War, but the Puritan movement had grown to such an extent that in 1627 Banbury refused to pay a forced loan required by the crown. At the time, Banbury's rebel leaders included William Fiennes, the Viscount Saye & Sele, of Broughton Castle, whose family also had held the lease on

Banbury Castle, Manor and Hundred since 1563 and who were among the most dignified families of the day.

In 1628, Lord Saye & Sele's continued opposition to the crown's taxes caused King Charles I to order soldiers to Banbury to raise the funds by force if necessary. During the soldiers' occupation of Banbury, a fire broke out that destroyed 103 dwellings, 600 bays or other buildings and 20 malt kilns. At the time of the fire, most of Banbury's leading citizens were in church, where Vicar William Wheatley, among the most celebrated Puritan divines of his time, urged his congregation to stay seated, thus preventing injury while the town burned to the ground.

As far as the Puritan Vicar was concerned the blaze was judgment and deliverance from Providence. Others saw there was more to be gained by blaming the fire on the King's troops. Hearings in Oxford and London dragged on for years trying to affix blame and assess damages, with the king's opponents using the episode to refuse to pay taxes and otherwise drive home the wedge that would soon turn the country to war.

The leader of this resistance in the Banbury area was William Fiennes, Lord Saye & Sele, known as the Godfather of the Puritan Party. Puritan meetings were held in Fiennes' Broughton Castle near Banbury, where he and his colleagues, including Lord Brook from Warwick Castle in nearby Warwichshire, plotted strategy.

In 1632, Lord Saye & Sele and Lord Brook obtained a license from their friend and neighbor, Robert Rich, the Earl of Warwick, who was then a proprietor of the New England Company as well as a religious and political ally. The license, known as the Warwick Patent, gave its proprietors permission to establish a plantation in the "territory that lay west from the Narragansett River, 120 miles on the sea coast, and from there in latitude and breadth to the South Sea (Pacific Ocean)."

In July 1635, Lord Saye & Sele and Lord Brook, through the influence of their friend Rev. Hugh Peter, appointed John Winthrop, Jr., son of the Massachusetts Bay governor, to be their emissary in the establishment of their plantation on the mouth of the Connecticut River (now Saybrook). The idea was that this settlement should be ready for emigrants if the Banbury Puritan leaders had to flee.

When Winthrop the Younger arrived in Boston in October 1635, he organized a company. The following month he sent a party of 20 men in a 30-ton vessel to the mouth of the Connecticut River to establish a fort and prevent the Dutch from going upriver. Early in 1636, Lion Gardiner, an English soldier who came from Holland to Boston, was sent by the new company to make improvements in the new settlement and prepare for the new colony to be organized by Lord Saye and Sele and Lord Brooke under the Warwick Patent. With news of the developments a daily topic in Banbury and Claydon and nearby villages and shires, immigration became likely. Many began the move. Mary Betts and her husband, **JOHN**, with their three children, became part of Rev. Hooker's Braintree Company, which settled in Newtowne in 1635.

John Betts was likely the descended from **RICHARD BETT** of Claydon, whose name appears in the Lay Subsidy list for Banbury Hundred in 1546. John may also have been mentioned in the will of John Bett of King Sutton near Banbury dated January 15, 1615. Other family records show that, in Clayton, the baptism of "John Bet, a sonne of John Bet and Mary his wyffe" was recorded May 5, 1627. This was likely John Betts, Jr., one the three children of John and Mary Betts. The other two children were Mary and Martha, who all emigrated to New England with their parents. Family tradition holds that John Betts died on the journey.

Mary and her children were among those in Rev. Hooker's company who made the overland trip to Hartford in 1636. Apparently John died before they reached Hartford because Connecticut records refer to Mary as "Widow Betts." She was the only woman among the original proprietors of the town. Widow Betts was granted four acres and "lots at the courtesy of the town" in 1639. She also was granted 12 acres on the east side of the Connecticut River. Mary supported herself and her children by keeping a school in her home, located on the north side of the bank of the Little River on the east side of today's Trumbull Street at the intersection of Wells Street. The schoolchildren called her "Goody Betts." Use of the titles "Mr." and "Mrs." was not yet common. Those forms of address were reserved for ministers, magistrates, those of station and their wives. The contemporary custom was to refer to fellow citizens as "Goodman" and "Goodwife." "Goody Betts" was a child's version of the title "Goodwife."

Mary, Hartford's first schoolteacher, taught for more than a decade, until her death during the 1647 flu epidemic. Her death was noted in a letter sent by Rev. Samuel Stone July 19, 1647, to Rev. Thomas Shepard, pastor of the Church of Christ in Cambridge, whose company had purchased much of Cambridge from Mr. Hooker's Company. The Rev. Stone wrote to Mr. Shepard that on July 7, 1647, the Rev. Thomas Hooker had died, adding:

> "...Mrs. Hooker was taken with the same sickness
> that night when I came to Hartford and was very

near death; she is yet weak and I hope recovering...
Mrs. Cyllick died that day when I came to Hartford.
Goody Betts, the school dame, is dead with some
others..."

John and Mary Betts had three children, including daughter
Mary [#30].

[5] REBECCA OLMSTED was born in Great Leighs,
Essex, a daughter of RICHARD and FRANCES (SLANEY)
OLMSTEAD.

Rebecca's earliest known ancestors were JAMES and ALICE
(HAWKINS or SORRELL) OLMSTED. James Olmsted, likely
of Braintree and Beatrice, Essex, was born about 1520 and died
between 1550-53 in the nearby community of Grand Leighs. Their
son, JAMES OLMSTED, JR., born in 1550, married JANE BRIS-
TOW on August 12, 1576. James and Jane (Bristow) Olmsted, Jr.,
would have 11 children, including Richard Olmsted, who was born
in Grand Leighs and baptized March 22, 1579. Richard Olmsted
would marry Frances Slaney. Among their six children was
Rebecca. Rebecca's mother, Frances (Slaney) Olmsted died in nearby Fairsted, Essex, and was buried September 10, 1630.

Two years later, Rebecca Olmsted sailed with Elder Goodwin
and the "Braintree Company" on the ship *Lyon* under the escort
of her uncle James Olmsted. The ship arrived in Boston September
16, 1632. Other passengers on that trip aboard the *Lyon* named
Olmsted, included Richard, John, Nicholas, Nehemiah, and Mrs.
Joyce Olmsted. All settled at first in Newtowne and migrated
with Rev. Hooker's company to Hartford. The relations of the
Olmsteds are uncertain, however it appears that Nicholas and
Nehemiah were sons to James Olmsted, who was uncle to niece
Rebecca, and nephew John, a physician, and Richard, later a cap-
tain of militia. James and Captain Richard and Dr. John Olmsted
were all later proprietors of Hartford in 1639. Rebecca's father,
Richard, stayed behind in Fairsted where he died and was buried
November 16, 1641. The family name has also been spelled
Holmsted, Hownsted, Hampsted and Holsted.

After arriving in New England, Rebecca married THOMAS
NEWELL, who had been born in Hertfordshire and first came to
Hartford. In 1640, Thomas and Rebecca were among the first
settlers of Farmington, who were attracted to the meadows along
the Tunxis (Farmington) River. The land was purchased from the
Tunxis Indians by 84 proprietors who divided the land among
themselves. At the time of the town's incorporation in 1645,

Farmington occupied about 15 square miles, and included land now included in the towns of Berlin, Bristol, Burlington, Southington and Avon.

Thomas Newell became a member of the Farmington church February 7, 1652/3, and his wife was listed on the church membership July 12, 1653. Thomas Newell's name was among the list of freemen in 1669. In 1672, Thomas Newell was one of the party sent to visit Mattatuck (now Waterbury) to survey the area for a potential settlement. He later signed a petition for the "liberty of planting" a settlement, but he never moved there. Thomas Newell died in Farmington September 13, 1689, leaving an estate of 700 pounds. Rebecca (Olmsted) Newell died in Farmington February 24, 1697/8. They had 10 children, including daughter Rebecca [#38].

[6] JOHN COIT was born in England and immigrated to New England where his name is recorded in 1632 in Dorchester as one of its earliest settlers. John Coit came to New England with his wife **MARY JENNERS**, who was born about 1596.

The Coit family was originally from Glamorganshire, Wales. John Coit's name was sometimes spelled Coyte, Goite Goyte, and Guoit. By April 17, 1635, John and Mary (Jenners) Coit apparently had moved from Dorchester, as land previously owned by him was divided by the Dorchester court between two other settlers "on the condition that he (John Goite) come not over to possess it the next somer."

Employed as a ship's carpenter, John Coit never returned to Dorchester, and instead moved to a home situated on a hill on the north shore of Marblehead Harbor which was better suited to his trade. He built a house in a place known for many years as "Coit's Cove." In November 1638, Salem granted John Coit three acres "on the neck." Mary Coit joined the Salem Church June 18, 1643, and the next month two of her children were baptized there. The baptism of their three children in 1643-4 was recorded in Salem. John Coit and family lived in Marblehead until 1647, when he sold his house February 9 to William Pitt and moved to Glouchester, where he was made a freeman that year and selectman in 1648. John had his Gloucester residence at the end of the neck of home lots now called Wheeler's Point, where, and on Planter's Neck, he had considerable land.

The Rev. Richard Blinman, who had been in Glouchester since 1642, was pastor of that community from 1649-50. But a dispute arose in his congregation and he relocated to New London. John Coit and a dozen other Glouchester families followed their clergyman to New London. Coit was granted land in New London December 19, 1650. They called the land "Cape Ann's Lane" after Cape Ann in Gloucester.

New London had been founded four years earlier by John Winthrop, Jr. Winthrop had been Governor of Saybrook under the Warwick Patent between June 1635 and June 1636. The Warwick lands were transferred to the Connecticut Colony in 1644 after it became clear that Lord Saye and Sele, Lord Brooke and the other organizers of the Saybrook Plantation would remain in England in hopes of a Civil War victory. With the failure of the Saybrook migration plans, John Winthrop, Jr., returned to Massachusetts, where he founded the town of Ipswich. After founding New London in 1646, Winthrop built a home and laid claim to a wide territory west of New London, including a large part of today's Lyme. Claims were disputed, yet Winthrop was able to gain title to some 12,000 acres of land east and northeast of New London. John Winthrop, Jr., was made an Assistant of the Connecticut Colony in May 1649, Magistrate in 1651, and Governor in 1657.

In 1653, Coit exchanged his original lot for a parcel at Close Cove on the Thames River, where he practiced his trade as a ship's carpenter for which he was widely recognized. The area where he worked is today called Ledyard. John Coit was joined in trade by his youngest son, Joseph, and two sons-in-law, Hugh Mould and John Stevens. After John Coit's death, these family members stayed in the trade for the rest of their lives. John Coit died August 29, 1659. Mary Jenners is recorded as a member of the New London Church in October 1670. She remained a widow for 16 years until her death January 2, 1676. This extended period of widowhood was unusual in those days, as single adults usually remarried after the death of a spouse. However, record show that Mary Jenners, widowed at age 64, was considerably older than her neighbors at that time. John and Mary (Jenners) Coit had seven children, three of whom remained in England. Among the five children born in New England, was a daughter, Martha [#56].

[7] WILLIAM CORNWELL, JR., was born and baptized May 25, 1609, in Terling, Essex, a son of WILLIAM and MARGERY (HAYWARDE) CORNWELL, and grandson of GEORGE and JOAN CORNWELL.

On September 27, 1632, William married Joane Ranke in the adjoining parish of Fairsted, where they lived until joining the Great Puritan Migration. The earliest record of William and

Joane (Ranke) Cornwell in Massachusetts is 1633, when their names are found among the members of Rev. John Eliot's congregation at Roxbury. Rev. Elliot lists them as "William Cornewell" and "Joane Cornewell, the wife of Willia Cornewell."

By 1639, William Cornwell, Jr., had moved to Hartford where records show that as proprietor of the town, he lived at No. 54, west of South Street, south from the Lane with eight acres of land in the village. Early Hartford records identify him as "William Cornwell, Sergeant-at-arms," which confirms family tradition that William Cornwell, Jr., was at one-time in the guard of King Charles I, though he became a Puritan, broke with the King and emigrated to New England. Tradition is that Joane (Ranke) Cornwell had died by 1639, and that by 1640 William had married a woman named **MARY**.

In 1650/1, Mary and William Cornwell, Jr., moved to Middletown, where he obtained a house and 15 acres in the center of the village at a place near today's intersection of Main and Washington streets. He eventually owned more than 900 acres in Middletown and also "a great lot over the Great River." He joined the church in Middletown on December 3, 1658, and represented Middletown as a deputy to the General Court in Hartford in 1654, 1664, and 1665. He was also a Middletown constable in 1664. The common spelling of the family name today is Cornwall, though in early spellings it was Cornwell. William sometimes spelled his name Cornell, which is how he signed his will. William, who died in Middletown February 21, 1677/8, and was buried in Riverside Cemetery, and Mary Cornwell, Jr., had eight children, including son John [#52].

[8] NATHANIEL FOOTE was born about 1593 in Shalford, Essexshire. Nathaniel was a son of **ROBERT FOOTE** of Royston, Hertfordshire, and **JOAN BROOKS**, who was a daughter of **JOHN** and **ELIZABETH (WHETMAN) BROOKS**, of London, who lived in Shalford. Robert, who died in London and was burned in Shalford February 16, 1608/9, and Joan (Brooke) Foote had nine children and possessed property in both Shalford and Royston. In 1615, their son, Nathaniel Foote, married **ELIZABETH DEMING**, who was born in 1595, a daughter of **JOHN DEMING**.

Family tradition holds the Deming family were of French Huguenot descent. Huguenots were French Protestants who emerged in the middle of the 16th Century, and who became a significant political and religious force dealt with harshly by French's Royals and their Roman Catholic supporters.

The persecution of Huguenots began in the 1520's and reached a climax in 1523 when the first Huguenot dissenters were burned at the stake. Inflammatory Protestant reform rhetoric continued to alarm Catholic public opinion to such an extent that, in 1534, many Protestants were forced to flee. Among those who left France were John Calvin, who found refuge in Geneva.

Protestantism continued to spread, even among the nobility. A synod at Paris in 1559 drew up a confession of faith. In 1562, the so-called Wars of Religion broke out in France and continued intermittently until 1598. The most notorious episode in this period was a massacre of Protestants in Paris August 23, 1572, when 3,000 attending a demonstration were killed during rioting on the eve of St. Bartholomew's Day. The rioting and vengeance continued, and nearly every prominent Huguenot in Paris was murdered; thousands more in the countryside were killed. These continuing terrors were punctuated by a succession of assassinations among the nobility and royal families until 1598 when Henry IV, a one-time Huguenot who turned Catholic upon his ascension to the throne, promulgated the Edit of Nantes, which gave Huguenots a measure of political and religious freedom.

The calm did not last long. Civil wars erupted again 20 years later under King Louis XIII. Eventually Huguenot armies in France were defeated and their political and military base destroyed. The struggle against religious persecution continued however. When Louis XIV revoked the Edict of Nantes in 1685, waves of religious refugees spilled into Europe. Historians say that more than 250,000 Protestants fled France during Louis XIV reign. Many French Huguenots joined the forces of the Dutch William of Orange, whose armies would defeat England's Catholic King James in Ireland, and who assumed the English throne as King of England, with his wife, James' sister, Mary, as Queen.

It is not known precisely when the Deming ancestors fled France for England. However, during this extended period of persecution in France between 1520 to 1688, hundreds of thousands of Protestants sought refuge in Holland, Prussia, England and later America.

Elizabeth, the daughter of John Deming, the Huguenot, was born in England in 1595 and married Nathaniel Foote in 1615. Nathaniel and Elizabeth (Deming) Foote immigrated with their six children to New England and settled in Watertown, where Nathaniel was made a freeman September 3, 1634, and owner of sixteen acres and a two-acre march.

Though Nathaniel continued as a proprietor in Watertown until 1642, he moved with his family in 1636 to the settlement of Wethersfield, on the Connecticut River, where he would own

a ten-acre home lot and various other tracks including the southern part of Pennywise Island. Also in Wethersfield at the time
was Nathaniel's brother-in-law John Deming, an early and
prominent settler of Wethersfield.

A skilled farmer, Nathaniel was best known for his ability to
raise stock, particularly swine. Nathaniel was one of the first two
men to have goats in the colony, and was a representative from
Wethersfield to the General Court from 1641 to 1644, the year
he died at age 51. His death was unexpected and he hadn't made
a will. Court appointed advisors valued his estate at 800 pounds,
making him the community's most wealthy man at the time.
Nathaniel Foote's fortune was left entirely to the administration
of his widow, Elizabeth (Deming) Foote, though her son was
aged 24 at the time of her husband's death, attesting to her
stature and independence. Nathaniel was buried in the rear of
the Wethersfield meeting house.

Two years after Nathaniel's death, his widow, Elizabeth
(Deming) Foote, married Thomas Welles, an original Hartford
proprietor who moved to Wethersfield where was also a proprietor and magistrate. Welles was Secretary of the Colony from
1640 to 1649, when he became a Commissioner of the United
Colonies. Welles was Governor of Connecticut in 1655 and 1658
and died January 14, 1659/60. Elizabeth remained one of the
colony's most prominent women until her death, at age 88, July
28, 1683. Nathaniel and Elizabeth (Deming) Foote had seven
children, including daughter Elizabeth [#17].

[9]   WILLIAM MEAD was born in 1600 in Elmdon,
Essex. Married in 1625, William and his wife and son in April
1635 sailed for Plymouth Colony aboard the vessel *Elizabeth*,
which left the Kent port of Lydd under Captain Stagg. The name
Mead is an English name translation of the Norman name "de
Prato," found in the records shortly after the Conquest, and
which means "of the meadow." Early Norman de Pratos found
in the era 1180-95 were named William, Robert, Matilda, Roger
and Reginald.

Accompanying William Mead and his family was William's
brother, known today only as "Goodman" Mead. Like Edmund
Lockwood [#1], Nicholas Knapp [#2], John White [#3], Rebecca
Olmsted [#5], William Cornwell, Jr. [#7], Nathaniel Foote [#8],
and others to follow, William Mead was from the area of
England called East Anglia.

For an understanding of East Anglia and its relationship to
the development of New England, I have relied on David Hackett

Fischer's illuminating work, *Albion's Seed—Four British Folkways in America*, throughout this narrative.

East Anglia comprises 7,000 square miles, about 8 percent of Britain and is located north and east of London in the counties of Essex, Suffolk, Norfolk, Cambridgeshire, Huntingtonshire and Lincolnshire and parts of Bedfordshire and Kent. For more than 1,000 years, the sea had exposed East Anglians to invasions by and trade with a variety of travelers, marauders, plunderers, and adventurers including Viking Danes, Germanic Angles, Jutes from Denmark or Dunkirkers from France.

These invaders often stayed with their ways. Overland travel and communication was hard and travel frequently dangerous. However, the sea linked East Anglia, Kent and Lincolnshire with each other and also with the Netherlands across the North Sea. This region developed special trading relations and also a common culture and religious outlook. East Anglians developed their own culture, speech and character; they were more like each other than the rest of Britain. Linguists trace New England's twang to East Anglia, and New England architecture had its roots in East Anglia. The pious, reserved, independent and perhaps tenacious ways of native New Englanders can be traced to East Anglia.

In the years leading up to the English Civil War, East Anglia was a densely settled, highly urbanized section of England. In 1630, Norwich was England's second largest city, whose population had tripled in 50 years. The region was dotted with small seaports and market towns. In 1600, there were some 130 little ports on the coast of Essex alone. In 1630, half of Essex adults were employed in the cloth trade. Suffolk, Norfolk, Cambridge and Kent were major textile centers, specializing in the manufacture of light woolens favored in Southern Europe. Called "Suffolk shortcloths," these garments were considered luxurious and worn by the Western World's elite.

Ideas and goods were traded with the Netherlands, then a center of commerce and religious toleration. In the years leading up to the Civil War, the area's economic depression was compounded by England's wars with Spain in 1625-30 and France 1627-29. At the same time, the 1629 corn crop failed. Farmers fled to the towns, pleading with authorities for work. East Anglia was a seat of Puritan dissent and the home to Oliver Cromwell, and the Parliamentarians' political base was at Cambridge, whose Emmanuel College was also the training ground of many learned Puritan divines.

East Anglia's religious traditions, the proximity of Cambridge and its intellectual fervor galvanized local dissent. During the Great Migration more than half the 129 university-trained ministers who went to New England had lived in East Anglia. More than three-fourths of New England's college-trained ministers and magistrates were born, bred, schooled, married or employed for long periods in the seven counties of East Anglia. Nearly half of these ministers went to three of Cambridge's colleges, Emmanuel, Magdalen and Trinity, with one-third of those having graduated from Emmanuel.

East Anglia emigrants were family-centered, better educated and more urban than their English countrymen. In general, the New England immigrants had occupied the middle strata of English society and arrived as parts of households. Women had standing in East Anglia. In a community where the practice of religion was central to the culture, records of church membership show that most of the members in New England—the elect— were women. In the general population itself, however, the ratio of men to women was 3 to 2. Only 11% of Winthrop's original fleet were identified as gentlemen, and less than 5% were listed as labourers. Most were craftsmen, yeomen, husbandmen, artisans, merchants and traders. One-third came from small market towns, one third from large towns (much greater than the English population as a whole), fewer than 30% from manorial villages.

To illustrate their relative wealth, records indicate that nearly 75% paid their own way, and only 25% traveled with servants. The price of a third-class passage was 50 pounds, with 60 to 80 pounds for minimal comforts. At the time the typical English yeoman earned 40 pounds a year, while a husbandman, who would gross 20 pounds a year, saved only 3 or 4 pounds after expenses. Nearly two-thirds of the emigrant men could sign their names, while in England only one third could do so.

New England emigrants were of keenest interest in these studies. However, some 80,000 fled England in the period before the Civil War. New England was the destination for only 20,000. Another 20,000 went to Ireland, 20,000 to the Netherlands or the Rhineland in Europe, and another 20,000 to the tropical trading islands in the Caribbean, such as Barbados, Nevis and St. Kitts in the West Indies, or Old Providence off Nicaragua.

In 1630, the first year of the migration to New England, 17 ships sailed to Massachusetts. During the next decade, 200 emigrant ships would make the crossing, each carrying 100 passengers, the migration slowing to a trickle in 1641 as the Civil War improved prospects for Puritans at home.

While William Mead's brother stayed in Massachusetts, William followed the migration from both Plymouth and Massachusetts Bay colonies to the River Towns along the Connecticut. William settled in Wethersfield, which was founded in 1634 by adventurer John Oldham and 10 men from

Watertown. Oldham had first come to the land along the long river in 1633 after hearing of Plymouth Governor Winslow's successful journey. Oldham himself found "many very desirable places...fit to receive many hundred inhabitants." Many Watertown citizens were eager for new beginnings in Connecticut, away from the stern rule of Plymouth and Massachusetts Bay. Oldham's report persuaded many to move.

After the settlement of Wethersfield, Windsor and Hartford, there were some 800 English settlers along the Connecticut River. The three River Towns continued to grow, and their prosperity caused concern about the Pequots, the strong and warlike Indians nearby. In April 1636, Rev. Hooker gave a sermon urging the River Towns to convene a General Court together. When the Deputies from each town met, leaders decided that the General Court itself, and not the Church, would be the supreme authority among them, and that two Deputies from each town would act together to rule their common affairs, mainly security.

The fears were well founded. That year, Wethersfield founder John Oldham was murdered off Block Island. Pequots gave Oldham's killers refuge.

Later, two traders named Stone and Norton were slain as they traveled up the Connecticut River. Oldham's murder enraged the population in Massachusetts, where he remained popular. A Massachusetts militia under Captain Endicott waged murderous reprisal raids on Pequot camps between Boston and the River Towns. Pequots avenged Endicott's raids with raids of their own on the small settlement at Saybrook. From Saybrook, Lion Gardiner, who had warned that Endicott's tactics in Connecticut would spread the bloodshed, wrote Endicott: "You come hither to rouse these wasps about my ears and then you will take wing and flee away." Finally in April 1637, the Pequots raided Wethersfield and killed six men, three women and kidnapped two young girls who were never seen again.

On May 1, the River Towns General Court ordered that 90 men be raised to make war on the Pequots. Command was given to Captain John Mason of Windsor, who raised a militia consisting of 42 men from Hartford, 30 from Windsor and 18 from Wethersfield. Several days later, 70 Mohegans, led by Uncas, long-time enemy of the Pequots, joined the militia. At Saybrook, the militia was joined by Captain Underhill from Massachusetts with a force of 30.

The main camp of the Pequots was at a fort in what is now West Mystic. Behind a wood fence 12 feet high, some 500 Pequot men, women and children lived in 70 wigwams scattered over several acres. Captain Mason's militia surrounded the camp and set fire to its outside. Aided by a rising wind, which the Puritans took to be an act of Providence, the entire camp was soon ablaze. Those Pequots who ran through the flaming gates were shot. Those inside burned to death. Only two militia members lost their lives. Pequots at the second camp at what is now Fort Hill tried to stop Captain Mason's militia but failed, soon fleeing west with the militia in pursuit. The forces finally met in July in a swamp in what is now Fairfield County, where the remaining Pequot warriors were slain or captured and sold into slavery to the Mohegans. The Pequots were wiped out.

The prosperity of the River Towns also posed political problems for the settlers. The Connecticut settlements, for the most part, were on land purchased directly from Indian sachems and thus did not have clear title under English law. Some simply assumed that the settlements were part of either Massachusetts Bay or Plymouth. However, this was unsatisfactory. The political, legal and religious control was too remote and not responsive to the wishes of the River Towns' leaders, particularly Rev. Hooker.

The General Court of the River Towns, flush with the success of their joint effort in the Pequot war, believed that joint action was possible apart from church authority. On May 31, 1638, Rev. Hooker gave a sermon in Hartford in which he reiterated his view that people should have a greater voice in their government, and that a General Council should be chosen by all. Suffrage would be based on property, not religion. Some of Hooker's ideas:

> "...The choice of public magistrates belongs unto the people by God's own allowance...the foundation of authority is laid, firstly, in the free consent of the people...in matters which concern the common good a General Council, chosen by all, to transact business which concerns all, I conceive most suitable to rule and most safe for relief of the whole..."

Rev. Hooker's sermon, containing ideas revolutionary in their implications, encouraged the River Towns' leaders to ask legal scholar Roger Ludlow to draft a charter. Called Connecticut's Fundamental Orders, Ludlow's document contained the practical outline of Hooker's notions, calling on freemen to form "one public state or commonwealth." The River Towns adopted it in January 1639.

Despite this step forward in public affairs, church affairs in Wethersfield were strained. There was a split in the congregation. Mediation by Rev. Hooker and Massachusetts Governor John Winthrop proved fruitless. Many leading citizens decided to relocate.

This dissension in Wethersfield coincided with development along the shoreline spurred by the New Haven Colony. Acting on behalf of New Haven, Captain Daniel Patrick and Robert Feake landed on a point of land near Dutch New Amsterdam called Monakewego. Within days of landing in July 1640, Captain Patrick signed a document, which agreed to pay local Indian sachems 25 coats for the land between the Asamuck and Patromuck Rivers. The land today is called Old Greenwich.

Soon, Captain Patrick dispatched another New Haven Colony agent, Captain Nathaniel Turner, a few miles northeast along the coast to explore the Ripowan area, today known as Stamford. Captain Turner purchased Stamford from Ponus, sachem of the Siwanoys. In November 1640, title to the land was transferred to Andrew Ward and Robert Coe, who acted on behalf of 22 families from Wethersfield looking for new land. Among them was William Mead.

In the spring of 1641, William Mead and the heads of 21 other Wethersfield families joined Ward and Coe in Stamford. On the list of 42 names of original proprietors of the Town of Stamford is William Mead, who in December was granted a home lot and five acres of land as his share in the purchase.

William Mead, who died in 1664, and his wife had at least four children, including a son, John [#40].

[10] JOHN LOTHROP, was born and baptized December 20, 1584, in Elton, East Riding, Yorkshire, the twelfth child of THOMAS and MARY (HOWELL) LOWTHROP. John entered Queens College, Cambridge, in 1601 and received his AB degree in 1605, and AM degree in 1609. He became a clergyman in the Established Church at a parish in Edgerton, Kent.

Family tradition holds that Lothrop ancestors came from Yorkshire since the 14th century, and family's name had a variety of spellings, including Lawthrop, Lowthrop and Lothrop. John's earliest known ancestor was JOHN LOWTHROP who, in 1545, was assessed twice as much as any other inhabitant in Cherry Burton, in Yorkshire. John Lowthrop's son ROBERT LOWTHROP, born in 1513 in Cherry Burton, married ELLEN ASTON, likely the daughter of THOMAS ASTON, of Fole, Checkley, Straffordshire.

In his will dated July 15, 1558, and proven at York October 20, 1558, after his death, Robert Lowthrop called himself a yeoman of North Burton and listed among his possessions a "jack" or coat of mail, and a "bill" or battle ax. His widow, Ellen (Aston) Lowthrop, who survived him for 14 years, was buried

March 8, 1572/3, in Cherry Burton. Her will was dated February 12 of that year. Robert and Ellen (Aston) Lowthrop had at least four children, including son Thomas Lowthrop born June 19, 1536, in Cherry Burton.

Thomas Lowthrop's first wife, a widow Elizabeth Clark, died and was buried in Elton July 29, 1574. On September 2, 1574, Thomas married Mary Howell, a daughter of **JOHN HOWELL**. After Mary (Howell) Lowthrop's death and burial in Elton January 6, 1588, Thomas married a third time. By three wives, Thomas Lowthrop had 22 children. Thomas died and was buried in Elton October 9, 1606. Thomas and second wife, Mary (Howell) Lowthrop, had five children, including son, John Lothrop, our immigrant ancestor, who after entering the clergy became as, Rev. John Lothrop, a curate at Egerton.

On October 10, 1610, Rev. John Lothrop obtained a license to marry **HANNAH HOUSE (HOWSE)**, of Eastwell, Kent, the eldest daughter of **REV. JOHN** and **ALICE HOWSE**. Alice, who was born in 1572 in Eastwell, and John Howse were married in 1590. Rev. John, who died August 30, 1630, and Alice Howse had eight children. The family name was also spelled House.

This was a time of religious turmoil and over time Rev. John Lothrop's views changed. In 1625, he succeeded Rev. Henry Jacob as pastor of the Separatist church at Southward, London. In 1632, the persecution of Puritans reached a new level of intensity and Rev. John Lothrop was imprisoned at Newgate Prison for his beliefs, along with many of his parishioners. While her husband was in prison, Hannah (House) Lothrop died in London February 16, 1633. Rev. Lothrop was released from prison in 1634 only on petition of his orphaned children, and on the condition that he emigrate to America.

Rev. John Lothrop and his children sailed for Boston in 1634 on the *Griffin*; among his fellow passengers was Ann Hutchinson, who in time would be banished from Boston for her unorthodox religious views and flee to Rhode Island. Upon his arrival, Governor John Winthrop praised Lothrop, a fellow clergyman, as possessing "modesty and reserve of one who had so prominently, so ably, so fearlessly upheld the Puritan faith."

Rev. John Lothrop settled in Scituate September 27, 1634, with many of his parishioners, and became a minister. He married a widow, Ann Hammond, February 17, 1636/7, who would bear six children. They moved to Barnstable, Massachusetts in October 1639. Rev. Lothrop ministered in Barnstable, where he died November 8, 1653. His widow died February 25, 1687/8. Rev. John and Hannah (House) Lothrop had nine children, including son Samuel [#12].

[11] TIMOTHY STANLEY was born and baptized May 22, 1599/0, in Ashford, Kent, England, a son of **JOHN** and **SUSAN (LANCOCK) STANLEY**. In May 1634, Timothy and his wife, **ELIZABETH**, came to New England with their year-old son, Timothy, Jr., who died soon thereafter. Joining Timothy Stanley on the voyage were his brothers, Thomas and John.

John Stanley died on the voyage, leaving behind a widow and two children. The son was raised by his uncle, Thomas, while Timothy and Elizabeth took niece, Ruth. Timothy and Elizabeth Stanley settled in Newtowne (Cambridge), where he was made a freeman March 5, 1635. In 1636, Timothy Stanley and his family followed Rev. Thomas Hooker to Hartford, where he was an original proprietor. Other Hartford proprietors included Thomas Stanley, Samuel Greenhill, Simon Willard, and William Pantry, who also emigrated on the same ship as Timothy Stanley and also had settled first in Newtowne.

Timothy Stanley's home lot was on the west side of Front Street, near the road to the landing, the second lot north of present-day State Street. Timothy Stanley was chosen a juror in 1641, a selectman in January 1642/3 and served on several town committees. He died in Hartford in April 1648. His widow, Elizabeth, married Andrew Bacon in 1661 and lived in Hadley, Massachusetts until his death October 4, 1669. Elizabeth returned to Hartford, where she lived with her son, Caleb, until her death February 23, 1678/9 at about the age of 76. Timothy and Elizabeth Stanley had six children, including daughter Abigail [#49].

[12] SAMUEL LATHROP was born in February/March 1622/3, in England, a son of Rev. John and Hannah (House) Lothrop [#10]. Samuel's mother died in England about 1633 and he came to New England with his father in 1634, settling first in Scituate and then Barnstable.

Samuel Lathrop became a house builder by trade, and worked for a time in Boston. In Barnstable, November 28, 1644, Samuel married **ELIZABETH SCUDDER**, born about 1622, a daughter of **THOMAS** and **ELIZABETH (LOWERS) SCUDDER**.

Thomas Scudder, born in 1591 in Groton, was a son of **REV. HENRY SCUDDER** who presided over a convention of clergymen appointed by the King at Westminister in 1643. Thomas Scudder came to New England aboard the ship *James* from Groton, England, in 1636 with wife Elizabeth (Lowers) of Daruth, Kent, and children, John and Elizabeth. The Scudders settled in Salem, where Thomas Scudder died in 1657. His son,

John Scudder, moved to Barnstable where he lived next door to the Lathrop family. John's sister, Elizabeth, lived with him. Apparently Elizabeth had married Henry Bartholomew in Boston where she was a member of the First Church. She was dismissed from the First Church November 10, 1644. What happened to her first husband is unknown. However, on November 28, 1644, just a fortnight after leaving Boston's church, she married Samuel Lathrop, in his father's home in Barnstable, where Rev. John Lathrop was pastor.

In 1648, Elizabeth and Samuel Lathrop moved to New London where Samuel was one of the builders of the meeting house. The following year, Samuel was appointed a magistrate in New London. In 1668, they moved to Norwich. Elizabeth died about 1688. Two years later, Samuel married Abigail, a daughter of Deacon John Doane. Abigail (Doane) Lathrop would die in 1734/5 at age 104 years. Samuel Lathrop was Norwich constable in 1682 and selectman in 1685, and died in Norwich February 29, 1699/1700. Samuel and Elizabeth (Scudder) Lathrop had nine children, including daughter Martha [#63].

[13] JEFFREY FERRIS was born in 1610 in Leicestershire, and came to New England in 1635. Leicestershire was the birthplace of Rev. Thomas Hooker. Family history reports that the family is descended from the Norman French de Feriers, who first were granted land in Leicestershire by William the Conqueror.

Jeffrey married MARY in England. With their first child, Jeffrey and Mary Ferris came to New England in 1634, with Jeffrey being made a freeman in Watertown the following year. He soon moved to Wethersfield, where he stayed for four years.

In 1640, Jeffrey Ferris and seven others were present on July 18 when Captain Daniel Patrick and Robert Feake, acting as agents for the New Haven Colony, landed at Greenwich Point and purchased land from the Indians for the first settlement of Greenwich. Some report that Jeffrey Ferris had been with the pre-landing party, having previously negotiated with Indian sachem Keoferram before Patrick and Feake arrived.

Jeffrey Ferris was one of the first landowners of Greenwich. In fact, the name Greenwich has been attributed to Ferris's family, because in 1590 an adventurer named Richard Ferris served as a messenger in the court of Queen Elizabeth, whose favorite summer resort was Greenwich on the Thames, where her yacht lay alongside the wharf in front of the palace. Records show that Jeffrey was in Stamford in 1641, which at that time was part of Greenwich, and is listed as one of the 59 Stamford pioneers in

1642. On February 4, 1664, Jeffrey is listed as one of the proprietors of Greenwich.

Mary Ferris died in 1658. In 1659, Jeffrey married Susannah (Norman) Lockwood, widow of Robert Lockwood, daughter-in-law of Edmund Lockwood [#1] and sister-in-law of Elinor (Lockwood) Knapp [#2]. Susannah (Norman) (Lockwood) Ferris, a native of Salem who had moved to Fairfield with her husband, would die in 1660, a year after her marriage to Jeffrey Ferris. Another Ferris-Lockwood connection was the 1662 marriage of Jeffrey's daughter, also named Mary, to Jonathan Lockwood, the son of her late stepmother, Susannah (Norman) (Lockwood) Ferris, and thus her stepbrother.

Jeffrey, who died in Greenwich May 31, 1666, and Mary Ferris had five children, including Joseph [#45], Peter [#46] and James [#47].

[14] PAUL PECK was born about 1618 in England. Family tradition holds that Paul Peck sailed from Essex to Boston aboard the *Defence* arriving in 1635. Paul Peck migrated to Hartford, where he was a proprietor by 1639 "by courtesy of the town."

Paul Peck married **MARTHA HALE**, who was born in 1621 in England, and whose two brothers, Samuel and Thomas, were also proprietors of Hartford. Both Samuel and Thomas served in the Pequot War in 1637 for which they granted land. Samuel received a lot in "soldier's field" and was a Hartford juror twice in 1643. Samuel later moved to Wethersfield and later to Norwalk, from which he was a deputy to the Connecticut General Court in 1656, 1657, 1658, and 1660. Samuel returned to Wethersfield in 1660 where he lived for the next three decades.

Brother Thomas was made a freeman in Roxbury in 1634, a proprietor of Hartford in 1639 and resided in Hartford on the west of the road from Seth Grant's to Centinel Hill. Thomas Hale married Jane Lord of Roxbury in 1640 and was later granted 50 acres of land for his service in the Pequot War. He was one of the original "planters" of Norwalk and moved there in February 1651. He lived there until at least 1655. Family tradition holds that Thomas later moved to Charlestown, Massachusetts, where he died.

Paul and Martha (Hale) Peck's homelot in Hartford was on the "road from George Steele's to the Great Swamp." He was named a surveyor of highways in 1658 and 1665, a selectman 1661, 1668, chimney-viewer in 1667, and was a deacon of the

First Church in 1691. Governor John Winthrop, Jr., a physician, took note of Martha (Hale) Peck's health (good) and age (45) in his medical journal March 23, 1666. Deacon Paul Peck died in Hartford December 23, 1695. His widow subsequently felt compelled to sue her two sons, Paul, Jr., and Samuel, for refusing to pay rent on land due her at the bequest of her husband. Deacon Paul and Martha (Hale) Peck had 10 children, including a daughter, Martha [#52].

[15] WILLIAM PECK was born in 1601 in London, where he became a merchant. In 1622, William Peck married ELIZABETH in England. The Peck family with their children arrived in Boston on June 26, 1637, aboard the ship *Hector* in the company of Governors Theophilus Eaton and Edward Hopkins, Rev. John Davenport and the son of the Earl of Marlborough.

Eaton, born October 31, 1590, in Stony-Stratford, Oxfordshire, was a wealthy international merchant, having worked in the Eastern trade along the Baltic coast of Northern Europe, and as the king's agent in Denmark. In London, Eaton was active in St. Stephen's Church, whose vicar was the Rev. John Davenport, Eaton's schoolmate at Coventry Free School years earlier. Davenport was born in April 1597 in Coventry, Warwickshire and was educated at Oxford. In 1616, Davenport was a chaplain at Hilton Castle near Durham, arriving at London's St. Stephen's in 1624.

St. Stephen's became a center of religious nonconformism among London's middle class. As early at 1629, Rev. Davenport had shown interest in gaining a charter for Massachusetts Bay. The following year, the Earl of Warwick signed the Warwick Patent granting Lord Saye and Sele, Lord Brooke and others the right to establish a plantation in southern New England. Davenport, a Warwickshire native, was among those intrigued with the notion of emigration.

As Davenport's commitment to Puritanism continued, his liberty was threatened. In 1633 he fled to Holland, where, with the Rev. Hugh Peter and George Fenwick, he purchased supplies for the proposed Saybrook Plantation. Rev. Peter also persuaded his step son-in-law, John Winthrop, Jr., the son of the Massachusetts Bay governor, to become governor of the new Saybrook Plantation. A year after John Winthrop, Jr., left England for Boston, Davenport returned to England from Holland disguised as a country gentleman to prevent his arrest and imprisonment by Anglican Archbishop William Laud, the Puritans' chief persecutor and key supporter of the king.

While Davenport was away in Holland, Eaton, distressed by his friend and pastor's exile, also had seen the commercial possibilities of a New England plantation. By the time of Davenport's return in 1636, Eaton had advanced his idea for an immigrant company to the point where he was ready to act. The Eaton/Davenport company left London April 13, 1637, arriving in Boston June 26. They were warmly received. Many believed their stay in Boston would be permanent, but Eaton had other ideas.

Within weeks of their arrival, the militia that had made war on the Pequots returned to Boston. Captain Stoughton of the militia told Eaton of the land the militia had seen while pursuing the Pequots along the Connecticut coastline. The spot that particularly impressed Stoughton was a place inhabited by the Quinnipiacs and which Dutch explorer Adraean Block years before called Rodeberg, or Red Hills. The Quinnipiac territory had an excellent harbor and lush hunting grounds. Such a place fit Eaton's plans. In August, Eaton and a team of scouts sailed around Cape Cod into Long Island Sound and to the Quinnipiac territory. Eaton found it ideal. Leaving behind a number of pioneers, he returned to Boston and assembled his company. On April 10, 1638, the Eaton/Davenport company of 200 arrived to join the pioneers. The Quinnipiac sachem, Momauguin, sold Eaton the land comprising today's New Haven, North Haven, Wallingford, Cheshire, Hamden, Bethany, Woodbridge and Orange for 23 coats, 12 spoons, 24 knives, 12 hatchets and some scissors and hoes.

That spring was the occasion of Rev. Hooker's sermon in Hartford that led to the adoption of Connecticut's Fundamental Orders. Eaton, Rev. Davenport and other leaders of New Haven Colony were aware of their uncertain legal status. On June 4, 1639, six months after the River Towns adopted their new charter, 11 leaders of Davenport's congregation met in a barn owned by Robert Newman and adopted a Plantation Covenant that held that the Word of God would be the absolute authority in the New Haven Colony. God's Word as contained in the Laws of Moses was to be interpreted by a New Haven council of Seven Pillars, a title derived from Proverbs 9: 1:

> Wisdom hath builded her house;
> She hath hewn out her seven pillars.

New Haven was an ambitious colony. Eaton laid out a very large town by New England standards, a square almost a half mile on each side, divided into nine squares of 16 acres each. Today one of those squares is the New Haven Green. Despite his vision in town building, Eaton's commercial ventures were never very successful. Agriculture was poor, and the colony's strict theocracy stifled trade and growth. The colony's economic fate was sealed early, when 70 of the ablest citizens, together with all the available capital of 5,000 pounds, and all goods boarded a "Greate Shippe" in 1646 and set sail for England. The ship and all aboard disappeared without a trace.

William Peck was one of the founders of the New Haven Colony in 1638, signing the fundamental agreement in 1639. He was admitted as a freeman October 29, 1640. William, his wife, Elizabeth, and their sons Jeremiah, John and Joseph were baptized in New Haven May 7, 1643. In New Haven he was a merchant, and was a trustee, treasurer and general business agent for the Hopkins Grammar School. From 1659 until his death in 1694 at age 93, William Peck was a deacon in Guilford. Elizabeth died December 5, 1683, while visiting her son Joseph in Lyme. William, who died in 1694 (also at Joseph's home in Lyme) at age 93, and Elizabeth Peck had four children, including a daughter, Alice [#39], and son Jeremiah [#41].

[16] **THOMAS KIMBERLY** was born and baptized June 24, 1604, at Wotton-Under-Edge, Glouchestershire, a son of **ABRAHAM** and **KATHERINE (HOWE) KIMBERLY, JR.** who were married October 4, 1602, and who had three children. Abraham, born in 1558, was a son of shoemaker **ABRAHAM KIMBERLEY, SR.** and became a tradesman in Wotton-Under-Edge, a thriving market town.

On August 28, 1628, Thomas Kimberly married **ALICE ATWOOD** of the neighboring parish, King's Stanley. Less than ten years later, Thomas and Alice (Atwood) Kimberly and their family emigrated to New England, where on January 2, 1637/8, Thomas was granted an acre of land in Dorchester. The family moved with the company of Rev. Davenport and Theophilus Eaton to New Haven, where Thomas was one of the original signatories of the Fundamental Agreement June 4, 1639.

Thomas, literate and articulate and able to quote scripture against heretical views, was an active member in Rev. Davenport's congregation. In 1642, Thomas, a tailor, was chosen a corporal of the New Haven train band and, at various times, was a marshal, a selectman, and constable of the New Haven colony. Alice (Atwood) Kimberly died October 10, 1659. Thomas Kimberly married widow Mary (Seabrook) Preston. In 1668, Thomas sold his New Haven house, barn and home-lot and, on December 28, 1668, bought three acres in Stratford, where he died about

January 1672/3. Thomas and Alice (Atwood) Kimberly had six children, including a daughter, Abiah [#55].

[17] ELIZABETH FOOTE was born about 1616 in England and came to New England in 1634, settling in Wethersfield in 1636 with her parents, Nathaniel and Elizabeth (Deming) Foote [#8]. In 1638, Elizabeth married **JOSIAH CHURCHILL**, who was born about 1616 in England.

Some say Josiah Churchill's father lived in London, others say the family came from Devonshire. Josiah's names were sometimes spelled Josias and Churchell. An early settler of Wethersfield, the first time his name on record is Josiah's 1638 marriage to Elizabeth Foote. His first real estate holding in Wethersfield— six acres on the Connecticut River—was noted April 28, 1641. His homestead was on the east side of High Street, slightly south of his first home, on land formerly belonging to Charles Taintor. In 1670, Josiah was granted 18 acres of land in the town's Western Division.

Josiah held several offices in town, including constable in 1656 and 1669, and surveyor in 1666 and 1673. One history labeled Josiah Churchill as "a gentleman of more than a medium estate for the time in which his lived, and of reputation in the colony."

Josiah wrote his will November 17, 1683, and his estate's inventory was taken January 5, 1686/7, indicating he died a few days before. At the time he owned two home lots and 110 acres of land. Elizabeth (Foote) Churchill died in Wethersfield September 8, 1700. Josiah and Elizabeth (Foote) Churchill had at least eight children, including daughter Hannah [#50].

[18] EDWARD SHEPARD was born in England and married **VIOLET STANLEY**, born about 1605, a daughter of **THOMAS** and **BENEDICTA (SHEPARD) STANLEY**. Edward, a mariner, and Violet (Stanley) Shepard came to New England in the Great Puritan Migration.

Edward Shepard's name first appears in Cambridge (Newtowne) records in 1639 when he purchased a house from James Herringe, and was made a freeman May 10, 1643. Violet (Stanley) Shepard died January 9, 1648/9. Edward married Mary Pond, the widow of Robert Pond of Dorchester. Edward Shepard died about 1680. Edward and Violet (Stanley) Shepard had five children, including daughter Elizabeth [#31].

[19] RICHARD WATTS was born in England and emigrated to New England where his name is first noted in Hartford in 1639, when records show he was granted land by "courtesie of the town." His home lot was on the west side of the "road from George Steele's to the Great Swamp." Richard was married to a woman named **ELIZABETH**, who had a cousin in Banbury, Oxfordshire, named Mary Smith.

Richard Watts' will was dated and October 29, 1650, and inventory taken March 20, 1654/5. Elizabeth Watts' will was dated February 28, 1665/6 and her inventory taken April 17, 1666. Richard and Elizabeth Watts had four children, including daughter Elizabeth [#20].

[20] ELIZABETH WATTS was born about 1616 in England, a daughter of Richard and Elizabeth Watts [#19]. She came to New England with her parents and was married in Hartford in 1640 to **GEORGE HUBBARD, JR.**, who was born in England in 1601, and had migrated to New England. His name first appears in Hartford in 1639, when he was one of 12 deputies to Hartford's first General Court. There were others named Hubbard—George, William and Thomas—in Hartford and Wethersfield at that time and it isn't clear how or if they were related. Family tradition holds that George Jr.'s father, also named George Hubbard, lived in Milford and Guilford.

Whatever the relations, ancestor George Hubbard, Jr., married Elizabeth Watts in Hartford in 1640 and 10 years later sold his home-lot and land on the east side of the Great River and moved to Middletown with the first settlers. George Hubbard was made a freeman in 1654. George and his neighbor, Thomas Wetmore, the father of his future son-in-law, donated land for the second meeting house. George was selected as "keeper" of the first meeting house and, in December 1666, was allowed 40 shillings for tending the meeting house and "keeping the glass" —watching the hour glass, or time piece. George's eldest son, Thomas, was also mentioned for beating the drum to assemble the congregation and for standing guard as an Indian lookout during services.

George Hubbard, Jr., was commissioned by the General Court to act as an "Indian agent and trader for the Mattabessett district," a position requiring some prudence. His judgement was later questioned, however, when he was once fined 10 pounds for exchanging a gun with an Indian.

Elizabeth, who died in 1702, and George Hubbard, Jr., died March 18, 1684/5, and who both were buried in Middletown

Riverside Cemetery, had eight children, including Mary [#37] and Richard [#70].

[21] JOHN MOSS was born in 1604 in England and was in the New Haven Company of Theophilus Eaton and Rev. John Davenport. His name first appears in New Haven records when he is listed as the 37th member of the First Church of Christ (New Haven) in 1639. John Moss was married to **ABIGAIL CHARLES**. In 1640, he was fined for cutting down trees. In 1642, he was appointed a corporal in the New Haven Train Band. In the years that followed, John Moss' name is frequently mentioned in subsequent records of New Haven General Court, serving on many town committees, representing individuals in the community and as the colony's agent in various land transactions with the Quinnipiac Indians.

In 1664, he was deputy in the General Court of New Haven Colony, and, from 1667 to 1670, in the years immediately following New Haven's incorporation into Connecticut, he was deputy from New Haven to the General Court in Hartford.

As early as 1667, John Moss is mentioned in Hartford and New Haven records for his exploration of the area known today as Wallingford. His name is mentioned in various deeds and other land records in transactions with Indians to procure the land for colonial settlement. In 1670, while John Moss was still a deputy from New Haven, he is recorded as arguing before the Hartford General Court to incorporate the land and to name it Wallingford, which was approved in May 12, 1670, with John Moss as one of its founders. During this period, on various deeds dealing with land transactions with the Quinnipiacs in the General Courts of Hartford and New Haven, John Moss is listed with Rev. Samuel Street, Lt. Nathaniel Meriman, John Brocket, and Sgt. Abraham Doolittle as the proprietors of Wallingford. On November 30, 1687, 99 acres of land were recorded to him, which he later passed on to his son, John, Jr.

John Moss remained active in Wallingford for nearly three more decades as its representative to the General Court. His home lot was located at the south of the village. John Moss, who died at age 103 in 1707, and his wife, Abigail, had at least 11 children, including John, Jr. [#63].

[22] **JOHN CLOSE** was born about 1600, probably in Yorkshire, and married **ELIZABETH** in 1633. They emigrated to New England with their family about 1642, settling in Fairfield. The first reference to John Close is found in the will of William Frost of Fairfield, dated January 6, 1644, and filed in Hartford, in which he is called "Goodman Close."

Close come from the Saxon name Cloughes, meaning cliff or valley. Close is a common name in agricultural districts of North Yorkshire, where a close or cloughes can be any piece of ground enclosed with hedge or wall. The word cloister has the same root.

Saxon naming patterns have roots in 3000 BC, with simple meanings, such as Edward which means rich guardian. After the Norman Conquest in 1066, Saxon patterns faded and a few Norman names appear, among the most common were William, Robert and Richard. There were so few names, the church in the late Middle Ages introduced the practice of adding saints' names such as Stephen, John, Mary, Thomas, Elizabeth, and James to the Norman names in use. When the community wanted to distinguish, say, one Thomas from another, a second identifying name would be used, often describing personal characteristics or place names, such as Thomas le sauvage, or Rogerus de lockwood. By 1200, it was common to find in England a mixture of Saxon, Norman and Christian names. It wasn't until the 13th century that the practice of adopting surnames began and it wasn't common until two centuries later. These English names were an occupation—Potter [#25]; place—Knapp [#2], Close [#22] or Lockwood [#1]; relationship—Johnson [#26]; characteristic—Savage [#35]; or color—White [#3] or Brown [#24].

John and Elizabeth Close settled in Fairfield, where John died about 1653 aged about 53. Among John and Elizabeth's children was Thomas Close, who became one of Greenwich's most prosperous landowners. Elizabeth died in Stamford September 4, 1656, at about age 50. John and Elizabeth Close had five children, including a daughter, Hannah [#48].

[23] **ROBERT HIBBARD** was born in 1613 and baptized on March 13 in St. Edmund's Parish, Salisbury. He was the son of **JOHN HIBBARD**, who is listed in parish records as a labourer. Robert and his wife, **JOAN**, came to Salem in the Great Puritan Migration of 1635-39. He was admitted to communion in May 1646 in the First Church of Salem, where his 10 children were baptized. Robert was employed as a saltmaker, brickmaker and bricklayer. His residence in Salem was on land that is now part of the town of Beverly. At the time of his death, Robert

owned 34 acres of land, a home and barn, orchards, meadows and salt marshes near a mill. His property was valued after probate at 281 pounds, 6 shillings. Robert, who died in May 1684, and his wife, Joan, had 10 children, including a son, Robert, Jr. [#61].

[24] PETER BROWN

was born in 1610 in Hastings, England. A baker, Peter was a member of the immigrant company organized by London merchant Theophilus Eaton and the Puritan divine, Rev. John Davenport. Peter Brown was one of the signatories of the New Haven Plantation Covenant on June 4, 1639.

Peter Brown was one of many townsmen to seek opportunity elsewhere after the failure of the Greate Shippe. In 1647, Peter moved to Stamford. Peter, who died in 1648, and his first wife had at least one son, Hackaliah [#51]. Peter's second wife, Unity, widowed, later married Nicholas Knapp [#2] in Stamford.

[25] WILLIAM POTTER

was born in 1609, came to New England in the Puritan migration, and probably stayed in Watertown until 1642. His name frequently appears in Stamford records. His homelot appears on record in 1650. In 1656, William Potter asked the New Haven General Court to be relieved of military training and duty because of physical weaknesses. The court agreed but said if he got better he must resume his service. He appeared as a court witness in 1684 and told Justice Jonathan Bell he was 75 years old. By that time, William Potter had become a considerable landowner in Stamford and owned what is today Shippan Point. His will is dated March 9, 1684. He left the Stamford congregation five pounds to "be improved for the use of the Lord's table...the silver cups now in the service of the table of the First Congregational Church are still witnesses to this bequest." William also left bequests to the three sons of Mr. Bishop, the minister, and to each of his 11 grandchildren, the children of his daughter Hannah.

William Potter had at least two children, including Hannah [#40].

[26] ROBERT JOHNSON

was born in 1599 in Yorkshire and arrived in New Haven in 1640 with his wife, their four sons and Robert's brother, Thomas. Robert and Thomas Johnson came to join their other brother, John, who had come to

New Haven earlier with the Eaton/Davenport company. John Johnson was one of the signatories of the June 4, 1639, Plantation Covenant.

Shortly after their arrival, Thomas drowned in New Haven Harbor. Robert's name appears in New Haven records of a court hearing held November 3, 1641, when Robert claimed the home and lot of his brother, John. John gave Robert his New Haven property in payment of a loan made earlier in Yorkshire. John had moved to Massachusetts Bay and settled in Rowley, near Ipswich, where he was later murdered by Indians.

At the time of the November 3, 1641, court hearing, Robert was unsure whether to stay in New Haven. Yet in 1644 he was still a resident; records show that the colony's court appointed him to assess the damage done by cattle and hogs in the town's Yorkshire Quarter. In 1646, Robert was granted six and a half acres of land in "the Necke." He also purchased 52 acres of upland from resident Thomas Yale.

In 1648, Robert was appointed to a town committee to devise a method of "protecting freemen from animal damage." A year later he was appointed to another committee to determine "what quantity of corn every man hath sown or planted this year that he is to be paid for." That same year, he asked permission to dig a well in the street near his house. Robert died in 1661. His will, probated at a value of 400 pounds, 4.3 pence, begins: "I bequeath my soul to Jesus Christ, And my body to the Dust..." Robert and his wife had at least one son, John Jr. [#36].

[27] JOHN REYNOLDS was born in England in 1612 and married SARAH, who was born in 1614. John and Sarah Reynolds came to New England about 1633, settling in Watertown, where records list him in 1635. They moved to Wethersfield, and then in 1641 to Stamford, settling finally in Greenwich in 1650. Sarah, who died August 21, 1657, and John, who died in 1660, had at least three children, including two sons, John and Jonathan, whose name is sometimes listed in Greenwich as Renalds (See Benjamin Mead III [#100]), and a daughter Elizabeth [#46].

[28] MATTHEW BECKWITH was born about 1612 in Essex and came to New England, perhaps as early as 1630, as a merchant trader with a group from Essex that first settled in Watertown and later in Windsor, Weathersfield and Hartford.

Hartford Public Records show that on August 1, 1639, Matthew Beckwith was aboard a "pinnace," or small schooner, with other members of the vessel's crew. These schooners were used as trading ships, bringing supplies to the settlements along the Connecticut River in exchange for beaver skins of value in Boston, Providence and New Amsterdam.

In 1641, Matthew married **MARY**, who was born in 1625. The couple didn't acquire a home lot until four years later. Hartford records show that Mary and their first child, a daughter Mary born in 1643, resided with the household of B. Barnard in Hartford, indicating that Matthew traveled and lived on his vessel. In 1645, Matthew purchased land in Hartford from a proprietor, William Platt. In 1650 he bought more land in Hartford from another proprietor, Thomas Porter. In the spring of 1651, Matthew was given a home lot in that section of New London known today as East Lyme. Matthew traveled from port to port, keeping his home port in Lyme in a section of waterway that became known as Beckwith Cove.

Matthew and Mary had at least seven children, and many of them traveled with their father as youngsters. A son and two daughters found their spouses in distant port towns, indicating they were well traveled and familiar with people far from home. One daughter married a sea captain.

Matthew died in the spring of 1682. Records report that "Matthew Beckwith, age abt. 70, missing his way in the very dark night, fell from a ledge of rocks about 20 or 30 feet high and beat his brains against a stone he fell upon." His widow Mary married Samuel Buckwall (Buckland). Mary died June 30, 1694. Among Matthew and Mary Beckwith's seven children was a son, Matthew Jr. [#62].

[29] JOHN PARMALEE arrived in New Haven with the congregation of the Rev. Henry Whitfield in 1639. John was accompanied by his wife, **HANNAH**, and their three children. Family tradition holds that John's son, also named John, had come to New Haven four years before. The Whitfield congregation signed a Covenant among themselves aboard ship June 1, 1639, and settled east of New Haven in a plantation they called Guilford. John, one of the 40 original proprietors of Guilford, was made a freeman May 22, 1649.

Family tradition holds that John Parmalee was from the parish of Ochly of Guernsey Island, in England, and that his family was of French Huguenot descent. John signed his name to his will Parmly, a common name in Tyrol and in Holland. After the death of his wife, Hannah, John moved to New Haven, where he married Elizabeth Bradley. John died in New Haven where his will was probated November 8, 1659. John and Hannah Parmalee had at least three children, including a daughter, Hannah [#36].

[30] SAMUEL BOREMAN was born in Banbury, Oxfordshire where he was baptized August 20, 1615, a son of CHRISTOPHER and JULIAN (CARTER) BOREMAN. Samuel Boreman's earliest known ancestor is named WILLIAM BORE-MAN, whose name appears in the Lay Subsidy List of Banbury Hundred in 1525, the only Boreman named in the area. William's son, THOMAS BOREMAN, was born about 1519 in Banbury Hundred, where his name appears in the Lay Subsidy List in 1546 for Claydon, a nearby farm village. Thomas, a Claydon farmer, is called "the elder" and taxed three pounds and three pence on his goods. Thomas, who was buried in Claydon in December 9, 1579, and ISABEL Boreman, had nine children, including a son, THOMAS BOREMAN, JR., "the younger," born probably about 1560 in Clayton.

On February 16, 1579/80, Thomas "the younger" married DOROTHY GREGORY. Thomas, who was buried June 13, 1587, and Dorothy (Gregory) Boreman, Jr., had at least two children, including a son, Christopher Boreman, who was born in Claydon and baptized December 1, 1581, his parent's only son. On November 19, 1604, Christopher married Julian Carter, born in Claydon and baptized December 20, 1583, a daughter of FELIX and MARGARET CARTER.

After their marriage, Christopher and Julian (Carter) Boreman moved to Banbury, a market town, where Christopher became a tradesman. Christopher and Julian (Carter) Boreman had eight children. Julian (Carter) Boreman's father, Felix Carter, a yeoman, was one of only two in Claydon who owned land by his own right, not by leasehold. Toward the end of his life, Felix Carter urged his daughter and her family to return to Claydon, and when they did, Felix Carter gave his son-in-law some land. Felix Carter died in 1630. Christopher Boreman died in Claydon and was buried April 1, 1640. By this time, Samuel Boreman was in New England and his mother, Julian (Carter)

Boreman, moved to London to live with her married daughter, Elizabeth (Boreman) Middleton, with whom she lived for another two decades.

Samuel, like many residents of Banbury, was greatly influenced by the religious and political changes around him; emigration was in the air. His cousin, Felix, who was considerably older, was employed in 1628 as an armorer or cutler on Fleete Lane near St. Paul's Cathedral in the heart of London. On March 17 of that year, Felix was paid 4 pounds, 12 shillings, for 25 swords he sold to the Massachusetts Bay Company. The goods were likely part of the outfit of Rev. Francis Higginson's company, which left to settle in Salem that spring.

Samuel, a cooper by trade, came to New England aboard the *Nicholas*, which left London April 26, 1638, with 164 passengers, a crew of 48, 300 tons of goods and 20 cannon. Accompanying Samuel were his wife and an indentured servant who got into some trouble on the voyage. In an account of the voyage written by John Joselyn Gent and published in 1675, Samuel's servant's fate was described:

> "On the eighth day of the voyage, one Boreman's
> man, a passenger, was dunked at the main yard arm,
> for being drunk with his master's strong waters which
> he stole, thrice, and fire given to two whole sacree
> (canons) at that instant..."

Samuel settled first at Ipswich, which had been established by John Winthrop, Jr. On August 22, 1639, Samuel was granted a home lot and one acre at the west end of town, six acres of planting ground beyond Muddy River and 10 acres elsewhere. The following year Samuel's wife died.

Her death came at a time when land values were dropping and commerce was slow. After about a decade of immigration, which had brought some 20,000 to New England, the wave of population was slowing, land prices were dropping and money was scarce and business poor. Many in Massachusetts decided to relocate to the River Towns in Connecticut or return to England, where prospects for Puritans were improving.

In 1641, Samuel sold his Ipswich property to Francis Jordon for 17 pounds and moved to Connecticut. That year he married **MARY BETTS**, born in 1623 in Claydon, the daughter of John and Mary Betts [#4], and who was living in Hartford with her widowed mother. The Boreman and Betts families had been Oxfordshire neighbors.

Of peripheral interest, Mary's brother, John Betts, Jr., had moved to New London from Hartford where he married Abigail

Elderkin, who was born in Dedham, Massachusetts September 13, 1641, and who had migrated to New London. In 1662, Abigail (Elderkin) Betts was tried in New London for blasphemy and "whipped upon the naked body" for "lascivious conduct." John and his "lascivious" wife, Abigail, were divorced ten years later. John married a second time to the widow Abigail Adams and, in January 1680, moved to the Long Island plantation at Huntington, where he died 10 years later.

Samuel and his bride, Mary, moved to Wethersfield, where the first of their 11 children, a son, Isaac, was born February 3, 1642. At that time, Wethersfield already was a large producer of pipe staves and Samuel, a cooper, easily found employment. By 1641, laws were already on the books in Connecticut Colony governing the manufacturing of pipe staves, providing for an inspector in each town. By 1649, Wethersfield was the largest producer of pipe staves in Connecticut, exporting 30,000 a year, compared with Hartford and Windsor where production was limited by the General Court to 20,000 each. The staves were shipped to Barbados for barrels to hold molasses, sugar and rum. The north end of Wethersfield (today's Newington) had so many pipe stave makers, one section was called Pipe Stave Swamp and a waterway was called Pipers' River.

Samuel prospered. On April 9, 1649, he purchased a home lot of three acres, a barn and cellar on the east side of Broad Street, just north of Plain Lane. Later he purchased six additional home lots. On November 3, 1659, Samuel purchased from Nathaniel Dickinson three acres on the west side of Broad Street on the south side of Fletcher's Lane, extending to Wethersfield's Main Street. Dickinson sold out to move to Hadley with Elder Goodwin's party from Hartford. The property on Broad Street was home to the Boreman family for five generations.

Samuel was active in civic affairs. At times, his name was spelled Boardman and Bowerman. In 1649, the Connecticut General Court appointed him as Town Sealer of Weights and Measures, and in 1659 appointed him Wethersfield Customs Master. He was made a Wethersfield juror on October 1, 1646, and held that post until 1662. He also was a Grand Juror between 1660 and 1662. Samuel was first selected as Wethersfield deputy to the Connecticut General Court October 1, 1657, and held that post for 18 terms, being present at 34 sessions. Samuel was also appointed by the General Court to a number of colonial committees to settle church differences, lay out the town of Haddam (including its purchase from the Indians), settle estates, lay out bounds of Middletown and help settle differences with Indians there, and lay out the bounds of the proprietors at Nanbuck.

On February 5, 1641, shortly after his arrival in Wethersfield,

Samuel Boreman's mother, Julian Carter Boreman in Banbury wrote her son:

> To hervery loving Sonne Samuel Boreman at Ipswich
> in New England give this with trust
>> Good Sonne
>> I have received your letter whereby I understand
> you are in good health for which I give God thankes
> as we are all prayed be God for the same: whereas
> your desire is to see your brother Christopher with
> you he is not proviced for so great a Journey neither
> doe I thinke that he dare take uppon him so danger-
> ouse a voyage your Five Sisters are all alive & in
> good health & remember therie loves to you your
> Father hath been dead almost this two yeares & thus
> troublling you noe further at this time I rest praying
> to God to blesse you and your wife unto whome we
> all kindly remember our loves
>> your ever loveinge
>> Mother
>> Julian Boreman

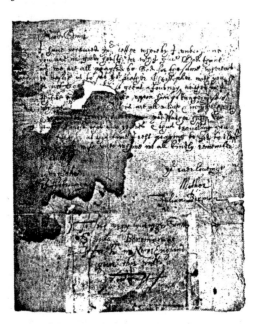

This letter arrived in Wethersfield five years after it was written. By that time, the English Civil War, which would lead to the
execution of King Charles 1, had nearly consumed Banbury. The
first armed encounter in Banbury occurred in July 1642, when
Lord Brook, the parliamentary commander of the Warwick
Militia, tried to retrieve six cannons from Banbury Castle. Just

as Brook and his 100 men were moving the cannon, they were stopped by a royalist force led by Spencer Compton, the Earl of Northampton and the King's commissioner for Warwickshire.

Rather than fight, the two forces agreed to a truce whose conditions included the return to Banbury Castle of the cannons. Both sides dug in. Meanwhile, support troops for both parliamentary militia and royalist forces arrived, turned Banbury dwellings and the surrounding countryside into a military camp and prepared for a siege, preparing roads and building earthworks. Nearby the Fiennes family raised more militia.

Finally, the king's army turned its attention to Banbury. On its way there, the royalist force on October 23, 1642, met at Edgehill, eight miles northwest of Banbury, and five miles west of Claydon, where the first great battle of the English Civil War was fought with forces loyal to parliament. The armies, though both were bloodied and battered, were still intact. The king moved to high ground, saw Banbury and ordered his forces to take the Banbury Castle.

His forces laid siege and soon the Parliamentarians inside surrendered. Built by Alexander, the Bishop of Lincoln, the castle had remained the property of the Roman Catholic Church until 1547, when it was taken over by the crown. In 1563, the Castle and Hundred were leased to the Fiennes family, who were now in open rebellion against the king. The castle was of the motte-and-bailey type and occupied 11 acres, with an open area of about three-quarters of an acre within an inner way. Now the castle was in the king's control and was turned over to the Compton family, nobility from Northamptonshire which fielded a royalist army under the command of Spencer Compton, the Earl of Northampton. Spencer's 18-year-old son, William, was given command of Banbury Castle, which would remain in royalist hands for four years.

During that time, Banbury families housed, fed and put up with hundreds of soldiers from both armies, as royalists periodically shored up the castle's defense, and alternately parliamentary armies laid siege to royalist defenders inside. Fire destroyed up to 200 dwellings in 1643 alone, and the following year, more than 40 homes near the castle were burned. Looting and burning were common. Murder and treachery were common. Suspected spies for either side were executed on sight. Finally, when the royalist forces learned in 1646 that Charles I had fled to Scotland, the royalists surrendered Banbury Castle. The town by then was devastated. The Fiennes family did not object when townspeople raised the castle and used its stones to rebuild the community.

Banbury, said one account in 1647, "scarce the one-half standing to gaze on the ruins of the other." King Charles I was executed January 30, 1649. After the failure of the Cromwell dictatorship, the monarchy was restored. On May 2, 1661, Samuel Boreman in

Wethersfield received a letter from his sister, Elizabeth (Boreman) Middleton, who wrote from London about the end of Cromwell's reign and the crowning of Charles II.

> "...Charles 2 went through the city from the Tower of London to White Hall in a very greate state with all noble men and their attendants, which was a most glorious show and the next day he was crowned at Westminister, God be praised, we are all in Peace now, the Lord continue it to us..."

Samuel left an estate showing he owned 350 acres, with a value of 742 pounds, 15 shillings. Samuel, who died in April 1673, and Mary (Betts) Boreman, who died in August 3, 1684, had 11 children, including a son, Isaac [#55].

[31] ELIZABETH SHEPARD was born about 1629 in England and came to Massachusetts with her parents, Edward and Violet (Stanley) Shepard [#18], and settled first in Newtowne (Cambridge). Before 1648, Elizabeth married THWAIT STRICKLAND, who was born about 1625, and was an early settler of Dedham, Massachusetts.

Thwait and Elizabeth (Shepard) Strickland moved to Hartford, where they lived with Gregory Wolerton, before moving to Glastonbury. Thwait Strickland died in Glastonbury in 1670. An inventory taken in Hartford showed his estate amounted to 55 pounds, six shillings. His widow, Elizabeth, subsequently married Gregory Wolerton, who died four years later, leaving her 30 acres of land in Hartford. Elizabeth then married Nicholas Disborough [#80], a widower, whose first wife was Mary Bronson of Hartford. Thwait and Elizabeth (Shepard) Strickland had six children, including a son, John [#60].

[32] EDWARD GRISWOLD was born in 1607 near Kenilworth, Warwickshire, a son of GEORGE GRISWOLD and grandson of FRANCIS GRISWOLD of Solihull, a nearby village. In 1638, Rev. Ephraim Huet, a minister at Wraxall, near Kenilworth, was persecuted by Anglican authorities for neglecting the ceremonies of the established church. The following year Rev. Huet organized a company to immigrate to New England. Accompanying Rev. Huet were Edward and his wife, MARGARET, their four sons and Edward's brothers, Matthew

and Thomas. They settled with Rev. Huet in Windsor. Edward's brother, Thomas, eventually returned to England after the Puritan revolution made life more bearable there. The return of Thomas and hundreds like him caused New England land values to drop. Edward's brother, Matthew, relocated to Saybrook, in land now in the town of Lyme. Edward's two sons, Francis and George, also moved to Saybrook, joining their uncle in 1655.

Edward stayed in Windsor until 1663 when he and Margaret moved to a new area west of Saybrook they called Killingworth, after their home in Warwickshire. Killingworth was the name used for Kenilworth in England in Elizabethan times. Today the area of Killingworth, Connecticut, where Edward and his family settled, is called Clinton.

Edward was a deputy from Killingworth to the Connecticut General Court in 1667 and a Commissioner of Killingworth that year. On August 23, 1670, Margaret died. Three years later, Edward married the widow of James Bemis of New London. In 1674, Edward was granted 200 acres at the north end of the Lyme bounds. From 1678 through 1689, Edward served again at Killingworth's deputy in the General Court. In 1678, he was appointed to a committee to establish a Latin School in New London. He also was the First Deacon of the Killingworth Church. Edward, who died in 1691, and Margaret Griswold, who died August 23, 1670, had at least 10 children, including a son, Francis [#58].

[33] JOHN COWLE was born in England and immigrated to New England where his name appears in Hartford in 1640. John's wife was named HANNAH. John and Hannah Cowle moved to Farmington where he served as selectman in 1652, and was a deputy to the Connecticut General Court in 1653, and 1654. John moved to Hadley, Massachusetts and settled in Hatfield in early 1660/1, where he was listed as a freeman in 1666. John Cowle probably died in Hatfield March 1676 during King Philips' War. His wife, Hannah, returned to Hartford, where she died March 6, 1683, at age 70. Hannah Cowle was buried at the Center Church in Hartford. John and Hannah Cowle had seven children, including son Samuel [#49].

[34] EDWARD BENTON was born in 1628 in Wiltshire and immigrated to New England where his name is first recorded in Guilford when he was admitted as a freeman in 1650. Benton's wife, MARY, was born about January 1642/3. Before 1669, Benton and his family joined 50 others in moving to Wethersfield, where he purchased 150 acres of land from the Indians for three shillings and three pence. Edward, who died at Wethersfield February 20, 1698, and Mary Benton, who died in Wethersfield August 8, 1702, had seven children, including daughter Rebecca [#78].

[35] JOHN SAVAGE first appears in Connecticut colonial records in Hartford on the occasion of his marriage on February 16, 1652, to ELIZABETH DUBBIN (Dublin). The details of John Savage's immigration are unknown; however, the name Savage appears several times in the parish records of Banbury and Claydon in Oxfordshire in the late 16th and early 17th centuries. Could John Savage have been like Connecticut immigrants Mary Betts and Samuel Boreman, who left Banbury and Claydon in the first migration of religious dissidents in the 1630s and 1640s?

There is no proof but evidence of a Banbury connection to John Savage is strong. In Banbury, records show that Thomas and Margaret Savage had at least three sons, Bennet, John and Thomas, Jr. Elder Thomas Savage was baptized March 29, 1572, and was buried the following September 17. On July 4, 1574, his widow, Margaret, married Thomas Harrys, a prosperous yeoman of nearby had at Calthrope. Thomas and Margaret (Savage) Harrys had a son, Matthew, who was born and baptized February 22, 1576/7. These relationships became known as a result of Bennet Savage's will, which was proved after Bennet's death June 29, 1593, in which he left bequests to John Savage, Thomas Savage, and Matthew Harrys, who he identified as his brothers. We also know that in 1594 Margaret (Savage) Harrys died in Calthrope and remembered her son, "John Savadge of Ladbrooke," and his four children with a legacy of "four stryke of barlie."

Could our ancestor, John Savage, be among the descendants of Thomas and Margaret Savage, whose son, John Savadge of Ladbrooke, was identified in his mother's will in Banbury in 1594? One possible time that John Savage could have arrived in America is 1636. George Wyllys, a prosperous Puritan from Fenny Compton, near Claydon, employed 20 indentured servants from the Banbury area under the command of William Gibbins to go to Hartford and build a home and prepare for the Wyllys family's arrival in 1638. The 20 men built the Wyllys family estate, where George Wyllys resided in 1638, the year he became Magistrate in Hartford. He became Governor in 1642. Subsequent generations of Savage sons were given the name Willis. Despite the different spelling, this may have been in memory of an early patron.

However he arrived, John Savage was among the first settlers of Mattabesset, today's Middletown. His name in Middletown colonial records appears with several spellings, including Savig, Savige, and Savidg. The spelling of his wife Elizabeth's last name is sometimes D'Aubin and Dublin. Their marriage record in Hartford spells the names Savage and Dubbin.

A family historian from a previous generation, James Francis Savage of Lowell, Massachusetts, wrote that in 1707 John Dublin petitioned the Rhode Island Assembly for compensation for a gunshot wound to the head he received when he served with Col. John Wanton and their vessel was seized by French pirates. J. F. Savage wrote that he believed John Dublin of Rhode Island was a nephew of Mrs. Elizabeth (Dubbin) Savage of Middletown, Connecticut.

The name Savage is of Norman origin, owing to the French word sauvage, meaning beast or wild one. It was likely given to William le Sauvage, who was among the Normans with William the Conqueror. William le Sauvage received his rewards and his descendants spread throughout England and Ireland.

The ancestor we know in New England as John Savage first appeared in Hartford with his marriage record in 1652 and later when he was made a freeman in Middletown on May 18, 1654. Middletown first appears in colonial records August 15, 1639, when the General Court in Hartford ordered a group of 100 men to go to Mattabesset to deal with Sowhead, the Indian sachem, who was suspected of harboring Indians who had murdered English settlers. The name Mattabesset means "a place at a great brook."

On October 30, 1646, the General Court appointed a committee to look into settling Mattabesset. Three years later the committee reported that lands on both sides of Little River could support 15 families; the first families arrived in 1650. Choosing a section of land some 50 feet above the western banks of the Connecticut River, the settlers built shelters in a wide area they cleared to prevent a surprise attack by the still unpredictable Sowhead, who had his headquarters on what is today known as Indians Hill.

The settlers built crude houses. The women cleared patches of land to plant food. A large elm tree served as the settlers' first meeting house until 1652, when a 20-by-10-foot shelter was constructed inside a palisade of upright timbers forming a wide circle for protection. Worshipers were summoned to meeting by a drum, which signified that the area was clear of Indians. During the early meetings, armed guards stood outside to watch for attack.

Each of the new families was allotted a house plot of five acres. In time, John Savage and other settlers branched from the center of the village into the area across the marshes of Little River to the north on the Connecticut River shore, an area called Middletown's Upper Houses, today's Cromwell. Among other towns of today included in the original Middletown domain are Berlin, Middlefield, Portland, East Hampton, Haddam and Westfield. On September 11, 1651, the General Court in Hartford decreed:

> ...it is ordered, sentenced and decreed that
> Mattabesset shall be a Town, and that they shall
> make a choice of one of their inhabitants, according
> to order in that case, that so he may take the oath of
> Constable the next convenient season...

The name Middletown was adopted in 1653. The following year, the freemen of Middletown decreed that John Savage was of sufficient means, character and piety to be "mayd free." Thereafter, he could take part in town affairs as a voting member. According to the political practice of the time, to be a freeman one had to be an adult male, possessing an enterprise earning 50 shillings a year or real property valued at 40 pounds, and according to one historian be "honest and civil in conservation, quiet and peaceable in behavior" and be regarded as such by a majority of the town's freemen.

John Savage was a sergeant in the Middletown Train Band (militia), and on September 4, 1668, was one of the founders of the First Congregational Church of Middletown. In 1657 and again in 1674 he was chosen one of the town's two selectmen. In 1674, John Savage possessed 1,207 acres of land. At the time of his death in March 6, 1684/5, John Savage held some 1,254 acres of land and possessions valued at 480 pounds, 12 shillings. John and Elizabeth (Dubbin) Savage had 11 children, including sons John, Jr. [#64], and William [#65].

[36] JOHN JOHNSON, JR., was born in England,

a son of Robert Johnson [#26], and came to New Haven with his parents and three brothers in 1640. On September 30, 1651, John married **HANNAH PARMALEE**, a daughter of John and Hannah Parmalee [#29], who was born in Guilford. John Parmalee and his daughter had moved to New Haven after the death of his wife.

John Johnson, Jr., lived, according to New Haven records, as a "husbandman," witnessing New Haven Colony's growth from its beginnings to its annexation by Connecticut Colony in 1664. During that period, New Haven's commercial ventures had fared poorly, and political events were taking place in England, in the Connecticut River Towns to the north and in Dutch New Amsterdam to the south that would overwhelm the fundamentalist colony.

Compared with New Haven Colony, the Connecticut Colony was prospering. The Fundamental Orders, a reasonably liberal charter by standards of the day, had been adopted in 1639. The effects of these Orders encouraged growth and commerce along the river. Connecticut also gained a veneer of legality under English law with the acquisition Saybrook and its Warwick Patent in 1644, and later New London, which was led by the politically astute John Winthrop, Jr. The Dutch, moreover, were expelled from Hartford's House of Good Hope in 1654, eliminating any Dutch threat.

Following the execution of Charles I in 1646, both Connecticut and New Haven Colonies operated independently of Cromwell's England and, to a large extent, from each other. The exception was the confederation of 1643 called the United Colonies of New England, when Connecticut, New Haven, Plymouth and Massachusetts Bay established a method for their common defense against Indian threats, the French to the north and the Dutch to the south. Despite this alliance, the four colonies guarded their independence. Yet for Connecticut, concern over its legal status grew after the monarchy was restored in England in 1660.

Connecticut Governor John Winthrop, Jr., sailed for England that year intent on securing the future of his colony in the eyes of England's new king, Charles II. Details of the negotiations are sketchy, yet envoys from New Haven were also lobbying the crown, and back home Connecticut and New Haven were negotiating their future as well. However, Winthrop was a skilled politician and knew many in the English Court. Using the Warwick Patent for Saybrook, which was now part of Connecticut, as the basis for his appeal, Winthrop succeeded in persuading Charles II to grant, on April 26, 1662, a royal charter to the Connecticut

Colony, which, in effect, endorsed with few changes the corporate government already in place under the Fundamental Orders.

Ironically, the charter granted nearly full self-government to Connecticut at just the time the new monarch was seeking to establish greater royal control over England's colonial affairs. The charter was similar to the provisions of a private joint-stock trading company, providing that men of sufficient property and reputation (freemen) could choose their own governor, deputy governor, council and house of representatives, which at the time was called a General Court.

The royal charter was forwarded to Connecticut, where it was read to freemen in Hartford October 9. Among its consequential provisions were that the boundaries noted in the charter ignored the boundaries of New Haven Colony. Connecticut had been granted exclusive right to the land south of Massachusetts, west of Rhode Island to the Pacific Ocean, then called the South Sea.

When details of the boundary provisions became known, New Haven's Rev. John Davenport and his followers were enraged. At one point, residents of New Haven's outer communities took up arms and threatened to make war on Connecticut to prevent their annexation into the colony of the River Towns. But New Haven was in a bind. Negotiations had failed. The charter was valid, signed by the king. Moreover, to the south was Dutch New Amsterdam. The Dutch and English had been adversaries for years, having been to war three times since 1648, primarily over colonial competition. During the last of these conflicts, Charles II on April 2, 1664, sent four English frigates under the command of his brother James, the Duke of York, to the harbor of New Amsterdam. The king granted James all the land between Maine and New Amsterdam Bay, as well as land south to Delaware Bay that was not already settled and occupied by English settlers under a valid charter. The Duke of York's forces arrived in August and by September 9 the Dutch in New Amsterdam had surrendered. On September 24, the Dutch at Fort Orange, today's Albany, surrendered without firing a shot. On October 4, the name of New Amsterdam was changed to New York.

In the months following James' capture of Dutch New Amsterdam, the new leaders of New York contended that their domain went north to the Connecticut River. The New Haven Colony was in peril. Unless Rev. Davenport agreed to Connecticut's annexation of his colony, he might, in his words, fall into the grip of New York's "Royalists, Romanists, and Stuarts." On December 13, 1664, Rev. Davenport, declaring that "Christ's interest in New Haven Colony was miserably lost," agreed to the union with Connecticut Colony.

John and Hannah (Parmalee) Johnson were among the New

Haven colonials who thus became members of the Connecticut Colony. John, who died in 1687, and Hannah (Parmalee) Johnson, who died about 1693, had nine children, including a son, John III [#76].

[37] THOMAS RANNEY was born in Scotland in 1616 and came to New England where his name first appeared in Middletown in 1658 when records note that Thomas Rany was granted a house lot. In May 1659, Thomas married MARY HUBBARD, born in Hartford, January 16, 1641/2, the eldest daughter of George and Elizabeth (Watts) Hubbard [#20].

The name Rheny is common in Scotland. In 1698, a Scots lawyer in Middletown named Alexander Rollo, who had married a daughter of a local citizen, witnessed a will wherein a man he identified as "Thomas Rheny" gave his son, Ebenezer, a parcel of land. Some family members would use that spelling. However, when Ebenezer's brother obtained adjoining land, he spelled his last name Rany. Ranney family descendants believe Rollo correctly identified their ancestor as a fellow countryman, choosing the common Scots spelling Rheny for the name at that time. The name however took many forms; over the generations it has been spelled Rany, Rheny, Renny and Rainie.

Thomas Ranney was not a member of the church, but served on various town committees and took an active and influential part in community affairs. Ranney called himself a husbandman, and in the census of 1670, when the inhabitants were rated, Ranney was rated as possessing 105 pounds, the ninth in a list of 52 proprietors. Given Ranney's lack of church affiliation, his Scots background and subsequent prosperity, it is possible that Ranney came first to Hartford and then to Middletown in a military capacity and his rewards for service gave him standing in community life.

In his will, George Hubbard gave to his daughter "forty shillings out of my Estate, but on further consideration instead of that forty shillings I give my sayd daughter the on halfe of my halfe Mille Lott on the East side the Great River by the List of 1673." George Hubbard's Middletown homestead was on Main Street extending south from what is now Rapello Avenue to the Connecticut River.

Thomas, who died June 25, 1713, and was buried at the Second Church of Christ in that portion of Middletown today called Cromwell, and Mary (Hubbard) Ranney, who died December 18, 1721, had 11 children, including daughter Mary [#64].

[38] **REBECCA NEWELL** was born in January 1643, the oldest child of Thomas and Rebecca (Olmsted) Newell of Farmington [#5]. Rebecca married **JOSEPH WOODFORD**, who was born in England, and came to New England where he was proposed as a freeman in Farmington in 1663. Rebecca (Newell) Woodford died in Farmington March 29, 1700. Joseph Woodford died in Farmington where the inventory of his will was made October 25, 1710. Joseph and Rebecca (Newell) Woodford had nine children, including Elizabeth [#73].

[39] **BALTAZAR DE WOLFF** first appears in colonial records in the 1640s in Connecticut. Tradition holds that Baltazar came from Livonia on the Baltic Sea. Baltazar married **ALICE PECK**, the daughter of Deacon William Peck and his wife Elizabeth [#15].

How Baltazar came to New England has been researched by family members for generations. The most recent and best account was written by Carol S. Maginnis, who established Baltazar's links to pre-colonial Europe in her 1992 volume, *Dolphs & DeWolfs*, published by Richard Dolph.

The first de Wolff was Louis de Saint-Etienne, an attendant of King Charles V, who accompanied the French king on a hunt in 1370. During the hunt, a wolf cub crossed the king's path. After the king threw a lance to kill the cub, the wolf cub's mother rushed the king. Before it could harm the king, Louis killed the she-wolf. For this, Charles V knighted him as Louis de Loup. (Loup is French for wolf.) In 1423, Margrave Frederick the Warlike, of the Meissen House of Wettin, was made governor of Elector Saxony. His eldest son was to marry Princess Mathilda of France, and one of her attendants who made the trip to Germany was Emile de Loup, a grandson of Louis. Once in Saxony, Emile became a favorite of the Saxon court and in 1427 was rewarded with the title of baron and granted estates, after which he changed his name from the French de Loup to the German de Wolff.

Emile's grandson, Frederic de Wolff of Saxony, was commissioned in 1517 by the Prince of the House of Saxe to settle the boundaries of various principalities with the Imperial Diet. Emperor Maximilian was so pleased with his work, he made Frederic a baron of the Holy Roman Empire. Baron Frederic I and his son and grandsons, II and II, continued to prosper in Saxony, serving as diplomats, envoys and negotiators; De Wolffs were ambassadors to various courts in France and England in the 16th 17th and 18th centuries.

Maximilian de Wolff, the second son of Baron Frederic I,

was the apparent ancestor to Baltazar, the American immigrant. Emperor Charles V granted Maximilian land near Ghent in Belgium. After receiving his grant Maximilian was made a baron; he took up residence in Belgium in 1534. In this era, a member of Maximilian de Wolff's family made his way to a Saxon stronghold on the Baltic Sea called Livonia.

Livonia entered the Saxon world three centuries before when Saxon merchants from Lubeck and Bremen came to the area now called Latvia and Estonia and began trading with the inhabitants of Finno-Ugrian stock (people of north Russia) along the Dvina River who called themselves Livs. Soon missionaries joined the traders, and in time both required protection.

In 1202, the third Bishop of Livonia, Albert von Buxhoevden, founded the Order of the Brothers of the Sword. Their main duty was to protect the church conquests in Livonia and convert local tribes to Christianity. The Livonian Knights were an organization of these crusading knights who conquered Livonia between 1202 and 1237. Consecrated by the pope in 1204, the Livonian Knights assumed the code of the Knights Templar, who were sworn to obedience, poverty and celibacy. Members of the order included soldiers, artisans and clerics. By 1206, the order was firmly established as the dominant power in the land of the Livs, who lived between mouths of the Dvina and Gauja rivers. By 1217, the Livonian Knights had conquered not only the neighboring Latvian tribes north of the Dvina but also southern Estonia. The Knights then began the conquest of the lands south of the Dvina but encountered resistance from the Kurs and Semigallians.

In 1236, the Livonian Knights were defeated. Because of this defeat and its interest in booty, not conversions, the pope disbanded the order the following year and reorganized it under the Teutonic Knights, whose main base was in Prussia.

The Teutons, a Germanic people from Jutland (Denmark and Scandinavia) had first clashed with Romans before the birth of Christ, and had come to dominate today's north central Europe. Teutons were cousins of the barbarian Jutes, Saxons and Angles, who in the fifth century migrated to Britain.

By the 11th Century, as the Roman church became stronger and wishing to counter the rising Islamic Turks, the European tribes organized a series of Crusades to retake the Holy Land of Jerusalem and Syria from the Muslims. The Third Crusade began in 1189 with Emperor Frederick I Barbarossa marching his Germanic armies toward the Holy Land. When he drowned after his victory June 10, 1190, in the River Saleph, his son Duke Frederick of Swabia led the army to the city of Acre near Jerusalem, where he too was killed. England's Richard I (the Lion-

Hearted) and Phillip II Augustus of France assumed leadership of the warriors who took Acre. The siege ended with an armistice with the Turk Saladin, who ceded the coastal strip of Tyre and Jaffa to the Christians as well as pilgrimage rights to Jerusalem.

A consequence of this crusade was the founding of a series of religious military orders, including the Knights of St. John, the Knights Templars and the Teutonic Knights. Each combined the vows of the monk (poverty, chastity, and obedience) with the chores of the knight (protection of the oppressed). The Teutonic Knights were founded in 1190 before the conquest of Acre, as a fraternity to serve the sick. Eight years later the Teutonic Knights became a chivalric military order.

As Saxons, the Teutonic Knights were called to Transylavania but were expelled in 1225 by the Hungarians. With the Germanic expansion to Prussia, the Teutonic Knights ventured there in 1309 to protect the Saxon settlements along the Baltic Coast from a base in Marienburg. Their authority lasted more than a century.

Over the next 50 years, the order exterminated most of the indigenous Prussians and took over the land. One third of the territory was given to the church, the order developed the region by establishing castles and inviting Germans to settle the territory. They monopolized the grain trade. By 1309, the order's grand master established the base at Marienburg, and the order expanded its control over Prussia, moving eastward into the Baltic lands of Courland, Livonia and Estonia. Over the next century, the order continued to extend its power by land purchase, unsuccessfully trying to conquer and convert Lithuania but also actively protecting the cities of the Hanseatic League.

During this time, Germanic traders along the Baltic formed a commercial federation that became known as the Hanse League. Originating in the island town of Wisby on Gotland between today's Estonia and Sweden, the Germanic traders followed the Knights throughout the coastal Baltic and established a "hanse" or group that instituted modern bookkeeping, sales on credit and agents' commissions in a series of coastal and river towns, as well as immigration embarkation points for settlers to Livonia and Prussia.

By 1358, the League gave traders certain benefits: storage rights and the ability to maintain inventories, unified actions such as boycotts or embargoes. Ultimately more than 200 cities and towns were part of the Hanse League, which lasted for more than 200 years. Among its port towns were London, Hamburg, Bergen in Norway and Riga in Livonia.

In 1525, Albert of Brandenburg of the Hohenzollern line converted to Protestantism, resigned as grand master of the Teutonic Knights, dissolved the knights in Prussia, transformed the order's territory into a Polish duchy and made himself a Duke. In 1561, his successor in Livonia, the landmeister of the Livonia branch, Gotthard Kettler, also dissolved his order, distributed Livonian lands among Poland, Lithuania and Sweden and became a secular duke of Courland, which was made a fief of Poland.

It was during this turbulent time that a son of Maximilian de Wolff found his way to Riga and into the service of Landmeister Kettler, who granted the de Wolff adventurer large estates and made him a baron of Riga. But in the late 16th century, the Russians, Swedes, Poles and Danes all attempted to gain advantage in the former Livonia, making the Baltic region unstable and perilous but providing commercial opportunity. Baron de Wolff thrived.

For a time the Teutonic Knights were able to hold out against the Russians, but Russians allied with Tartars destroyed Livonia and nearly destroyed Riga before they themselves were defeated by Polish armies. By 1561, the Livonian Knights had disbanded and Jacob Kettler, Gotthard's grandson, who had inherited the grand master title, developed Livonian resources by building ships to transport the products of Kurzeme and Livonia to the world. Kettler's shipyards constructed a maritime fleet of 59 men-of-war and 60 large merchant ships, at a time when, for example, Sweden had 30 ships and France 18. Kettler's shipyards also constructed ships for England and Venice, and he established two colonies in Africa and trade routes for his vessels between a variety of ports in Europe and America.

Despite this maritime prosperity, the Livonian agriculture and forestry business was at a standstill and life in the next century a chaotic misery. Castles and large estates fell in ruin. Denmark, Russia and Sweden, still eager to absorb Livonia for themselves, turned the area into a continuing battlefield. Kettler wrote the Council of Revel on December 22, 1560:

> "...news is reaching us of some young noblemen who attack and kill poor peasants coming into town and raid the country, ravaging and plundering pleasant farms..."

The conflict of the Protestant Reformation added to the chaos, with followers of Luther clashing with forces loyal to Rome. Disease took its toll, with a plague in 1610 killing peasants in huge numbers. In 1618, the Riga Town Council reported that the situation in Livonia was

> "...very regrettable as battles, fires, and destruction have devastated her. The king's soldiers seek only

food for themselves and work on the land has stopped."

Finally, in 1621, with Poland distracted elsewhere, Sweden's Gustavus Adolphus seized Riga. German nobles from the more than 170 landed proprietory families from Livonia petitioned the Swedish king for their rights. Though they failed to obtain full rights under Sweden, they maintained control of Livonia. Sweden's rule was reasonably benign, with Gustavus founding a university at Dorphat in 1632 for the study of Protestant theology and schools to educate the peasants of Riga, Taryu and Tallin. For the German nobility, they maintained hunting and fishing rights, even on peasant farms, as well as the rights to all industrial and commercial enterprise, including the lucrative forestry trade, in which Baltic timber was eagerly traded on the Baltic Exchange in London.

It was around the time Sweden took control of Livonia that one of the younger sons of the Baron de Wolff of Riga was born. De Wolff family histories in Livonia report that this son, well-educated and seeking adventure, sailed away from Livonia with an English trader or with a captain from Kurzeme. The Livonian family never heard from this young man again.

De Woff family historians in America, however, believe the young man's name was Baltazar De Wolff, a well-educated attorney, drafter of contracts and deeds, and business agent who appeared in Connecticut in the 1640s and would make his living among the prosperous in New London, Lyme, Saybrook, Hartford, Middletown, Wethersfield, Guilford, and New Haven.

Baltazar De Wolff married Alice Peck, the daughter of William and Elizabeth Peck [#15]. He was probably married to Alice Peck and residing in Middletown when his name first appeared in Hartford public records on March 5, 1656. He was among those "p'sented for smoaking in the streets contra to the law by Will Marcum, constable for Mattabesick (Middletown)..." Baltazar and the others were fined six pence each. Family tradition report the perhaps-apocryphal tale that Baltazar paid his fine, lit his pipe and walked out.

Six months later, the Wethersfield court authorized Baltazar De Wolff as an attorney empowered to collect on behalf of Charlestown merchant Matthew Price any debts owed him by residents within Connecticut or New Haven's jurisdiction. Despite his brush with smoking laws in Middletown, Baltazar was often cited in records for such work. He was an agent for his father-in-law William Peck, then a New Haven merchant; for William Masuer [#59], a merchant from Wethersfield and Lyme, and for Major William Whiting, one of Hartford's most prosperous commercial promoters.

Baltazar also was a breeder of riding horses, with Saybrook records indicating he sold horses with not only town markings or brands, but also cut ears indicating pedigree and ancestry. It also appears that Baltazar had detailed knowledge of carpentry and timber, as he and his sons and grandsons all were known as carpenters, joiners and sawyers in Lyme, and in the operations of lumber mills. The origins of these skills likely came from Livonia's forestry and lumber works.

Norwich was created as a result of an act of gratitude by Uncas, the Mohegan sachem who in 1659 sold a nine-square mile tract to several Saybrook men for 70 pounds. Two years earlier Thomas Leffingwell had delivered a canoe full of provisions to the Mohegan fort while it was under siege by warring Narragansetts. A number of Saybrook families moved to this new area, called Norwich, taking with them their minister, Rev. James Fitch, the town clerk and their meeting book. Jeremiah Peck [#41], Baltazar's brother-in-law, was asked to move from Guilford to Saybrook to assume the duties of pastor in 1661 and given land as an inducement. Jeremiah's father, William, was among the wealthiest men on the coast and with a few others he purchased a great deal of the available land in Saybrook. William Peck gave his daughter Alice, Baltazar's wife, her own dower in her own name, believing that women should own property in their own right. Baltazar paid 100 pounds for the right to land on the east side of the Connecticut River in 1661.

Baltazar and his wife Alice were living in East Saybrook in 1661 when their youngest child died. Feelings against sorcery and witchcraft were running high. In 1657, the General Court in Hartford reported "Suspicions about Whitchery" in Saybrook. Two years later, the Hartford General Court sent Samuel Wyllys to Saybrook to help Major Mason investigate and take whatever action was necessary. In time, the death of Baltazar and Alice's child persuaded the court to act:

> "Hartford Quarter Court of September 5, 1661:
> The Inditement of Nicholas and Margaret Jennings:
> Nicholas Jennings, though art here indited by the
> name of Nicholas Jennings of Sea Brook for not
> haueing the feare of God before thine eyes; thou hast
> enterteined familiarity with Satan, the great enemy of
> God and mankind, and by his help hase done works
> aboue the course of nature of ye loss and ye lives of
> several psons and in p'ticuler ye wife of Reynolds
> Marvin with ye Child of Baalshar de Wolf, with other
> Sorceries, for wch according to ye Law of God and ye
> Established Laws of this Common Wealth though
> deservest to die..."

On October 9, 1661, a 12-man jury including Samuel Boreman [#30] couldn't reach a unanimous decision. Jennings stayed in jail, however, until the following spring when the court disallowed the testimony of the Saybrook constables and declined to pay the lawmen's travel expenses to Hartford to clarify the facts. Jennings life was spared, but he was bankrupted while in prison and had to sell his goods. Some of these sales were arranged by Baltazar or witnessed by him, indicating he continued in his role within the legal bureaucracy despite the fact that his child's death was one of the points at issue.

East Saybrook, located on the east side of the Connecticut River, broke away from Saybrook after more than 30 families and their minister applied to the General Court in Hartford, which agreed to the proposition May 9, 1667, to call the new town Lyme. Baltazar and his wife Alice were both landowners in Lyme at the time, making Alice the only married woman in 1667 to own property in her own name, which derived from the Peck family's point-of-view that a woman needed to have independence and security of her own. Thereafter, Baltazar and his wife and their children appear numerous times in public records dealing with land transactions.

One episode not involved with land transactions was the narrative about Baltazar's dispute with Nathaniel Collins. Hannah De Wolff, Baltazar and Alice's daughter, had gone to work for Collins for a year, but Baltazar tried to take Hannah away before her year was up. Collins refused. The dispute became so heated Collins and Baltazar took each other to Hartford Court. The court found that Baltazar had spoken and written too harshly about Collins.

> "March 23, 1668: ...we find some expressions not
> well agreeing with truth and many expressions where-
> in he hath in a most vaine manner used the scripture
> thereby endeavoring to scandalize Mr. Collins & to
> make him odious to all that should see & hear the
> same, fore which offense we see good reason to binde
> him to his good behavior...doe declare that we find
> that Hannah the Daughter of the sayd Baltazer is still
> Mr. Collins his servant till her year is out..."

The Court ordered Baltazar to pay the court a fine of 10 pounds. Baltazar was elected a Lyme townsman in 1672, and served in that post with his son, Edward. He also was given a license by Lyme to operate a public house on Lyme Road, known as an ordinary, where liquor could be sold. He held that license from March 31, 1674, until December 23, 1678, when the license was given to William Masuer [#59], who later became father-in-law to Baltazar's son, Edward, after his marriage.

Twenty years later, when James II succeeded his brother Charles II on the British throne, James II banded the New York, New Jersey and New England colonies into one province with Edward Andros as governor. Andros dismissed the Massachusetts assembly, abolished colonial courts and forced framers to pay a fee for titles to the land allotted to them by their towns as well as a tax on the lands. On December 27, 1688, Baltazar was listed as a yeoman and taxed 40 pounds for his son Peter (under 16 years of age), house and land, four cows, two yearlings and a mare. Alice died in early 1689. The following year, Baltazar gave the rest of his land at Duck River Swamp to his son Edward, who sold half to another son, Simon. Baltazar died in 1696. Among Baltazar's and Alice's children, was a son, Edward [#59].

[40] JOHN MEAD was born in 1634 in Elmdon, Essex, a son of William Mead [#9], and immigrated with his family to New England, settling in Stamford in 1641. In 1657, John married **HANNAH POTTER**, a daughter of William Potter [#25], who at the time owned Shippan Point. The year of their marriage, John and Hannah moved to Hempstead, Long Island Plantation, which the New Haven Colony established in 1644. On October 26, 1660, after three years in Hempstead, John and Hannah returned to the Connecticut shoreline to purchase "several score" acres, some buildings and livestock from Richard Crab in Elizabeth Neck, today's Old Greenwich.

Old Greenwich was settled in 1640; the land was purchased from the Indians by agents of New Haven Colony, whose claim to the land was disputed by the Dutch in nearby New Amsterdam. In 1650 the Dutch ceded all Greenwich claims to Connecticut Colony. In 1656, Greenwich became part of Stamford and thus returned to the jurisdiction of New Haven Colony. In 1660, a second tract of land was purchased in an area between the Bryam and Mianus Rivers now included in the town of Greenwich. On February 5, 1664, the 27 Proprietors of Old Greenwich selected seven men to consider the fairest way to apportion the new land among themselves. John Mead was among the seven, who divided the common lands "by the rule of proportion." The following year on May 11, the Connecticut General Court declared that Greenwich shall be a township itself, "provided they can procure and maintain an Orthodox Minister." In 1672, John Mead was among the 27 Proprietors of Greenwich who purchased land from the Indians, then called Miosehasseky or Horseneck, in the western section of today's Greenwich. This transaction earned John

Mead and the others the title "the 27 Proprietors of 1672."

John Mead was a prosperous and self-possessed man with a strong character. A family story related how he tolerated little nonsense. One day he was riding through the Greenwich countryside to a mill when he came upon a Quaker struggling under the weight of a sack of grain, his destination also the mill. John offered the Quaker a ride, suggesting to the pedestrian that he hoist the sack of grain up in front of him, and then himself behind.

"I will do no such thing," the Quaker said. "I can read a man's mind, and you want to steal my grain and leave me here."

Put off by the accusation, John rode on. A short distance ahead, he came to a stream, swollen from the rain. John stopped his horse and waited until the Quaker came to the stream and watched as the Quaker contemplated his peril at crossing the waterway. Again John offered the Quaker a ride. This time, seeing that crossing the waterway might be too dangerous on foot, the pedestrian reconsidered and accepted John's offer of help. John quickly hoisted the Quaker's grain sack in front of him and pulled the Quaker up behind him on the horse.

Midway across the stream, which rose to just below the riders' feet, John stopped his horse and bent over as if to adjust his stirrup. Instead of grabbing the stirrup, John grabbed the Quaker's boot and, with a jerk, pulled the passenger's leg up. The Quaker fell backwards into the chilly water.

When the Quaker reappeared, John shouted: "That will teach you to accuse me of trying to steal your grain. You said you could read a man's mind. Well, when I offered you the ride the first time I did so in kindness. The second time I meant to throw you in the river, as I have just done. Next time you will think twice before accusing another, and boasting you can read a man's thoughts." John left the Quaker in mid-stream to consider the lesson and rode to the other side of the waterway where he threw the sack of grain onto the ground.

John Mead was chosen a deputy from Greenwich to the Connecticut General Court in 1679, 1680 and 1686. John, who died in 1699, and his wife, Hannah (Potter) Mead, had 11 children, including three sons, Ebenezer [#68], Benjamin [#69] and Samuel [#71].

[41] JEREMIAH PECK was born in 1623 in London and came to New England at age 14 aboard the *Hector* with his parents, William and Elizabeth Peck [#15], in 1637. Jeremiah moved with his parents to New Haven and attended Harvard. He first taught school in Guilford, where he met and on

November 12, 1656, married **JOHANNAH KITCHELL**, a daughter of **ROBERT KITCHELL**. Jeremiah and Johannah had their first child, Samuel, in Guilford in January 18, 1659. Jeremiah taught school in Guilford from 1656 to 1660. In 1660, he became the first schoolmaster of the Hopkins Grammar School in New Haven, founded at the request of Governor Edward Hopkins. In the autumn of 1661, Jeremiah Peck was invited to preach in Saybrook, where he was ordained and remained as a minister until 1666, when he returned to Guilford.

It was about this time that Rev. Jeremiah Peck's fundamentalist Puritan faith began to conflict with the increasing liberalization of church practices. Reform was causing the various congregations to wonder about the rites of baptism and conversion. Fundamentalists believed that salvation could be attained only through an emotional experience involving complete submission to God's will, that such an experience was necessary for admission to church membership and that only the children of church members were eligible for baptism. Others believed that no such experience was necessary for church membership and that anyone who professed faith should be baptized. But because of strict fundamentalist rules, many parents were not being admitted to church congregations, and an entire generation of children was growing up outside the church. Since town governments were integrated with church memberships this trend was causing considerable problems. In 1657, a synod in Boston recommended a compromise called the Halfway Covenant, which said anyone who professed belief in church doctrines could be admitted to partial church membership, and his children could be baptized, but the professor could not participate in full communion. Connecticut's River Towns adopted the Halfway Covenant in 1662, but New Haven Colony refused to go along until its forced union with Connecticut Colony in 1665.

Jeremiah, a fundamentalist, opposed the Halfway Covenant. When New Haven joined Connecticut, he and his father-in-law, Robert Kitchell, and their families in Guilford joined a movement led by Rev. Abraham Pierson of Branford to move to New Jersey. This group was among the first settlers of Newark in 1666. Jeremiah did not preach in Newark, but in 1669 or 1670 preached in nearby Elizabethtown, N. J.

Greenwich, for its part, was told by the Connecticut General Court in 1669 that in order to become part of Connecticut it had to "procure and maintain an Orthodox Minister." Plans began immediately and a preacher was sought. Jeremiah and his family returned to Connecticut and became one of the original 27 Proprietors of Greenwich in 1672. On September 3, 1678, Rev. Jeremiah Peck was invited to become the first minister of the First

Society of Greenwich. He stayed for 11 years and was dismissed, again, when his Puritan spirit ran afoul of reform.

Said one account:

> "His pastorate was a very quiet and useful one and only disturbed by his refusal in 1688 to baptize children of non-communications allowed by the Halfway Covenant..."

Another account explained:

> "...a controversy arose in 1688 among the members of the Society upon the subject of infant baptism, and the Rev. Mr. Peck refused to baptize the children of non-professors, because he claimed to be unable to find any biblical command authorizing such a practice. He was for a time supported by a majority of the members of the Society."

The matter was brought before a town meeting held on May 21, 1688. The Society heard the protest:

> "We John Mead, Se. [#40] and Jun., Nathaniel Howe, Francis Thorne, Thomas Close [#22], John Hubbe, Sen. and Jonathan Heusted [#89], do enter our protect against ye above sd., rendering this our reason, which is as followeth, that his cause is not according to the ye rules of ye gospel Mr. Jeremiah Pck refusing to baptise our children. Secondly, ye above sd John Mead's reasons are because sd Jeremiah Peck hath given him John Mead offence...".

Rev. Jeremiah Peck received a vote of support from a majority that night. However, after another year of preaching, so many new members had taken offense that Rev. Jeremiah Peck was dismissed at the end of 1689, his 11-year career in Greenwich over. He was invited by Waterbury residents to settle with them in the ministry and given a house and lot, a propriety of 150 pounds, and the full benefit of all town divisions, plus an annual salary of 60 pounds, of which 50 was to be paid in provisions and 10 in wood.

Rev. Peck served Waterbury as an Orthodox minister until a short time before his death in June 1699 at age 77. His wife, Johannah (Kitchell) Peck died in Waterbury in 1711. Jeremiah and Johannah had six children, including a son, Samuel [#66].

[42] JOHN WAKEFIELD arrived in New England were his name first appears in Watertown in 1646. Family tradition holds that John Wakefield lived before and after that date in New Haven, where he is referred to as "the miller," was married to **ANN** and possessed considerable property. At one time John Wakefield employed Edward Grannis [#57], who one day would become his son-in-law. John Wakefield died in 1660 and an inventory of 116 pounds, three shillings were proved in his will December 4, 1660. After his death, leaving three daughters, his widowed wife, Ann, married James Clarke in New Haven October 17, 1661. John and Ann Wakefield had three daughters, including, Hannah [#57].

[43] ROBERT ROYCE and MARY SIMS of Long Sutton, Somersetshire married June 4, 1634 in Martock, Somersetshire. The couple immigrated to New England where Robert Royce is listed as an early settler in Stratford, Connecticut who moved to New London in 1657.

In New London, Robert Royce was a constable in 1660 and a deputy from New London to Connecticut's General Court in 1660. Robert Royce died in New London before September 22, 1676. Mary (Sims) Royce died about 20 years later in Wallingford. Robert and Mary (Sims) Royce had seven children, including son Samuel [#50].

[44] NATHANIEL WHITE was born about 1629 in Chelmsford, Essexshire, a son of John and Mary (Levit) White [#3], and came to New England with Rev. Thomas Hooker's company, settling in Hartford in 1636. In 1650, Nathaniel moved to Middletown and was one of its original proprietors. He settled in Middletown's Upper Houses, where his home was located in the lower part of the village on a street now between the Middlesex Turnpike and the Connecticut River in Cromwell.

May 24, 1653, records in Middletown show that Nathaniel's father, John White, also was granted "30 acres of upland, and joining his homelot, being his proportion of Sowhead fields." Records also indicate that on that day, John White was granted "his second and third divisions at Wongonk."

Nathaniel held various town offices and was a captain in the Middletown Train Band (militia). From 1659 to 1710, Nathaniel was selected a total of 85 times to be Middletown's deputy to the Connecticut General Court in Hartford. In 1669, the

General Court selected him magistrate and commissioner for Middletown, and in 1684 the same offices for Middletown, Haddam and Meriden, where he held court.

Nathaniel's, sister, Sarah White, born in Hartford, had moved in 1659 to Hadley when her parents, John and Mary (Levit) White [#3]. By the time her parents returned to Connecticut in 1671, Sarah had made a life for herself in Hadley. Her first husband, Stephen Taylor, died and was buried in Hadley September 8, 1665. Sarah, a mother of at least one child, married Barnabas Hinsdale in that segment of Hadley called Hatfield on October 15, 1666.

Hatfield originally was that segment of Hadley founded on the west side of the Connecticut River. Within a few years however, difficulties of conducting business across the river—church services and town meetings, etc.—caused the "west-siders" to ask the General Court for their independence. On May 31, 1670, the west side was incorporated as Hatfield.

Sarah (White) (Taylor) Hinsdale moved with her husband and his family to a new community called Pocumtuck (Deerfield), where the family prospered until tragedy struck September 18, 1675, at what is known today as the Bloody Brook Massacre during King Philip's War. She and the others on the frontier of colonial New England experienced King Philip's War, one of the turning points in the history of North America.

For an understanding of the Bloody Creek Massacre and King Philip's War, I have relied on Richard Melvoin's excellent work, *New England Outpost—War & Society in Colonial Deerfield* for the descriptions that follow.

The community they called Pocumtuck had first been occupied by Indians of that name who were wiped out in June 1664 by a raiding party of Mohawk from the western Iroquois nations, as part of the continuing struggle among the native tribes in American northeast.

Pocumtuck, known today as Deerfield, is located just a mile below the Great Falls in the Connecticut River where the today's Deerfield River enters into the Connecticut in central Massachusetts. Nestled in a valley of the Berkshire Mountains, the flood plane of this confluence of rivers created an ideal settling for farming and fishing and had encouraged a local tribe named Pocumtucks to establish a village there. The natives grew corn, hunted deer for meat and fished for shad, salmon and alewife.

The Pocumtucks were one of the many Algonkian Indian tribes that inhabited New England. At the time of first English settlement, there were some 100,000 Indians in what is now New England. Thousands of Algonkians lived in the Connecticut River valley.

Among their Indian neighbors were Wappinger and Nipmuck

north up the valley, the Massachusetts tribes to the east, and, to the southeast, the Wampanoags and Narragansetts, New England's largest tribe. West of the Pocumtucks were the Mahicans, neighbors of the Wappingers, and still further north were the various western Abenaki bands. Directly south to central and southern Connecticut were the Pequots and their long-time enemies, the Mohegans, who came to ally themselves with the English not only against the Pequots, but also against their other traditional rivals, the Narragansetts.

Early colonial settlers got along amicably with the Pocumtucks and other Algonkian neighbors. A year after Hartford was established, the Hartford General Court in 1637 considered itself responsible for the land occupied by the "Pacumtucketts" and sought to have the tribe pay wampum for protection. By this time, there was a well established trade and variety of routine interactions between Indians, both as individuals and as tribal groups, and any number of English, Dutch and French pioneers, traders explorers and settlers. Treaties, commercial contracts, and a variety of alliances, partnerships and agreements had been made over the years as a regular feature of life on the frontier.

But the pioneers who first interacted with the Algonkians brought death, no matter their behavior or intentions. During the time Hartford, Windsor and Wethersfield were being established, waves of disease, such as measles and smallpox, swept through the native villages eradicating whole tribes.

Despite this pressure from the colonials, the key relationship among the Indians, particularly after the destruction of the Pequots by the English-Mohegan alliance in the Pequot War in 1637, was the rivalry between the Narragansetts, New England's largest tribe, and the Mohegans, and their leader, Uncas. This conflict, which broke out into war in 1640, continued for years. The Pocumtucks, seeking to navigate between these two rivals, allied themselves with the Narragansetts, and suffered Mohegan raids as a result.

With a few exceptions, the colonial settlements were able to steer clear of these fights for much of this period, seeking to remain neutral in these native disputes. Though a few colonial leaders tried to leverage influence for political advantage, for the most part, the colonials' role was on the sidelines.

To the west, however, the Mohawks of the Iroquois confederation sought to exploit the situation and exert their influence toward the tribes and colonials. The Mohawks were long feared throughout New England for their ability and willingness to make war. However, war and disease had decimated their ranks; one technique favored by Mohawks to replenish their tribe was to take captives during war and absorb them into their tribe.

Mohawk diplomatic emissaries went to the Pocumtuck

village in June 1664 to talk about the shifting alliances with their Algonkian allies and were murdered by the Pocumtucks who feared a Mohawk trick. In retaliation later that year, the Mohawk swept down the Connecticut River valley into Pocumtuck and wiped out the Algonkian tribe.

By coincidence, it happened that a few months after the Mohawks destroyed the Pocumtuck village, colonial explorers from the town of Dedham to the east were looking for a settlement site for pioneers. They found the just-abandoned Indian village ideal. The Dedham explorers were trying to take advantage of a land grant from the Massachusetts General Court awarded to remedy a problem created by the early and eager missionary work being done by Rev. John Eliot in converting Indians.

Rev. Eliot, like many of the New England clergy was from Essexshire, in East Anglia and been educated at Cambridge. In 1645, Rev. Eliot trained himself to speak the Algonkian language and launched a serious-minded evangelical effort. He lectured, raised funds and helped established the Society for the Propagation of the Gospel in New England. One technique was to establish "praying towns" where Christian Indian villages could be built on an English scale and pattern. Rev. Eliot's first "praying town" for Indians began at Natick in 1651 on the Charles River, 18 miles from Boston. In the next 25 years, Rev. Eliot's evangelizing efforts produced 14 towns inhabited by more than 2,500 Indians.

Not everybody liked these towns. For Dedham the problem was that part of Natick, as established by the General Court, was actually on land set aside for Dedham and owned by that town's proprietors. From 1650 to 1662, Dedham had been in litigation about who owned what. Finally Dedham's proprietors petitioned the leadership of Massachusetts Bay to settle their claim. The General Court agreed Dedham had a proper claim and on May 27, 1663, granted Dedham 8,000 acres of land "at any convenient place..." in compensation for the colony's earlier error.

By the fall of the next year, Dedham scouts had found and plotted the abandoned Indian village called Pocumtuck located 12 miles from Hadley, which Sarah (White) Hinsdale's father, John White, Elder William Goodwin, and other "engagers" had founded in 1659.

The Massachusetts General Court approved Dedham's plan to "make a toune of it, to majntejne the ordinances of Christ there once within five yeares." The owners of the new land would be the 79 proprietors of Dedham who would divide the land among themselves according to property and standing. Some sold their parcels, but little action was taken to actually move to Pocumtuck.

At a Dedham town meeting May 18, 1669, Samuel Hinsdale of Hadley told the court he had laid out the town, had purchased a parcel in Pocumtuck from a Dedham proprietor, had plowed a parcel for planting and "demanded the layeing out of the Rights (as a proprietor of Pocumtuck) he had so purchased...that he might settle himselfe upon it..."

It would take time to get the land parcels and ownership issues settled. Samuel Hinsdale appeared again at another Dedham town meeting May 22, 1670, as proprietors settled their interests. By that time, only 30 of the Pocumtuck's original owners remained, among them Samuel Hinsdale, and his father, Robert Hinsdale, an original settler of Dedham and Medfield.

Dedham proprietors soon had sold off most of their interests to settlers and speculators and in February 1673 Samuel Hinsdale was selected the village's first constable and as a representative of Pocumtuck residents in negotiations with Dedham and the Massachusetts General Court. Finally the General Court officially separated Dedham and Pocumtuck permitting Pocumtuck "the liberty of a touneship," increasing its land area from 8,000 acres to a track equal to seven square miles, and authorizing them to hire an orthodox minister.

By November 1673, 24 men had signed their names or marks at the first Pocumtuck meeting. Concerns of the meeting included roads, rights to woodlands, support for the ministry, property lines. Subsequent meetings chose town officers and established procedures to handle boundary disputes, how newcomers to town could purchase more. Pocumtuck already had settled a border dispute with Hatfield its neighbor to the south.

By 1675, within six years of its original settlement by colonials, the town was independent and had some 200 residents. The Hinsdales were the town's largest family, with one fifth of the town's couples Hinsdale relations. Samuel had been the town's first settler, arriving in 1669 at age 26 with his eye on a future plantation. He now possessed enough land to handle 46 cattle and three sheep.

His father, Robert Hinsdale, had moved to Pocumtuck with his second wife, Elizabeth, the widow of John Hawks of Hadley, and mother of a daughter-in-law. Other Hinsdale family members included 36-year-old Barnabas, his wife Sarah (White), and their four children who had given up their "Mansion house" in Hatfield before the move; Experience and Mary (Hawks) and their two children; John and his family; and a son named Ephraim. Robert's daughter, Mary, also had moved to town with her husband, Daniel Weld.

The population of the town was relatively young, and populated by families starting over. Of the new residents, 68 were adults, with the 39 men and 29 women with average at 35 years old. At least 29 of the husbands, like Barnabas Hinsdale, were married a second time. Seven of the 29 women, like Sarah (White) Hinsdale, were married to their second husbands.

Two thirds of the settlers of Pocumtuck came from the three Connecticut River towns to the south, Northhampton, settled in 1654, and Hadley and Hatfield, which began community life in 1659 as one settlement.

By June, 1675, with Pocumtuck possessing a resident population of 200 and on the frontier of colonial settlement in New England, fighting broke out between Indians and colonials in southeastern Massachusetts, 100 miles away.

The conflict had its origins in the earliest days of English settlement. Between 1600 and 1675, the population of Indians in New England had shrunk from 100,000 to about 10,000, primarily because of the disease created by the native's inability to withstand the bacteria and virus brought by the immigrants. Generations of urban life had immunized the English with antibodies Indians did not possess. As a result, the germs brought by the settlers, traders and missionaries decimated the native populations, creating tremendous social pressures on the Indians and their way of life. Furthermore, the beaver trade had created a heated economy with a cycle of boom and bust for Indian traders, and also had introduced alcohol as a commodity. All these factors created tensions jealousies, anxieties, fears and resentments.

As 1675 grew near, the colonial settlers become the focus of an ever-growing anger and resentment. In 1671, a young sachem named Metacom, of the Wampanoag tribe in the Narragansetts, described his feelings when speaking about his father, Massasoit, originally a great and loyal friend of the settlers.

> "When the English first came, my father (Massasoit) was a great man and the English as a litell Child, he constraened other Indians from ranging the English and gave them coren and shewed them how to plant and was free to do them ani good and had let them have a hundred times more land, than now the King had for his own people."

The speaker, who became known as King Philip, became the leader of a 15-month Indian uprising against the settlers that had profound impact on the Indians, the English settlements and destroyed forever tribal resistance in colonial New England.

The conflict began after a Christian Indian named John Sassamon, who worked for Metacom, told Plymouth authorities in January 1675 the Wampanoags were planning an uprising.

When the Wampanoags found out what Sassamon had said, he was murdered. Three Indians were convicted of killing Sassamon and executed. Distrust and suspicion between the settlers living near the Wampanoags in southeast Massachusetts caused English settlers to move women and children away from Swansea in the Mt. Hope Peninsula. Indians plundered and burned homes near Swansea June 20 and four days later open warfare broke out with nine colonial settlers killed.

Within days, the conflict known as King Philip's War had broken out and both sides organized to mobilize their forces. Of the estimated 11,000 natives in New England, some 2,900 men joined under King Philip's leadership to fight the English colonials. The raids and counter-raids in Rhode Island, Connecticut and Massachusetts continued for nearly two years. Virtually every community was affected, thousands were killed and homes, crops and stores of supplies were destroyed. During the war, one-tenth of the English men were killed, wounded or captured. All but a few hundred Indians warriors were killed.

The conflict, which began in June, widened and spread to other Indians and to the west, with the center of conflict moving toward Pocumtuck. In early August, the hamlet of Brookfield, 40 miles to the south, was destroyed. After similar Indians attacks, the village of Northfield, 15 miles away, was destroyed.

On September 1, Indians struck the colonial settlers at Pocumtuck. One soldier was killed, driving fleeing settlers into two fortified houses. The Indians burned 17 outlying houses and bars. Soon, the women and children of Pocumtuck were sent under guard to stay with friends and relatives in safer towns down the Connecticut River valley. Some 50 men, who included both townsmen and soldiers, tried to hold the town.

An attack September 12, resulted in more death and destruction in Pocumtuck. For the English, the village of Pocumtuck not only was the northern edge of the pioneer's settlement in New England, it also held stores of grain settlers throughout the area needed to survive. Knowing the stakes, the regional authorities ordered the Pocumtuck garrison to bring the grain supplies south.

Under a guard of 50 soldiers led by Captain Thomas Lathrop, 15 Pocumtuck villagers—including Barnabas Hinsdale—were recruited to drive the wagons of grain out of town Saturday morning, September 18. About five miles south of town, the convoy slowed to cross the stream called Muddy Brook. The men, not fearing attack, had their weapons lying on the wagons. A few men began to pick fruit from the trees along the stream bank. At that moment, a war party made up of hundreds of Wampanoags, Nipmucks and Pocumtucks attacked in a movement so swift and complete, victory was total. More than 60 colonials were killed; of the 15 Pocumtuck settlers only one survived.

The impact on Pocumtuck was devastating. One third of the men of the town were killed in the attack remembered today as the Bloody Creek Massacre. Nine women became widows that day, almost a third of the wives in town. Each was left with between two and eight children. In a town of 200, 40 children lost their fathers that day. The dead ranged in age from 20 to 58 and included Robert Hinsdale, his sons Samuel, Barnabas, John and a sister's husband, Joseph Gillett.

Pocumtuck widows moved to Hatfield, Hadley and Northhampton. Sarah (White) Hinsdale returned with her children to Hatfield, where she remained for the rest of her life.

In the days after the ambush, colonial authorities ordered the garrison at Pocumtuck abandoned, leaving the remaining buildings to be burned and destroyed by Indians. In all, 30 houses, plus barns and outbuildings, all lands and much of the harvest were destroyed. The property at once held no value. Fortunes and investments were lost.

The shock of the Bloody Creek Massacre galvanized colonial resistance to King Philip's uprising and ensured that the war fighting from that point on would be total. The settlers' Puritan religious leaders took the massacre as a sign from God that their way of life was depraved and degenerate. Only a closer adherence to their strict Puritan faith, and victory, would ensure salvation. This apparent sign of God's judgment destroyed within the Puritan community any lingering instinct for mercy.

The Indian implements of war—fire, axes, clubs, knives, tomahawks—meant the brutality of the fighting was horrible. Maiming, beheading, hacking, burning and torture were common. Prisoners were burned at the stake. Heads of victims were placed atop pikes for all to see.

The brutality was on both sides. In the fall of 1675, a captured Indian woman fell into the hands of English soldiers. After interrogation, a report by Captain Samuel Mosely, stated: "This aforesaid Indians was ordered to be torn to peeces by Doggs and she was so dealt with." Settlers adopted Indian tactics, raiding Indians camps and destroying their families, food supplies, and communities of support. A major assault by colonial militia on Narragansetts in December 1675 at the Great Swamp Fight ended with the death of nearly 1,000 men, women and children and virtually whipping out the Narragansetts.

Captain Thomas Savage, commander at Hadley, argued in April 1676 that colonials needed to shop "following the enemy up and down in the woods in which they can take advantage of us," and instead should attack Indian settlements where "they plant and fish on the river." Days later, just north of Pocumtuck, colonials attacked an Indian encampment at Turner's Falls in May 1676, killing of hundreds of elderly and women, and children.

King Philip and his allies had other problems too. While King Philip's forces were raiding Hadley and the other Connecticut River Valley towns throughout the first half of 1676, the Mohawks of the western Iroquois were raiding Algonkian camps.

One account read: "The Mohawks came upon their Head-Quarters, and smote their women and Children with a great Slaughter, and then returned with much plunder." A Pequot sachem told Connecticut authorities the only force capable of defeating King Philip were the Mohawks, whose role proved decisive. Mohawks continued war on their Algonkian adversaries meant that King Philip was forced during 1676 to fight a two-front war.

In terms of proportion of suffering in a population, King Philip's War remains the most destructive in American history. It would rage throughout Massachusetts and Connecticut until August 12, 1676, when King Philip was killed near his base camp at Mt. Hope ending the organized warfare.

As for Sarah (White) Hinsdale, she would marry a third time, and have more children. Sarah died in Hatfield and was buried August 10, 1709.

Meantime, in Middletown, Nathaniel White's wife ELIZABETH had died in 1690 at age 65. Nathaniel later married Martha (Coit) Mould [#36], who was also the mother-in-law to his two sons, Daniel and Joseph.

Nathaniel White, who died August 17, 1711, was Middletown's second largest landowner, leaving an estate of more than 1,500 acres of land and property valued at 927 pounds, 11 shillings, five pence. Nathaniel's will showed that he gave one fourth of his share in the common land to "the schools already agreed upon in the town of Middletown forever." When the first school was opened in that part of town now called Cromwell, the town voted unanimously to name it "The Nathaniel White Public School." Nathaniel and Elizabeth White, who are both buried at Riverside Cemetery, Middltown, had eight children, including a son, Daniel [#77].

[45] JOSEPH FERRIS was born in 1638 in Watertown, a son of Jeffrey and Mary Ferris [#13], and moved with his parents to Greenwich. On November 20, 1657, Joseph married RUTH KNAPP, born in 1640, a daughter of Nicholas and Elinor (Lockwood) Knapp [#2]. Joseph and his father Jeffrey

were among the seven men selected from the 27 Proprietors of Greenwich on February 5, 1664, to divide the common lands among the proprietors. Joseph was also among the men who signed the petition submitted to the Connecticut General Court that spring requesting that Greenwich be given township status. Joseph, who died in 1699, and Ruth (Knapp) Ferris, who died in 1687, had at least one son, Joseph, Jr. [#74].

[46] PETER FERRIS was born in 1636 in Watertown, a son of Jeffrey and Mary Ferris [#13]. Peter Ferris moved with his family to Stamford. On July 5, 1654, he married ELIZABETH REYNOLDS, a daughter of John and Sarah Reynolds [#27]. Peter, who died in Stamford September 28, 1706, and Elizabeth (Reynolds) Ferris had 10 children, including a daughter, Ruth [#66].

[47] JAMES FERRIS was born in 1643 in Greenwich, a son of Jeffrey and Mary Ferris [#13]. James, who died in 1736, and his wife, MARY, had at least one son, James, Jr. [#75].

[48] JOSHUA KNAPP was born November 5, 1634, in Watertown, a son of Nicholas and Elinor (Lockwood) Knapp [#2], and moved with his parents to Stamford in 1648. On June 9, 1657, Joshua, a weaver like his father, married HANNAH CLOSE, born in 1638, a daughter of John and Elizabeth Close [#22] of Greenwich. In 1663, Joshua and Hannah moved to Greenwich, where he was one of the seven of the 27 Proprietors chosen February 5, 1664, to divide the common lands of Greenwich. Joshua became a member of the Established (Congregational) Church in 1669 and became a freeman that year. Joshua, who died October 17, 1684, and Hannah (Close) Knapp, who died in 1696, had at least eight children, including a son, Joshua, Jr. [#67], and a daughter, Sarah [#68].

[49] ABIGAIL STANLEY was born in Hartford, a daughter of Timothy and Elizabeth Stanley of Hartford [#11]. On June 14 1660, Abigail married SAMUEL COWLES, who was born in 1639, a son of John and Hannah Cowle [#33] of

Hartford, Farmington, and Hatfield, Mass. Samuel Cowles was one of the 84 proprietors of Farmington in 1672, and joined the Church with his wife, Abigail, in 1690. Samuel, who died in Farmington April 17, 1691, and Abigail (Stanley) Cowles, who died about 1736, had 11 children, including a son, Joseph [#72].

[50] HANNAH CHURCHILL was born November 1, 1644, in Wethersfield, the third child and third daughter of Josiah and Elizabeth (Foote) Churchill [#17]. In New London on January 9, 1666/7, Hannah married SAMUEL ROYCE, a son of Robert and Mary (Sims) Royce [#43].

Family tradition holds that Samuel was born in New London. Samuel and Hannah (Churchill) Royce lived in New London for less than a decade, and then moved to Wallingford where her last four children were born. Samuel was an ensign of the Wallingford Train Band as early as 1697, and was a deputy to Connecticut General Court from May to August 1710. Hannah (Churchill) Royce died after the birth of her last child in March 1688. In Wallingford June 5, 1690, widower Samuel Royce married Sarah Baldwin, born Sept 25, 1655, in Milford, a daughter of John and Mary (Bruen) Baldwin. Samuel Royce died in 1711. Sarah Baldwin died in Wallingford January 11, 1729. Samuel and Hannah (Churchill) Royce had seven children, including Abigail [#72].

[51] HACKALIAH BROWN was born in 1645 in New Haven, a son of Peter Brown [#24], and in 1665, months after New Haven's annexation by Connecticut, moved to Rye, where he married MARY HOIT.

Family tradition holds that Mary is a granddaughter of SIMON HOYT, who was born January 20, 1590, in Upway, Dorchester, Dorsetshire, England. On December 2, 1612/13, Hoyt married DEBORAH STOWER, who was born in 1594. Simon and Deborah (Stower) Hoyt came to New England aboard the ship *Abigail*, which departed England September 6, 1628, and arrived in Massachusetts Bay. With Hoyt were his brother-in-law, Nicholas Stower, and the Sprague brothers, who were all of Upway. The Hoyt name was variously spelled Hoit, Hoite, Haight and Hight.

Simon and Deborah settled first in Charlestown and then moved to Salem, where in 1629 the Hoyts are listed among that community's first settlers. In 1630, the Hoyts moved to become among the first settlers of Dorchester, where he was made a freeman in 1631. The Hoyts moved to Scituate in 1633 where they joined the church. In 1639, the Hoyts moved to Windsor along the Connecticut River, where on February 28, 1640, Hoyt was granted four acres from the plantation for meadow and upland, which today is still called Hoyt Meadow. In 1649, Hoyt moved again. In March 1649, he was granted a house lot in Fairfield, and moved later to Stamford, where Simon who died September 1, 1657. Simon and Deborah (Stower) Hoyt had seven children, including sons Moses, Joshua, Samuel and Benjamin. Family tradition holds that one of these sons was the father of Mary (Hoit) Brown. Hackaliah, who died in 1710, and his wife Mary (Hoit) Brown had a son, Peter, Jr. [#80].

[52] **MARTHA PECK** was born about 1648 in Hartford, a daughter of Deacon Paul and Martha (Hale) Peck [#14]. On July 8, 1665, Martha married **JOHN CORNWELL**, a son of William and Mary Cornwell, Jr., born in Hartford April 1640 [#7]. Though the marriage occurred in Hartford, the records reside in Middletown where they lived. John Cornwell had moved to Middletown with his parents about 1650, where they were among the first settlers of town. He lived with his wife next door to his parents near the corner of present Main and Washington streets. John Cornwell was a sergeant in the town militia, and like his father, was commonly called Sgt. Cornwell. Martha (Peck) Cornwell died in Middletown March 1, 1707/8. Sgt. John Cornwell died in Middletown November 2, 1707. Sgt. John and Martha (Peck) Cornwell had ten children, including daughter Martha [#70].

[53] **JOHN COLE** was born in England, the son of **JAMES COLE**, and the father and son came to New England, where John's name appears in Hartford in 1655 when he was admitted as a freeman. John's wife was named **MARY**. Their last name was spelled Cole, Cowle, Coole, Coule, Colles, and Cowles. John Cole lived on Wethersfield Lane in Hartford, where his father also lived. In James' will, his property was left to his daughter and her husband, who soon died and in 1655 John bought out her interest.

John's daughter, Ann, became involved in a witch trial in 1662. According to a letter to Rev. Increase Mather in Massachusetts written by Rev. John Whiting in Hartford on

October 4, 1682, Ann Cole was bewitched by a next door neighbor who was later executed for witchcraft. Rev. Whiting said after the woman's execution, Ann Cole recovered from her fits.

John and Mary Cole, his wife, had seven children, including son John, Jr. [#54].

[54] JOHN COLE, JR., the oldest child of John and Mary Cole of Hartford [#53], settled in Farmington where he became one of the town's prominent citizens. He was elected constable in November 1657 and held office for two years. In May 1669 he was commissioner for the town. His wife was named RACHEL. John Cole, Jr. died in Farmington September 14, 1689. John and Rachel Cole, Jr., had four children, including a son, Nathaniel [#73].

[55] ISAAC BOREMAN was born February 3, 1642/3, in Wethersfield, the oldest child of Samuel and Mary (Betts) Boreman [#30]. In 1661, Isaac married ABIAH KIMBERLY, born in New Haven on December 19, 1641, a daughter of Thomas Kimberly [#16], and baptized by Rev. John Davenport. Abiah's older brother, Eleazer, was believed to be the first male born in New Haven. The year of her marriage, Eleazer moved to Wethersfield where he would serve as schoolmaster at intervals from 1661 to 1689.

On March 2, 1665/6, Isaac's father, Samuel, purchased for his son a house, barn and homelot of nearly four acres on the west side of Main Street in Wethersfield, a short distance from the church. Isaac and his family would spend their lives there, and it would later be occupied by his son, Thomas, and grandson, Thomas Jr. Isaac, a cooper like his father, later owned 40 acres of farm and pastureland. In 1684, Isaac was chosen a fence viewer, and five years later a surveyor of highways, sealer of weights and measures, selectman and constable. Isaac, who died May 12, 1719, and his wife, Abiah (Kimberly) Boreman, who died January 6, 1722/3, had six children, including a son, Isaac, Jr. [#78].

[56] MARTHA COIT was born about 1644 in Gloucester, the youngest child of John and Mary (Jenners) Coit [#6], and lived in Gloucester before moving with her parents to New London in 1650. On January 11, 1662, Martha married HUGH MOULD, a New London ship's carpenter who had moved to the port village from Barnstable, Cape Cod two years before. Hugh Mould worked with his brother-in-law in the ship building trade started by his wife's father. Hugh Mould died in New London in 1692. After Hugh Mould's death, Martha moved to Middletown's Upper Houses (Cromwell), where she married Nathaniel White [#44], the father-in-law of her daughters Susannah and Mary. Susannah was married to Daniel White [#77], while Mary's husband was Joseph White. Martha (Coit) (Mould) White died in Middletown April 17, 1711. Hugh and Martha (Coit) Mould had at least three children in New London, including two daughters, Christian [#65] and Susannah [#77].

[57] HANNAH WAKEFIELD was born and baptized in New Haven on December 29, 1644, a daughter of John and Ann Wakefield [#42]. In 1662, Hannah married widower EDWARD GRANNIS in Hartford. Grannis, born about 1630, had worked in New Haven at a mill operated by Hannah's father, John Wakefield.

Family tradition holds that Edward Grannis was of Norman origin and that he had been baptized in the Established Church in England. Evidence of this is in Hartford when on November 22, 1666, Edward Grannis joined other, former members of the Anglican (Established) Church, and asked for permission to become members of the First Church of Hartford, a Puritan congregation. This Norman view coincides with another family tradition that holds that the name Grannis was of Flemish origin and that many of that name reside in Belgium.

Whatever the origin of the name, the Edward Grannis who had been a member of England's Established Church first appears in colonial records in New Haven when, on October 2, 1649, the New Haven General Court fined him "18 d. for want of Worme, Scourer and Flints." At the time, all residents were required to bear arms and provide themselves with "a good serviceable gun and four or five good flints fitted for every firelock piece, all in good order and ready for any sudden occasion, service or view." Edward Grannis, at about 20 years old, was old enough to be armed.

Grannis' name appears again in March 1, 1652, when, as an employee of miller John Wakefield [#42], he was a witness in a case against Thomas Langden, who was accused of beating and threatening to kill his wife, and of killing and eating three hogs owned by Rev. Peter Prudden.

Grannis moved to Hartford where on May 3, 1655, he married Elizabeth Andrews of Farmington, a daughter of Hartford schoolmaster, William Andrews. Elizabeth died shortly after giving birth to their first child, Joseph, March 31, 1656. Grannis, a shoemaker by trade, was appointed leather sealer for Hartford on October 4, 1656. In 1662, Edward married Hannah Wakefield in Hartford, where their first child was born.

On March 18, 1671, Edward sold three parcels of land he owned in Hartford and moved to Hadley, Massachusetts, where, by new wife, Hannah (Wakefield), his second and third children were born. They were among the thousands of residents and refugees in the Connecticut River valley who lived through King Philip's War. They were also among those punished during the social repression imposed by Puritan laws enforced on the community in the war's wake to prevent the continued wrath of Providence.

Repressive social laws enacted in 1651 by the Massachusetts General Court made it an offense for a person whose estate did not exceed 200 pounds, or their dependents, to wear "gold or silver lace, gold or silver buttons, bone lace above 2 s. value a yard, or silk hoods or scarfs." The Puritan rationale of the day was that only the rich could wear such clothing and not be ostentatious. For those of modest means to wear such clothing was too great a demonstration of material pride and tempted God's wrath.

Hannah (Wakefield) Grannis was first in the family to run afoul of these rules in 1674, when she was fined 10 shillings in Hadley for "wearing a silk hood and scarf; though the articles were somewhat worn, (they) had been good silk."

Such rules were taken seriously. The connection between a community's behavior and God's wrath was, in the Puritan view, direct. In the aftermath of the September 1675 massacre of the Pocumtuck wagon train at Bloody Creek, the colony's religious leaders drew the lesson that, according to Rev. Increase Mather, "the Lord himself seemeth to be against us, to cast us off, to put us to shame." Rev. Mather, writing from Boston, said that "the sinful degenerate estate of the present generation in New England" was to blame. God had used the horrors of this massacre "as a heavy judgement which should come to punish the sin of men's unfaithfulness..."

The Massachusetts General Court labeled October 7 "a day of humiliation" of prayer and contemplation, and six days later decreed that proper religious practice be integrated into the military code. November 3, the Court, detailing the colony's failings, declared the colonists had "neither heard the word nor rod as we ought hence the righteous God hath heightened our calamity."

The court said sins that encouraged the God's wrath in war included "neglect of discipline in the churches" especially among children, "manifest pride openly appearing among us in that long hair, like women's hair, is worn by some men...either theirs or... periwigs." Both men and women were accused of "the evil of pride in apparel...vain, new strange fashions, both in poor and rich, with naked breasts and arms...Common swearing and cursing...the shameful and scandalous sin of excessive drinking, tippling and company keeping in taverns...and private unlicensed houses of entertainment (threatened the colony, as did) the sin of idleness." The court claimed shopkeepers were hiking prices too high and that men and women were riding from town to town "merely to drink and revel."

After the Bloody Creek Massacre and in the wake of the sieges of Hadley, Northhampton and Hatfield, many were charged with these crimes. In 1676, Edward Grannis' eldest son, Joseph, and 30 others were fined for "wearing silk, and that in a flaunting manner." The most severe punishment for the Grannis family came in March when Edward was identified as the leader of a group of nine men in Hadley charged with "participating in a riotous assembly," which was likely little more than singing or dancing in a public house or ordinary. A lower court sentenced Edward to be whipped with 12 strokes "well laid on," but another court set aside the punishment.

In the wake of King Philip's War, the Grannis family left Hadley in 1677 and returned to New Haven where they took up residence in a section of North Haven called Montowese. Edward and Hannah Grannis received more land and two more children were born.

In the fall of 1680, Hannah (Wakefield) Grannis, at age 36, was so afflicted with rheumatism she went to Stonington for treatment. On April 26, 1681, New Haven records declare "Goodwife Grannis was under infirmity and lameness, she had been before ye last winter in Stonington with a woman of skill to use means for her cure, and had some benefit by her going, but was to (go) again this spring in order to (obtain) a cure."

In 1695/6, Edward and his wife were permitted to resign their membership in the Hartford church and on June 28, 1696 were admitted as members of the First Church of New Haven. New Haven records identify Edward as a "cordwainer," a tanner and worker of leather. Hannah died in North Haven in 1711 and was buried in Montowese Cemetery, where a small red sandstone marker reads: HG 1711. Edward Grannis died in New Haven December 10, 1719 and is buried in Montowese Cemetery, where a red sandstone marker reads: EG Dec 10 1719.

Edward and Hannah (Wakefield) Grannis had seven children, including daughter Mabel (Mehitabel) [#76].

[58] FRANCIS GRISWOLD was born in Kenilworth, Warwickshire, a son of Edward and Margaret Griswold [#32], and came with his parents to New England in 1639, settling in Windsor. Francis moved to Saybrook, where his name is on town records in 1655 and 1656. Francis later moved to Norwich, where in 1660 he was one of the town's original proprietors. From 1661 to 1671, the year of his death, Francis was Norwich's Deputy to the Connecticut General Court.

Francis' uncle Matthew, a stonecutter, had moved early to Saybrook and later to Lyme. Matthew had a son, Matthew Griswold, Jr., who, though he was a first cousin of Francis, was considerably younger, born in 1653. Matthew, Jr. was active in civil affairs, as a Commissioner and a Deputy to the Connecticut General Court in 1704, 1707, 1708 and 1710. Matthew, Jr., was also a poet. A sample verse:

> Then find it true and not a lie
> He's thy best friend that speaks out plain:
> My dear, take heed,
> And make great speed,
> Lest though give God no Just offense;
> Then for my part
> A loving heart
> From thee shall be large Recompense...

Matthew, Jr., was a pious man and a correspondent of the Rev. Cotton Mather, the Puritan divine of Massachusetts Bay. On November 8, 1712, Matthew, Jr., wrote a lengthy letter to Rev. Mather about the fate of his son, Matthew, III. The letter tells of his son who five years earlier had run away from home, against his father's wishes, while the father was away in Hartford at the General Court.

> "I used utmost endeavors to recover him, but he got off from Piscatqua, leaving me sorrowfully to think what the event might prove, of a child's willful for-saking the Duty of his relation and the Means of Grace, and ingulfing himself into the Temptations of a Wicked World."

Matthew, Jr. told how his son was not long at sea before there was a ferocious storm. Matthew III was ordered aloft by the Captain to secure a yardarm. He slipped and fell, only to save himself from certain death by catching hold of a loose rope. After the ship arrived in Jamaica, Matthew III was pressed into service on a man-of-war, which then went to sea for months of hard service. Matthew III finally secured his release from duty at sea, only to be captured and put aboard a privateer.

> "...on board whereof he was exposed unto eminent hazard of his life, in an hot engagement, wherein many were killed, and the man that stood next unto him was with a chain-shot cut all to pieces...In the time of this fight, God caused him to take up Solemn Resolutions to Reform his life, which Resolutions he was enabled, through Grace, to observe.
>
> "And he then resolved that he would return as soon as he might be to his Father's house. After a skirmish or two more he was cast away. Then he was taken by the French, and turned ashore at the Bay of Honduras where he with 15 more was taken by a party of Spanish Indians who were led by a Spainard...Having their hands tied behind them and ropes around their necks, they were in that manner led unto a place called Paten, 600 miles distant from the place where they (were) taken, and very far within the land, having no food but water and the cabbage that grows upon trees.
>
> "My son had at that time the fever and ague very bad so that many times every step seemed as though it would be his last. Yet God marvelously preserved him, while three men much more likely to hold the Journey than himself perished on the road.
>
> "Upon their arrival to the end of their journey, they were fast chained, two by two, and so they continued eight months confined, and languishing in exquisite miseries. My son was visited with the small pox while he was in these wretched circumstances."

Matthew, Jr. wrote Mather that during this time, he was visited by friendly ministers who urged him to pray for his lost son. He later came to understand that as these prayer sessions took place, his son was suffering from smallpox in the Central American jungle. During this time, Matthew, Jr. wrote, the priests accompanying the enslaved men attempted to

> "...turn them Papists, sometimes promising them great rewards, at other times threatening them with the Mines, and with Hell. Some of these miserable men became Roman Catholics..."

Matthew, Jr. wrote that the slavemaster requested permission of the Spanish viceroy to sell the men into the mines. However, the governor took sympathy on the men and decided to return them to Spain, and thus to English authorities. The men were placed on Spanish ships as prisoners and set sail for Spain. Matthew III took a fever, and was treated by a ship's doctor. After that, Matthew, Jr. wrote:

> "...the Captain of the galleon told him he had no child, and, if he would embrace the Catholic faith and be baptized into it, and partake of the Mass, he would immediately give him 300 pounds, and put into as good a way to live as he could wish for.
>
> "Then the pious instructions of a Godly Mother, long since gone to a better world, were of precious use to him. For, though he was then lame (and not long after in danger of losing his leg) he was enabled to sleight all these Temptations, and put his trust in the Providence of God.
>
> "My son was landed at Cadiz. From thence, by the Good Providence of God, he got a Passage to Portugal. From thence to Newfoundland. From thence to Nantucket, and a cure for his leg...there a gentleman of Boston, who had some lameness in his knees...supplied him with money, and was very kind to him. At Nantucket several were exceeding kind to him, entertained him at their houses, gave him monies and garments.. When I resolve the Charity of these good people, it often makes me think of what we read Mark ch 14, v 8, 9. My son coming to Rhode Island got as passage home from thence by water.
>
> "Thus, after four years were expired, I received my son, the truest Penitent that ever my eyes beheld! This he freely manifested both in Public and Private."

Matthew, Jr. wrote that his son appeared healthy but was certain to die soon. The son wished to forgive those who past had wronged him, and did so. Matthew, Jr., quoted his son:

> "Sir, my business home was to make Peace with you and to die...My most dear Father, I will hide nothing from you. When I was in Irons at Paten, I had a clear Manifestation of the Love of God in Jesus Christ unto me. I had after this no burden remaining on my conscience, but only my wicked departing from you. For which cause I earnestly begged of God that I might live to see your reconciled face. This I now do and I bless God for it. Had it not been for that one thing, I would much rather have chosen at that time to have died than

to live. I could now desire to live, if God please to grant it, that I may Glorify Him, and be a comfort to you in your old age. But I think you will find it otherwise."

Mathew, Jr. wrote:

"He lived not long after this. His whole conversation for the 8 weeks (which was all the time he lived after his return home) was exceeding exemplary. Then the Lord was pleased to take from me a Son in whom I hoped to have enjoyed a blessing."

Matthew, Jr., encouraged Rev. Mather to use this story about his lost son as a teaching example.

"This account may quicken parents in well teaching their children in the fundamental Truths of Religion, and may admonish Children to take heed of running undutifully from their parents, and irreligiously from the Means of Grace, and may encourage those who do so, yet humbly, in their distress, to cry unto God, adhere his truth, and hope in him mercy."

The account so impressed Rev. Mather that he published the testimonial in Boston under the title "Repeated Warnings. Another Essay to warn Young People against Rebellions that must be Repented of...With a Pathetical Relation to What occur'd in the Remarkable Experiences of a Young Man who made a Hopeful End lately at Lyme, Connecticut." Today the letter is at Yale Library in New Haven.

Matthew, Jr., fathered five other children, including a son, George. George's son, Matthew IV, became governor of Connecticut. His name was given to Fort Griswold, known today as the site of the Revolutionary War massacre wrought by Benedict Arnold, after the war hero turned traitor.

Matthew, Jr.'s cousin Francis, who resided with his wife in Norwich, had at least one daughter, Deborah [#79].

[59] EDWARD De WOLFF was born in 1646 and came with his parents, Baltazar and Alice De Wolff [#39], to Lyme in 1661. Edward, a carpenter and millwright, built and operated two sawmills and a gristmill in Lyme. Edward received his first grant west of his father's home lot in 1670. His parents gave him half their land at the Head of Duck River for a home lot.

Edward married **REBECKAH MASUER**, a daughter of **WILLIAM MASUER SR.** of Wethersfield, who was also known as Measure and Measurer. Rebeckah's father, William Masuer, a widower, had moved to Lyme after marrying the widow of John Tinker who had a homestead on Lyme Road. Masuer was elected Lyme recorder of deeds in 1670, the year he was also elected a freeman. He served as Lyme magistrate in 1674, as well as townsman in 1675, 1676, 1678 and 1680. He was also Lyme's representative at General Court in Hartford in 1676. On August 6, 1678, Lyme chose William Masuer as treasurer to collect:

> "...money accruing to the Towne, The gathering of which hath been hitherto neglected, Excepting Those wch belong to ye Towne to be payd by rate...(The townsmen also voted)...that Mr. Measurer shall have free liberty to sell powder and Lead unto the friendly Indians according to the Law and the aforseaid Mr. Measurer doth hearby engage to keep and maintain a town Stand of powder and lead for the Towns nearby if need be and for to continue til this twelve month."

Later that year, on December 23, the townsmen also gave William Masuer a license to operate an ordinary on Lyme Road and sell spirits. He maintained that license for three years. In 1680s, Masuer was a witness to a number of land transactions and also was chosen to collect the minister's rate. Masuer died March 24, 1688.

Edward De Wolff was a respected member of the community at an early age. On October 24, 1672, though just 26, Edward was chosen a townsman in Lyme along with his father, Baltazar. On that date, he was also first chosen a fence viewer, a post he held again in 1675 and in 1676, when Lyme had 45 free voters. He was reelected townsman January 8, 1673, and in 1677 and 1678. In 1676, he served as surveyor, and in 1678 and 1679 as collector of the minister's rate.

Edward was a member of the Lyme Train Band (militia) and in late 1675 served with his brother, Stephen, in the Connecticut Volunteers, seeing action December 19 in the assault on Swamp Fort during King Philip's War.

The war had been raging throughout New England for 10 months when, in October, Governor Winslow, fearing an attack from the Narragansetts, marched with 1,000 men against their stronghold at Swamp Fort. The colonial force, including Edward De Wolff of the Lyme Train Band and the Connecticut Volunteers, attacked the Narragansett stronghold December 19, wiping out the Indians there, ending the Narragansett tribe's threat forever. The wars continued through the winter and into the following year. King Philip's death at his base camp on Mt. Hope Peninsula in today's Rhode Island, August 12, 1676, ended the organized warfare. In compensation for his service, Edward received Lot No. 1 in a six-square-mile plantation called Narragansett, later called Voluntown.

Edward was a skilled carpenter who built several mills in Lyme, repaired the 10-year-old Duck River Bridge, built a causeway over Mill Brook, shingled the Lyme meeting house and built Tillotson's barn, a Lyme landmark. His skill as a carpenter and man of the community was underscored in 1682, when he was asked to help settle the dispute between the people of New London with the contractor they had hired to build their new meeting house. Over the years, Edward built four homes, the first at Lieutenant's River, consisting of 10 acres of upland and swamp, was connected by roads to inter-New England thoroughfares and by the landing to Lieutenant's River and Long Island Sound.

In March 27, 1693, Goodman Edward De Wolff was elected by Lyme to find

> "some sutable person to Keep School and teach
> children to write and read both for time and price,
> and consider they appoint what children shall to be
> taught and what they ought to pay and what that
> Doeth make upe to pay the School master the towne
> to take up the rest, and wt they Doe miss to Declare
> to the Towne shall make a full obligation..."

At the time of his marriage, Edward owned only the 10 acres granted to him as the son of a town proprietor, including 7 acres of upland and three as meadow and swamp. On July 7, 1670, Lyme granted him five acres opposite Calves Island, as well as another grant on the west side of Lieutenant's River. Four years later Edward bought five acres on Great Island, bought stock and on June 3, 1675, registered an ear mark for use on all his animals except horses. In January 1677, Edward received another grant of 30 acres along Grate Point, and later 20 acres of upland in the Third Division of the Commons.

Edward was appointed by New London authorities in 1682 to arbitrate a dispute between the builders of a new church and the congregation. In May 1686, Lyme gave Edward 22 acres of land for his work in the building of a new meeting house. In 1688, Edward moved to land on Eight Mile River and was given permission to built a grist mill. He later built a second sawmill near his home on Eight Mile River, which was near the village of Laysville. Edward and Rebeckah (Masuer) De Wolff had five children, including a son, Charles [#81].

[60] JOHN STRICKLAND was born February 14, 1648, in Dedham, Massachusetts, a son of Thwait and Elizabeth (Shepard) Strickland [#31]. On Sept 1, 1676 in Wethersfield, Connecticut, John married ESTHER SMITH, daughter of RICHARD and MARY (WEED) SMITH of Wethersfield, who was born about 1659, and granddaughter of RICHARD and REBECCA (BUSWELL) SMITH. Esther's mother died in Glastonbury May 7, 1704, at age 86. Her father died June 1690 in Wethersfield at age 73. John and Esther (Smith) Strickland had seven children, including a son, Jonah [#83].

[61] ROBERT HIBBARD, JR. was born in 1648 in that part of Salem now called Beverly, a son of Robert and Joan Hibbard [#23], and was baptized March 7 in the First Church of Salem. Robert married MARY WALDEN of Wenham, Massachusetts where they settled, joining the Wenham Church in 1694. In 1700, Robert and Mary moved with their family to Windham, Connecticut. Robert, who died April 29, 1710, and his wife, Mary (Walden) Hibbard, who died March 7, 1736, had 11 children, including a son, Nathaniel [#82].

[62] MATTHEW BECKWITH, JR. was born about 1645 in Hartford, a son of Matthew and Mary Beckwith [#28]. In 1666, Matthew Beckwith, Jr., married ELIZABETH in Old Lyme, and they had eight children. Elizabeth died after 1685. In 1691 Matthew Jr. married another Elizabeth, the twice-widowed eldest daughter of Matthew Griswold [#58]. Matthew Beckwith, Jr., died June 14, 1727. Among the children of Matthew Beckwith, Jr., and Elizabeth, his first wife, was a daughter, Prudence [#81].

[63] JOHN MOSS, JR. was born October 12, 1650, in New Haven, a son of John Moss [#21] and baptized in the First Congregational Society in New Haven October 20. John Jr., moved with his parents to Wallingford in 1667. In December 12, 1676, John, Jr. married MARTHA LATHROP, born January 1657 in New London, a daughter of Samuel and Elizabeth (Scudder) Lathrop [#12]. On December 5, 1683, John Moss, Jr., was accepted as a planter and assigned a home lot. John and Martha (Lathrop) Moss, Jr. settled on a plot of land at the south end of Wallingford where a dwelling later known as the Beach

House stands. John, Jr., who died in Wallingford March 31, 1717, and Martha (Lathrop), who died in Wallingford September 21, 1719, had at least 10 children including Benjamin [#88].

[64] JOHN SAVAGE, JR. was born December 2, 1652, in Middletown, a son of John and Elizabeth (Dubbin) Savage [#35]. John, Jr., grew up in Middletown's Upper Houses and on May 30, 1682, married MARY RANNEY, born in October 1665, a daughter of Thomas and Mary (Hubbard) Ranney [#37], also of Middletown. John, Jr., a longtime member of the Middletown Train Band, was made an ensign October 10, 1700, and a lieutenant on October 14, 1703, and from May 10, 1711, until his death October 30, 1726, served as the militia's captain. John, Jr., died October 30, 1726, and left an estate valued at 905 pounds, 16 shillings, eight pence. John and Mary (Ranney) Savage, who died August 19, 1734, had 11 children, including a daughter, Sarah [#84].

[65] WILLIAM SAVAGE was born April 26, 1668, in Middletown, a son of John and Elizabeth (Dubbin) Savage [#35] and baptized at the First Congregational Church of Middletown on November 15, 1668. On May 6, 1696, William married CHRIST-IAN MOULD, born in New London on May 8, 1670, a daughter of Hugh and Martha (Coit) Mould [#56]. William was a Deacon of the First Congregational Church of Middletown and in 1719 was appointed a Captain in the Middletown Train Band. William was selected 13 times as Middletown's deputy to the General Court, where he served from 1715 to 1726, living their lives in that section now called Cromwell. William, who died January 25, 1726/7, and Christian (Mould) Savage, who died in October 16, 1719, had six children, including a son, William, Jr. [#84].

[66] SAMUEL PECK was born in 1659 in Guilford, a son of Rev. Jeremiah and Johannah (Kitchell) Peck [#41]. On November 27, 1686, Samuel married RUTH FERRIS, who was born in 1662, a daughter of Peter and Elizabeth (Reynolds) Ferris [#46]. When Samuel's father, Rev. Jeremiah Peck, moved to Waterbury after losing his minister's post in Greenwich in 1689, Samuel remained in Greenwich.

Well-educated, Samuel prospered in Greenwich and maintained the confidence of his community. He was Greenwich justice of the peace for 50 years. Ruth (Ferris) Peck died at age 83 in Greenwich on September 17, 1745, and Samuel died in 1746 at age 87. Samuel and Ruth (Ferris) Peck had nine children, all in Greenwich, including at least one son, Theophilus [#87].

[67] JOSHUA KNAPP, JR. was born in 1663 in Stamford, a son of Joshua and Hannah (Close) Knapp [#48], and moved with his parents to Greenwich that year. Joshua, Jr., whose first wife Elizabeth Reynolds died at age 23, married **ABIGAIL BUTLER**, a daughter of **WALTER** and **REBECCA BUTLER** of Greenwich and granddaughter of **EVAN BUTLER** of Cusopp, Hertfordshire. Joshua and Abigail moved to Stamford, where he became a proprietor, justice of the peace and member of the First Congregational Church. Joshua, who died before 1750, and Abigail (Butler) Knapp, who died June 1, 1710, had seven children, including a son, Jonathan [#89].

[68] EBENEZER MEAD was born in 1663 in Elizabeth Neck, a son of John and Hannah (Potter) Mead [#40], and moved with his parents to Horseneck, Greenwich. Ebenezer married **SARAH KNAPP**, a daughter of Joshua and Hannah (Close) Knapp [#48]. In February 1686, a group of 10 Indians sold land, in an area today called Indian Field, to Ebenezer. In 1694, the Town of Greenwich appointed Ebenezer to "keep a place of public entertainment for men and beast." Mead Tavern stood for almost 200 years.

In the early years, stern-minded Puritans often raided Mead Tavern, swinging clubs, to prevent dancing and drinking among travelers and residents. Taverns in Greenwich were centers of commerce, gossip and socializing, filled with customers waiting to take the weekly packet boats loaded with produce from Greenwich Harbor to New York. During the Revolutionary War, New York's royal governor, Major General William Tryon, tried to use Mead Tavern as his headquarters during one of his raids in 1779. As he and his aides were making themselves comfortable, a patriot shot through the tavern's clapboards. The ball whistled past Governor Tryon's head, struck the mantle above the fireplace and ricocheted into the floorboards. The incident caused Tryon and his group to go elsewhere. Mead Tavern was torn down in July 1886 to make way for the Presbyterian Church, now in the center of Greenwich on the Boston Post Road.

Ebenezer was selected to be Greenwich's deputy to the Connecticut General Court in 1694, 1699, 1702 and from 1711 to 1716. He was a justice of the peace for Fairfield County in 1703, from 1705 to 1709 and from 1714 to the year of his death in 1728. Ebenezer and Sarah (Knapp) Mead had nine children, including a son, Ebenezer, Jr. [#85].

[69] BENJAMIN MEAD was born in 1667 in Elizabeth Neck, a son of John and Hannah (Potter) Mead [#40], and moved with his parents to Horseneck, Greenwich. Benjamin married SARAH WATERBURY, born in 1667.

There are two reports about Sarah's ancestry. One is that she was a granddaughter of JOHN WASSERBURG, a native of Germany who came to Connecticut with the Puritans, perhaps as part of the Baltic Sea trade. The other, perhaps more likely version, is that Sarah was descended from JOHN and ROSE (LOCK-WOOD) WATERBURY. John Waterbury was born about 1620 in Sudbury, Suffolk, and came to New England in 1641. Also from Sudbury were WILLIAM and ALICE WATERBURY, who came with Winthrop's fleet in 1630 and were listed as the 35th and 36th members of the First Church of Boston. John Waterbury is believed to be the son of William and Alice Waterbury.

John Waterbury married Rose Lockwood, a daughter of Edmund and Elizabeth Lockwood, a niece of Elinor (Lockwood) Knapp [#2], and a granddaughter of Edmund Lockwood [#1] of Combs, Suffolk. Rose's father, Edmund, was born in Combs in 1594 and died in Cambridge in 1634. John and Rose (Lockwood) Waterbury's first child was born in 1641. They settled in Watertown, sold out in 1646 and moved to Stamford, where John Watebury was granted a parcel of land in 1650.

John Waterbury was one of three deputies from Stamford who in 1657 presented the paper from the inhabitants of Greenwich, in which they agreed to "fall in with Stamford and be accepted a part thereof." John Waterbury was a Stamford town judge in May 1657 and May 1658. John, who died in 1659, and Rose (Lockwood) Waterbury had at least five children, three sons and two daughters. Family tradition is that Sarah Waterbury was born to one of John and Rose's three sons.

Sarah's husband, Benjamin Mead, was a surveyor of Fairfield County from 1725 to 1727, and in May 1728 was commissioned an ensign in the Greenwich West Train Band. In 1728, Benjamin and Sarah moved to Quaker Ridge in North Greenwich, where he purchased land. In 1743, he purchased 68 more acres on Quaker Ridge, paying John Marshall, Jr.,

147 pounds. Later, Benjamin acquired still more land on Quaker Ridge, including some common land from the town. All of Benjamin's property was on the west side of Quaker Ridge Road, about a mile south of today's North Greenwich Congregational Church. Benjamin, who died in 1746, and Sarah (Waterbury) Mead had five children, including one son, Benjamin, Jr. [#86], and two daughters, Elizabeth [#87] and Hannah [#90].

The Mead home on Quaker Ridge, Greenwich

[70] MARTHA CORNWELL was born August 13, 1669, in Middletown, the second daughter and second child of John and Martha (Peck) Cornwell [#52]. Martha was married in Middletown March 13, 1692, to **RICHARD HUBBARD**, the youngest son and seventh child of George and Elizabeth (Watts) Hubbard, Jr. [#20], born in July 1655 in Middletown.

Richard Hubbard was the executor of his father's will and was left with home lot, house, barn and all other buildings there on and was "enjoyned to provide comfortably for his mother during her widowhood." Richard's own will on file in Hartford was dated July 14, 1731. He died in Middletown July 30, 1732. Richard and Martha (Cornwell) Hubbard had six children, including daughter Martha [#83].

[71] SAMUEL MEAD was born in 1673 in Elizabeth Neck, a son of John and Hannah (Potter) Mead [#40], and moved with his parents to Horseneck. Samuel, who died in 1713, and his wife, **HANNAH**, had at least one son, Peter [#90].

[72] ABIGAIL ROYCE was born November 24, 1677, in Wallingford, a daughter of Samuel and Hannah (Churchill) Royce [#50]. In Wallingford on July 13, 1699, she married JOSEPH COLE, a son of Samuel and Abigail (Stanley) Cowles [#49], who was born in Farmington June 18, 1677/8.

After Abigail (Royce) Cole died in Wallingford May 24, 1714, Joseph later married Anna (Peck) Yale, the widow of Nathaniel Yale, and daughter of John and Mary (Moss) Peck, of Wallingford. Their only child died after one month. Anna (Peck) (Yale) Cole died February 16, 1716. Joseph's third marriage was to Mrs. Mindwell Waples, widow of Ephraim Waples of Wethersfield, on May 29, 1718. They had a son, Ebenezer Cole, who would later have 16 children by two wives.

Joseph Cole lived out his years and died, November 30, 1760, at age 83, in the northern section of Wallingford called Meriden Farms, which would become a separate town, Meriden, in 1806. Joseph and Abigail (Royce) Cole had nine children, including a daughter, Abigail [#88].

[73] ELIZABETH WOODFORD was born about 1678 in Farmington, a daughter of Joseph and Rebecca (Newell) Woodford [#38]. On June 11, 1707, she married NATHANIEL COLE, a son of John and Rachel Cole, Jr. of Farmington [#54]. Nathaniel was born in 1678 and died in Farmington June 20, 1743 at age 65. Elizabeth (Woodford) Cole died June 19, 1749 at age 71, and was buried in Christian Lane Cemetery in Berlin. Nathaniel and Elizabeth (Woodford) Cole had seven children, including a daughter, Rachel [#93].

[74] JOSEPH FERRIS, JR., was born in 1683 in Greenwich, a son of Joseph and Ruth (Knapp) Ferris [#45]. Joseph and his wife, ABIGAIL, had at least one daughter, Martha [#86].

[75] JAMES FERRIS, JR., was born in 1699 in Greenwich, a son of James and Mary Ferris [#45]. James, Jr., who died in 1739, and his wife, MARY, had at least one daughter, Sarah [#91].

[76] MEHITABLE (MABEL) GRANNIS was born in 1666/7 in Hartford, a daughter of Edward and Hannah (Wakefield) Grannis [#57]. In 1670, when Mehitable was three, she moved with her parents from Hartford to Hadley, returning to New Haven during King Philips' War in 1676.

On March 2, 1684, 18-year-old Mehitable Grannis married **JOHN JOHNSON III**, who was born August 27, 1661, in New Haven, a son of John and Hannah (Parmalee) Johnson, Jr. [#36].

John and Mehitable lived in what is now New Haven's Westfield section. He later owned his grandfather Robert Johnson's [#15] home on York Street, given to him by his uncle Thomas. John Johnson III's will was written December 12, 1712/3, and probated after his death the following February. It begins:

> "In the name of God, Amen. I, John Johnson Senior of New Haven, being at this time sick and weak in my body yet of perfect mind and memory, thanks be to God for it, I do make and ordain this day my last will and testament. In manner and form following—firstly and principally I give my soul to God, hoping for acceptance and mercy through the merits and right-eousness of Christ Jesus, my Lord, and my body I commit to the earth to be buried decently at the dis-cretion of my executrix, hereafter name (Mehitable) and as concerning the disposing of all such temporal estate as it hath pleased God to bestow upon me I give and dispose thee as followith..."

Mehitable lived in New Haven until at least 1729. In 1732, she was living in Middletown with her son, Thomas, and in 1738 with her daughter, Mehitable, and son-in-law, Thomas Rose. John and Mehitable (Granniss) Johnson III, who died December 9, 1745, and is buried in Durham, had 10 children, including a son, Thomas [#95].

[77] DANIEL WHITE was born February 23, 1661/2, in Middletown, a son of Nathaniel and Elizabeth White [#44]. In March 1682/3, Daniel married **SUSANNAH MOULD**, born April 2, 1663, in New London, a daughter of Hugh and Martha (Coit) Mould of New London [#56]. After the death of Hugh Mould, Susannah's widowed mother, Martha, moved to Middletown, where she married her daughter's father-in-law, Nathaniel White [#44].

Daniel White was a selectman in Middletown in 1690 and a

constable in 1701, and an ensign in the Middletown Train Band. Daniel, who died December 18, 1739, and Susannah (Mould) White, who died in that part of town today called Cromwell September 7, 1754, had 11 children, including a daughter, Susannah [#95].

[78]
ISAAC BOREMAN, JR., was born July 21, 1666, in Wethersfield, a son of Isaac and Abiah (Kimberly) Boreman [#55]. On December 7, 1699, Isaac, Jr., married REBECCA BENTON, the eldest daughter of Mary and Edward Benton [#34], who was born in Guilford and had moved with her parents to Wethersfield.

A weaver, Isaac, Jr., was an invalid much of his life, dying May 9, 1719, at age 53, three days before the death of his father, Isaac. Isaac, Jr. left his widow, Rebecca, and their four children land valued at 134 pounds, five shillings. On his deathbed, Isaac, concerned about the death of his son, changed his will and left his fatherless grandchildren and their mother a homelot and several parcels of farmland. The will was dated May 12, 1719, the day he died. Isaac and Mary (Benton) Boreman, Jr., had four sons, including Josiah [#93].

[79]
DEBORAH GRISWOLD was born in 1664 in Norwich, a daughter of Francis Griswold [#58]. Deborah married JONATHAN CRANE, who was born in 1658. Jonathan, who died in 1735, and Deborah (Griswold) Crane, who died in 1704, had at least one daughter, Sarah [#82].

[80]
PETER BROWN, JR., was born in 1670 in Rye, a son of Hackaliah and Mary (Hoit) Brown [#51]. Peter, Jr., married MARTHA DISBROW, a daughter of PETER DISBROW (DISBROUGH) of Rye, who first settled Manursing Island, purchasing it directly from the Indians.

The Disbrow-Disbrough-Desbrough-Disborow-Desbrow family descended from NICHOLAS DISBROUGH, who was born in 1612 in England and who, in 1639, was a proprietor and early resident of Hartford. In 1640 Nicholas married MARY BRONSON, probably the sister of John Bronson, an early member of Hartford's First Church.

Nicholas was in Hartford in 1639 a proprietor "by courtesie

of the town." He was granted a home lot on the east side of the road to the Cow Pasture, today's North Main Street, not far from the present tunnel. Nicholas served in the Pequot War; for his service received a grant of 50 acres May 11, 1671. He was given a number of municipal assignments, including being chosen chimney viewer (fire inspector) in 1647, 1655, 1663 and 1669; and the surveyor of highways in 1665. Because of advancing years, Nicholas was relieved of his training duties in the militia March 6, 1672 at age 60. After Mary's death, he married Elizabeth Shepard [#31], daughter of Edward Shepard [#18] of Cambridge, and the widow of Hartford's Thwaite Strickland [#31]. Nicholas later moved to Farmington, where he died in 1680.

Peter, who died in 1752, and Martha (Disbrow) Brown, Jr. had a daughter, Hannah [#85].

[81]

CHARLES De WOLFF (Dewolph) was born September 18, 1673 in Lyme, a son of Edward and Rebeckah (Masuer) De Wolff [#59]. Lyme was a center of ship construction and merchant trade and, like Middletown to the north, a central market for farm produce and manufactured goods sold in exchange for West Indies cargoes.

Charles married **PRUDENCE BECKWITH**, a daughter of Matthew and Elizabeth Beckwith, Jr. [#62], who was born August 22, 1676, in New London (Lyme). Charles De Wolff operated mills with his father, Edward, in Lyme. As his family and debts grew over the years, Charles sold off parts of his Lyme property and that of his wife until 1716, when, now owning just a few acres of his homelot, he moved with his family to Lebanon, where he farmed.

Lebanon was originally called Poquechannug, Pomakuk or Poquedamseg. Its founders were the proprietors of Saybrook who had moved to a one-by-five-mile strip west of Norwich that had been granted to Rev. James Fitch in 1666. In 1692, a second piece of land five miles square, was granted to Captain Mason and three others by the Mohegan sachem, Oweneco, a son of Uncas, and confirmed by the General Assembly in 1705.

The name Lebanon was derived from an extensive cedar grove on a hill in the mile-deep grant given to Rev. Fitch. It reminded the Puritan founders of the Biblical reference: "I come up to the height of the mountains, in the sides of Lebanon; and I will cut down the tall cedars thereof." The name Lebanon was approved by the Assembly in 1697, and the town was incorporated in 1700.

The lot purchased by Charles De Wolff in 1716 was part of the Crank land lying on both sides of the Hop River in the northwest part of Lebanon. The first church in Lebanon was organized

November 27, 1700, and called Lebanon Crank, later set off as the town of Coventry. The De Wolffs baptized their son Joseph in the First Church of Lebanon in 1719. The southern part of the parish was set off as the Second Society of Lebanon Crank in 1720, and Charles moved his family to a new home on a tract to the south called Mile and a Quarter, which the court added to Coventry in 1723.

On January 2, 1724, Charles purchased the 90 acres on which he built his home and an additional 57 acres on Hop River at the Coventry boundary adjacent to his farm at Mile and a Quarter. Ownership of these two properties was transferred in Hartford and the deed recorded in Coventry in February. Prudence De Wolff transferred her membership to the Second Lebanon Crank Church on March 24, 1724.

Charles later gave much of this land to his children. In early 1731 he sold his remaining 80 acres in Lebanon for 32 acres in Glastonbury and 19 acres in Middletown that belonged to Rev. Thomas White. The Middletown property included a home, upland, meadows and a swamp in that portion of Middletown on the east side of the Connecticut River now called Portland. The White/De Wolff transaction occurred April 3, and Prudence joined the Portland church June 20, 1731. At his death in December 1731, the inventory on Charles' property was worth 409 pounds.

Charles, who died December 5, 1731, and his wife, Prudence (Beckwith) De Wolff, who died in June 1737, had at least 10 children, including a son, Charles, Jr. [#92].

[82] NATHANIEL HIBBARD was born in 1680 in Wenham, Massachusetts, a son of Robert and Mary (Walden) Hibbard, Jr. [#61], moving with his parents to Windham, Connecticut, in the fall of 1700. On April 16, 1702, Nathaniel married SARAH CRANE of Windham, daughter of Jonathan and Deborah (Griswold) Crane [#79]. Nathaniel and Sarah settled on land his father purchased along Christian Street near Beaver Brook in Windham. Nathaniel became known as "Sergeant Hibbard" owing to his service in 1712 as a soldier in a British colonial expedition against the French in Canada, service for which Nathaniel was paid four shillings, four pence. At the end of his life, Nathaniel possessed property and real estate valued at 700 pounds, nine shillings, six pence. Nathaniel, who died in the spring of 1725, and Sarah (Crane) Hibbard had 11 children, including a son, Jonathan [#94].

[83] **JONAH STRICKLAND** was born February 2, 1685/6, in Glastonbury, a son of John and Esther (Smith) Strickland [#60]. On November 21, 1711, Jonah married **MARTHA HUBBARD**, who was born January 3, 1692/3, In Middletown, a daughter of Richard and Martha (Cornwell) Hubbard [#70].

They were admitted into the communion of the Middletown First Church February 1, 1712/3. Records of the Middletown First Church called Jonah Strickland (or Strictland) a "covenanter" April 28, 1712, and "came from another place but subjected himself to the discipline of this church." He lived in Chatham until his death in July 1777. Jonah and Martha (Hubbard) Strickland had seven children, including daughter Esther [#97].

[84] **WILLIAM SAVAGE, JR.** was born September 18, 1699, in Middletown, a son of William and Christian (Mould) Savage [#65], and baptized at the First Congregational Church in Middletown October 29, 1699. On June 2, 1726 William, Jr., married his cousin, **SARAH SAVAGE**, born in that part of town today called Cromwell and baptized September 8, 1700, daughter of John and Mary (Ranney) Savage [#64]. William, Jr., was a deacon of the First Congregational Church in Middletown. William, who died in Cromwell April 5, 1744, and Sarah (Savage) Savage, Jr., who died August 10, 1782, had eight children, including a son, Elisha [#96].

[85] **EBENEZER MEAD, JR.** was born in 1692 in Horseneck, a son of Ebenezer and Sarah (Knapp) Mead [#68]. Ebenezer, Jr., married **HANNAH BROWN**, born in 1698 in Rye, daughter of Peter and Martha (Disbrow) Brown, Jr. [#80]. Ebenezer, Jr., was a justice of the peace in Greenwich from 1733 to 1758, and was selected Greenwich's deputy to the Connecticut General Court in 1733, 1734, 1737 and 1738. He was a member of the town's Train Band, commissioned a lieutenant May 9, 1728, and a captain May 11, 1738. Ebenezer, who died in 1775, and Hannah (Brown) Mead, Jr., who died in 1783, had 11 children, including a son, Jonas [#91].

[86] **BENJAMIN MEAD, JR.**, was born in 1701 in Greenwich, son of Benjamin and Sarah (Waterbury) Mead [#69]. Benjamin, Jr. married **MARTHA FERRIS**, born in 1708, daughter of Joseph and Abigail Ferris, Jr. [#74]. Benjamin, Jr., was a surveyor of Fairfield County in 1752, 1754 and 1755 and a member of the town's New Company Train Band, commissioned a lieutenant October 2, 1767. Benjamin, Jr., inherited 45 acres of his father's 207-acre estate on Quaker Ridge. Benjamin, who died in 1799, and Martha (Ferris) Mead, Jr., had 11 children, including a son, Benjamin III [#100].

[87] **THEOPHILUS PECK** was born in Greenwich, a son of Samuel and Ruth (Ferris) Peck [#66]. Theophilus married **ELIZABETH MEAD**, who was born in 1703 in Greenwich, daughter of Benjamin and Sarah (Waterbury) Mead [#69]. Theophilus, who died in 1783, and Elizabeth (Mead) Peck, who died in 1783, had at least one daughter, Eunice [#101].

[88] **ABIGAIL COLE** was born January 18, 1702/3, in Wallingford, a daughter of Joseph and Abigail (Royce) Cole [#72]. On March 28, 1728, Abigail married **BENJAMIN MOSS**, born February 10, 1702, in Wallingford, a son of John and Martha (Lathrop) Moss [#63]. Abigail and Benjamin lived in Cheshire, where Benjamin was a lieutenant in Train Band. Benjamin, who died June 10, 1761, and Abigail (Cole) Moss, who died February 11, 1794, and who were both buried at Hillside Cemetery, Cheshire, had 11 children, including a daughter, Eunice [#98].

[89] **JONATHAN KNAPP** was born in 1702 in Greenwich, son of Joshua and Abigail (Butler) Knapp, Jr. [#67]. Jonathan married **MARY HUSTED**, born in 1695, a granddaughter of **ANGELL** and **MARY (MEAD) HUSTED**, and great-granddaughter of **ROBERT** and **ELIZABETH HUSTED**.

Robert Husted was born in 1596 in Weymouth, Dorsetshire. Robert and Elizabeth married in 1620 and their son, Angell, was born later that year. The Husted family came to New England in 1636 and settled in Braintree. The family moved to Connecticut and is believed to have been in the area later called Greenwich as early as 1638. Robert Husted and his son Angell were witnesses to the signing on July 18, 1640, of the deed and land transaction between the Indians and Captain Patrick and Robert Feake. Robert Husted was one of the company granted a parcel of land in Stamford in 1640. Robert Husted's will dated, July 8, 1652, bequeathed to his son, Angell, all his lands and housing in Greenwich and to his other son, Robert, all his land and housing in Stamford. Robert Husted died in 1652 and his wife, Elizabeth, two years later.

Angell Husted, born in England in 1620, was among the first settlers of Greenwich. One of the 27 proprietors of Greenwich, Angell was one of seven among the proprietors, who, on February 5, 1664, were selected to divide the common land among all. Four of the other seven men were Jeffrey Ferris [#13], John Mead [#40], Joseph Ferris [#45] and Joshua Knapp [#48].

Jonathan Knapp was a member of Greenwich's Second Congregational Church. Jonathan, who died in 1799, and Mary (Husted) Knapp had two children, including a son, Joshua III [#101].

[90] **PETER MEAD** was born in 1700 in Greenwich, son of Samuel and Hannah Mead [#71]. Peter married his cousin **HANNAH MEAD**, who was born in 1706 in Greenwich, a daughter of Benjamin and Sarah (Waterbury) Mead [#69]. Peter and Hannah (Mead) Mead had at least one daughter, Anna [#102].

[91] **JONAS MEAD** was born in 1723 in Greenwich, son of Ebenezer and Hannah (Brown) Mead, Jr. [#86]. In 1750, Jonas married **SARAH FERRIS**, born in 1730, daughter of James and Mary Ferris, Jr. [#75]. Jonas died in 1783. His wife, Sarah (Ferris) Mead, died in 1752, shortly after giving birth to their only child, a son, Edmond [#103].

[92] **CHARLES DE WOLFF, JR.** was born in 1695 in Lyme, a son of Charles and Prudence (Beckwith) De Wolff [#81]. Lyme had become a center of trade with the French West Indies, and Charles, Jr., as a young man, followed the corridor of sea commerce to the French colonial island of Guadeloupe, where he established himself as a millwright and trader. On March 31, 1717, Charles, Jr. married **MARGARET POTTER**, a native of England who had moved to the West Indies with her father.

Charles and Margaret (Potter) De Wolff, Jr. had four children, including a son, Simon [#97].

[93] JOSIAH BORDMAN was born June 30, 1705, in Wethersfield, son of Isaac and Rebecca (Benton) Boreman, Jr. [#78]. Josiah changed the spelling of his name to conform to its common pronunciation. On August 5, 1734, Josiah married RACHEL COLE, who was born in Farmington January 17, 1712/3, daughter of Nathaniel and Elizabeth (Woodford) Cole [#73], who had moved to Middletown's Westfield Society. On November 29, 1737, Samuel Galpin of Kensington Society sold Josiah 50 acres of farmland in the northwest corner of Middletown. Josiah and Rachel were active members of the Kensington Congregational Church. On August 12, 1766, Josiah deeded land to his three sons. Josiah, who died January 29, 1781, and Rachel (Cole) Bordman, who died February 29, 1782, who were both buried at Old Highland Cemetery, Westfield, had 10 children, including a son, Nathaniel [#98].

[94] JONATHAN HIBBARD was born October 22, 1709, in Windham, son of Nathaniel and Sarah (Crane) Hibbard [#82]. Jonathan moved to Greenwich, where he married and had 14 children, including a son, Nathaniel, Jr. [#102].

[95] THOMAS JOHNSON was born January 12, 1689/90, in New Haven, a son of John and Mehitable (Granniss) Johnson III [#76]. As a young man, Thomas moved to Middletown, where in 1722 he is recorded as being a captain in the Middletown Train Band, and justice of the peace. On January 2, 1717/8, Thomas married SUSANNAH WHITE, born October 16, 1694, a daughter of Daniel and Susannah (Mould) White [#77]. Thomas, who died April 22, 1761, and Susannah (White) Johnson, who died September 28, 1786, had nine children, including twin daughters, Desire and Thankful [#96].

PART TWO

Militiamen, Merchants & Pioneers
1728–1818

[96] **ELISHA SAVAGE** was born December 9, 1728, a son of William and Sarah (Savage) Savage, Jr. [#84]. On May 6, 1755, Elisha married **THANKFUL JOHNSON**, who was born July 5, 1735, a daughter of Thomas and Susannah (White) Johnson [#95]. Church records show their community scolded them for the fact that their first child was born in September, four months after their marriage. Cromwell Church records show that on "October 26, 1755, Elisha Savage and Thankful his wife made Christian satisfaction for their sin of fornication & were accepted." Theirs was a forgiving congregation, however, as the situation in which the young couple found themselves was quite common. The following week, records show that "on November 9, 1755, Elisha Savage and Thankful his wife received their Baptismal covenants."

In 1767, Elisha was made an ensign in the 15th Company of the Connecticut 6th Regiment, established as part of the British colonial army for service in the French & Indian War.

During the Revolutionary War, Elisha, at age 49, was

commissioned a lieutenant in 1777 in Captain Shepard's Company, Colonel Belden's Regiment in the Brigade of General Erastus Wolcott. The regiment was raised to serve in Peekskill, New York, during a two-month campaign.

In the late 1780s, Elisha and his family moved to a section of Middletown called the Northwest or Third Division. The area was located in the northwest part of Middletown and had originally been settled in 1735 by Daniel Wilcox (1715-1789), a grandson of Sarah Savage (1658-1724), a daughter of John and Elizabeth (Dubbin) Savage [#35]. Daniel Wilcox, through his grandmother, Sarah (Savage) Wilcox, had inherited land in Middletown's Northwest Division called Savage Hill. Over the years, Daniel purchased land abutting his Savage Hill property until he eventually established an estate of one square mile. Over the course of the succeeding years, others moved to the area, including Elisha Savage, a great-grandson of John Savage [#35], who purchased 100 acres.

In 1785, the Northwest Division was set apart from Middletown and incorporated as the Town of Berlin, which five years later had a population of 2,465. As Elisha's sons grew, he acquired more land, dividing it into parcels, allotting to his son, Seth, some 25 acres for a homelot tract. Neighboring Seth's home was that of his brother, Selah, with Thankful and Elisha's homestead some distance to the south. Records indicate that the home of Elisha and Thankful was quarantined in 1794 because of a smallpox epidemic. All the homes were along the north-south road called Savage Hill Road, which, in pre-colonial days, had been a main trail used by Quinnipiac and Mattabesset Indians traveling between present-day Hartford and New Haven. In addition to the Savage family members, others who lived near Savage Hill were families with the names of Wilcox, Sage, Penfield, Hubbard, Buckley, Galpin, North, Shepard and Boardman.

Some 650 feet west of Seth Savage's home on Savage Hill was a stream called Spruce Brook, which ran along the valley dividing Berlin and East Berlin. Like most waterways in New England, Spruce Brook was turned into a source of power for mills. One such mill, located behind Seth Savage's home, was originally constructed in 1771 by David Sage, Jr., Daniel Wilcox, Jr., and Daniel's brother, Josiah. The mill was just south of Stantack Road, where a dam was laid across the brook, creating a mill pond next to which a mill house was erected. Called the East Berlin Mill, it was originally used to spin cotton and woolen yarns for blankets and clothing.

In 1798, the mill was owned by Roswell Woodruff. On January 2 Woodruff leased the mill and all water privileges to Elisha Savage and his heirs for 70 years.

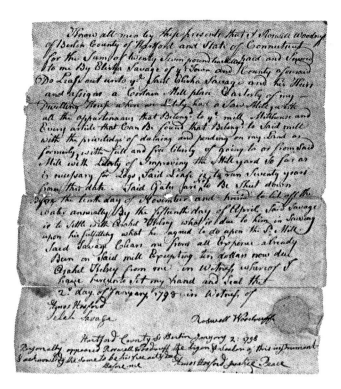

The deed assigning Elisha Savage the East Berlin Mill, 1798

Elisha was a pious man, contributing 15% of his income to the Berlin Congregational Church. Records show he was very frugal, watching every cent earned and spent. Elisha, who died January 24, 1807, and Thankful (Johnson) Savage, who died November 23, 1806, had 11 children, including a son, Seth [#99].

[97] SIMON DeWOLF was born in March 8, 1719, on the island of Guadeloupe, French West Indies, a son of Charles and Margaret (Potter) De Wolff, Jr. [#92]. As a boy, Simon was sent by his parents to live with his grandparents, Charles and Prudence (Beckwith) De Wolff [#81], who lived in Glastonbury. Simon moved with his grandparents to Middletown, where his grandfather opened a general store. On August 27, 1741, Simon married **ESTHER STRICKLAND**, who was born April 4, 1719, in Middletown and baptized in the First Congregational Church April 12, 1719, daughter of Jonah and Martha (Hubbard) Strickland [#83]. Simon, who died January 17, 1762, and Esther

(Strickland) DeWolf, who died May 12, 1761, had eight children, including a daughter, Esther Prudence [#99].

[98] NATHANIEL BOARDMAN was born November 12, 1742, in Westfield Society, Middletown, son of Josiah and Rachel (Cole) Bordman [#93]. On May 24, 1770, Nathaniel married **EUNICE MOSS**, who was born August 12, 1747, in Cheshire, daughter of Benjamin and Abigail (Cole) Moss [#88]. The marriage was performed in Cheshire Congregational Church before Rev. John Foote. Nine years later, Nathaniel was chosen a deacon of the Westfield Congregational Church, a position he held for 15 years. Nathaniel, who died April 9, 1807, and Eunice (Moss) Boardman, who died August 5, 1825, and who were both buried in Old Highland Cemetery in Westfield, had six children, including a daughter, Esther [#105].

[99] SETH SAVAGE was born September 8, 1755, in Middletown's Upper Houses, son of Elisha and Thankful (Johnson) Savage [#96], and baptized in November 9, 1755, the same day his parents also received Baptismal covenants at the Cromwell Church.

Seth grew up when Connecticut was struggling to decide whether to continue on the independent road it had followed since its origins more than a century before or remain loyal to an increasingly arbitrary Parliament and Crown in London. The turning point occurred in 1766 when colonial elections put into the Connecticut General Court and governor's office leaders from the rural and less developed eastern portion of the colony openly contemptuous of London's authority. These leaders and their supporters throughout the colony were able to intimidate or silence the merchants from the more prosperous western and Loyalist segment of the colony.

Any lingering Loyalist sentiment waned in Connecticut in the spring of 1775 when the London Parliament extended the ban, previously imposed only on Massachusetts, prohibiting merchants of all New England colonies from trading with any colony except through England. Later, when New England fishing fleets were barred from Atlantic fishing, nearly all-remaining Loyalist sentiment in Connecticut vanished.

After the closing of the Boston port and during the subsequent British occupation, Congregational churches in Middletown and throughout Connecticut organized drives to send clothing and food to the boycotted city. After the "Lexington alarm," when word spread about the fighting in Lexington and Concord April 19, 1775, Pomfret native Israel Putnam, the respected veteran of the French & Indian War and activist organizer of the convoy of supplies to Boston during the boycott, issued a colony-wide call for volunteers.

Among the Yankees to volunteer were Seth's 16-year-old brother, Selah, born January 9, 1759, and Seth's father's cousin, Abijah Savage, then 30. Abijah was born July 2, 1744, in Middletown, a son of Joseph (1711-1755) and Prudence (Sage) Savage (1713-1807). Abijah's father, Joseph, was a brother of William Savage, Jr. [#84].

Abijah was no stranger to war. His father, Joseph Savage, had been commissioned a captain in the 5th Company, 6th Regiment, in the colonial militia in 1754, serving in the British

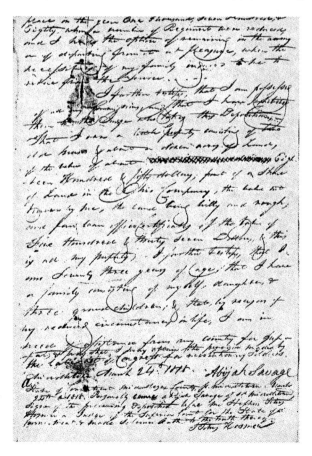

Capt. Abijah Savage recounted his service in pension records

forces during the early part of the French & Indian War until his death the following year. In 1761, Abijah, at age 17, with his brothers Joseph, Jr., Fortanus and Samuel joined the British forces and served in the French & Indian War until their discharge two years later. Owing to this service, his age and respectability, Abijah on May 1, 1775,was selected a lieutenant in the 4th Company of General Spencer's 2nd Regiment. Joining Abijah's company was his cousin Elisha's son, Selah.

Abijah and Selah and the others from Connecticut's Middlesex County and western part of the colony in Spencer's 2nd Regiment marched to Boston, joining thousands of other New Englanders who came to ring Boston in an arch from Dorchester to Chelsea, surrounding the British-occupied port town.

The evening of June 16, Lt. Abijah Savage, Private Selah Savage and others in the 2nd Regiment joined the troops in General Israel Putnam's command sent from Cambridge to dig earthworks in the hills high above Charlestown, where farmers Bunker and Breed grazed their livestock. All night the colonial militia dug trenches and erected barricades. The British guards across the harbor in Boston heard the commotion but didn't think it was important enough to awaken General Thomas Gage. By daybreak, the British awoke to see fully erected military earthworks, with more than 1,000 colonial troops still working on hills where only the day before a few livestock had grazed. Soon artillery from the *HMS Lively* and the *HMS Falcon* pounded Charlestown and the colonials. General Putnam and the other officers kept the men working on the fortifications. By mid-morning Charlestown was ablaze, and the Redcoats were boarding longboats for the trip across Massachusetts Bay to Charlestown.

More than 2,000 British troops formed for the assault on Breed's Hill. The colonials, behind their barricades, held their fire until the first line of Redcoats came within 15 feet of their line— until they saw the "whites of their eyes." Then the Americans unleashed a barrage of musketry. The first British assault failed. Twice, then a third time the Redcoats came. Finally, the Redcoats' overwhelming forces fought hand-to-hand through the colonial line, forcing the Americans to withdraw, first to Bunker's Hill and then across a narrow strip of land to Cambridge, leaving the Charlestown peninsula in British hands. The British suffered 2,000 casualties that day; the Americans lost hundreds. Among the survivors were Abijah and Selah.

The battle of Breed and Bunker Hills was a turning point in the conflict; too much blood had been shed to turn back. About two weeks later, General Washington arrived in Boston. On July 2, he assumed command. He began to mold the diverse and independent group of New Englanders and their colonial allies into a unified army. Life in the camps was crude. Washington found conditions unsanitary, discipline lax. He ordered drills. Strict military command was instituted.

The days when the New England militiamen could select or appoint their own officers were coming to a close. Washington was building a national army.

Selah's cousin, Daniel Wilcox, Jr., who had helped build the East Berlin Mill on Spruce Brook, was among the militiamen surrounding Boston. During the summer from his camp in Roxbury, he wrote a letter home:

Ever Loving Wife:

After my tender regards for you and my dear children,
I take this opportunity to write unto you. Hoping
these few lines will find you all well, as through the
Divine Goodness of God they leave me at present.

I would like to inform you that Brother Isaac, yet
remains very weak and low, but in the whole I've reason to think that he is considerably better, but not yet
able to ride. I hope that by the Goodness of God to
him, that he will a few days be able to go home, if
the Doctor and Officers will give him Liberty, which
is not altogether certain.

The camps are sickly. Ensign Rite is and Sergeant
Gillet and Sergeant Booth and some others are all
unwell, John Wilton Hibbeg yet remains very dangerous. Likewise Jonas Hubbard is sick and gone into
hospital.

Furthermore, I would inform you that I have this
day had the opportunity to hear a number of cannon
fired. The Regulars at first fired one gun from their
floating battery, then our men fired upon them, and
the number of cannon which was fired from the
breastworks and from the floating battery was 27 cannon, and have two bombshells over into Roxbury and
struck a barn upon the roof and went down through a
scaffold and through a stable floor and then broke,
but hurt nobody although there was one man in the
barn and several nearby. The others they struck in a
cornfield, but I have not seen it. Only as I stand some
distance from it and saw the smoke of it when it
burst; further more there was only one man wounded

by one of the enemy's ball; but I hope not mortally. One of their balls went right over my head and afterward was picked up by our men; and another ball struck a large limb of a fine tree nearby where was a great number of our men stood, but hurt nothing.

Likewise there is a number of vessels to the number of 13 or 14 sail vessels, now appearing in sight, supposed to be the same that went out of the Harbor of Boston sometime ago; our men fired but four or five of their canon, but they fired some field pieces at the Enemy. The Enemy did not march out but I do wish that they had. God being on our side we need not fear them. So no more at the present, but I remain your loving friend, a comfort until Death.

Daniel Wilcox, Jr.

While the siege around Boston continued, the Continental Congress in Philadelphia endorsed Washington's plan for an assault on Canada. Washington ordered General Robert Montgomery in Canada to take Montreal and move his forces northeast toward Quebec where they would be joined by the forces to be sent from Boston under the command of Connecticut native Benedict Arnold. Only months before, Arnold had successfully seized Fort Ticonderoga at Lake Champlain in upper New York with Vermonter Ethan Allen and his Green Mountain Boys.

In Boston, Washington called for volunteers to join Arnold's expedition. Among those to volunteer was Abijah Savage. In all, Arnold would get 1,000 men, including three companies of riflemen from Pennsylvania and Virginia, and 10 companies of New Englanders. Arnold and the expeditionary force left Cambridge and sailed September 19 from Newburyport to the Maine coast and north to Kennebeck. The troops had 350 miles to travel through the thickest woods in the northeast in the chill weather of the late fall and early winter.

The trek north was hard. Rain ruined supplies. Sickness spread. Arnold and his officers bickered. Some of the troops were forced to eat boiled rawhide. Men starved. The snows came. Finally, six weeks after the start of the expedition, Arnold's men joined at Pointe aux Trembles above Quebec with Montgomery's army December 2. Arnold had lost 350 men on the march, from starvation, disease and desertion. Montgomery had but 400 men. Together their joint force was 1,000 troops, many weakened and in no condition for the coming assault.

The Arnold-Montgomery joint assault on Quebec called for Montgomery to attack from the west, Arnold from the east on December 31. A blizzard began December 30, and continued the day and night of December 31. Despite the blinding storm, the assault went ahead. It was a disaster. Montgomery's assault from the west failed. He was killed. Arnold's drive from the east also failed. He was seriously wounded. More than 100 Americans were killed and some 300 others were captured, among them Lt. Abijah Savage, who spent nearly 13 months in a British prison before his release in an exchange January 10, 1777.

Meanwhile, around Boston, Washington was trying to build his army. Among the 15,000 troops ringing the city, all but a handful had enlisted for only the year. Their enlistments would expire December 31, 1775. Washington was able to convince only 3,500 colonials to join his Continental Line Army. The others, tired of camp life and many of them ill, wanted to return home. Among those who went home January 1, 1776, was Selah Savage.

Selah would later serve as a private in militia assignments throughout the rest of the war. These included two months in the summer of 1776 with Captain Roger Riley's Company, Colonel Matthew Talbott's Regiment, in the march to New York; for three months in the winter of 1776-77 as a private in Captain Blackman's Company, Colonel Enos' Regiment, in a march to White Plains and, Selah said in his pension record, "sundry other places above and about New York"; another week with Captain Riley in a march to New Haven; another two months with Captain Sage in Guilford, and another two months with Captain Riley at Fishkill on North River when Essopus was burned by the British. In 1779 Selah served for more than two months with Captain Riley at East Haven, and again in September 1781 with the militia in Guilford and Killingworth.

The enlistment problems in the Continental Line Army in 1776 caused Washington to ask the colonial general assemblies to raise more troops. Connecticut sent three more regiments of volunteers to the Boston area. Among them was Seth Savage, Selah's brother, who volunteered early in 1776 and was made a private in Captain Heart's 3rd Company, Colonel Erastus Walcott's Regiment.

In the early months of 1776, Washington's forces in Boston got a big break. The seizure of Fort Ticonderoga the previous spring had enabled a force led by General Henry Knox, in a heroic effort, to bring nearly 60 cannon from the fort over land and water to Boston in the early months of 1776. The British held Boston and Charlestown, but had done nothing to secure Dorchester Heights to the south. In March, using the Knox cannon train, Washington ordered his forces to fortify Dorchester with the newly acquired artillery. A second letter from Daniel Wilcox, Jr., to his wife shows the pace of camp life at this time:

Loving Wife:

After my love to you, I kindly take this opportunity
to write a few lines to you hoping these will find you
all well. Through the Goodness of God they leave me
in good health. Please to remember any duty to my
honored parents and love to my brethren and sisters
for I hain't time to write in particular to them.

Our company are all well, all others sickly.
I would inform you that Sergeant Maget is dead
and Jubez Meiller is dead, and I am informed that
Nathaniel Mill and Lt. Rite is very sick. William
Meiller is weak and low and may have dismission
if he could get home.

Eliphelet had got the mumps but isn't bad;
Simeon Linston had got them again—Furthermore,
I would inform you that I have seen Brother Samuel
Gibson and Brother Solomon Sage and Brother
Porter and they are all well and I am informed that
Brother Sage has behaved very well ever since he left
home.

Furthermore, I would inform you that our men
last night took three Regulars at a place called
Brown's Chimney—furthermore, I would inform you
that our troops are in gay spirits and hundreds of our
men are sent every day to cut fences in order to erect
breastworks as I suppose on Dorchester there is great
preparations for something or other from reports—
think it will not be long we shall make a trail for
Boston, which I hope God in his Providence will
prosper our attempts and for which I ask an interest
in your prayers to God for wisdom and direction and
protection.

I would inform you that we live well. We have
good provisions and as for my own part, I have plenty of business for I have received Regimental orders
for to turn out our men—those that are not on duty
in the forenoon and in the afternoon—and the
Regiment are to meet three times a week for exercise,
and I have the men to warn on Duty and to make a
morning report and a weekly in return, and for to
receive orders every day, sometimes very long, sometimes I take most of a sheet of my paper for to write
them down.

I live very contented although I have more business than any other sergeant in the company, but I lie
and take my rest every night, but I hain't had any

time to go and see Myron Clarke but Abraham Sage
says that he understands that Lt. Rite sold the gun
that did belong to Brother Isaac a few days before I
came down and I cain't leave any business at present
to see anything about it, as I am so busy. I hain't time
to write any more at present, so I remain your friend
and husband until Death.

Daniel Wilcox, Jr.

By the morning of March 5, the work done by the colonials
on Dorchester Heights referred to by Daniel Wilcox, Jr., persuaded British General Howe, now in control of Boston, that
his position was impossible. On March 17, the British evacuat-
ed Boston.

Washington began to concentrate on a possible British assault
on New York City. Some decided to stay on duty around Boston,
while others volunteered to go to New York with the Continental
Line Army. Seth Savage volunteered to serve in Captain Edward
Eell's 7th Company, Colonel Sage's 3rd Battalion, Wadsworth's
Brigade, which was sent to Brooklyn Heights on Long Island,
across from Manhattan. Daniel Wilcox, Jr., decided to stay in
Boston, where he died several months later from illness and was
buried in Roxbury.

Washington had been building his forces in New York since
the spring. British forces, after a delay caused by a failed attack
on the port city of Charleston, South Carolina, finally arrived in
New York Harbor in August. Washington had split his army,
part in Brooklyn, part in Manhattan and part in New Jersey,
near today's Fort Lee. The army of General Howe landed south
of Brooklyn and marched north over Long Island toward the fortified Brooklyn Heights, threatening to trap the American forces
there. After a fierce assault the first day, the cautious Howe
delayed two days before attempting another mass assault. This
delay saved the revolution. On the foggy night of August 29-30,
Massachusetts fishermen under the command of Col. John
Glover of Marblehead ferried 9,500 Americans, including Private
Seth Savage, across the East River to Manhattan, with their baggage, guns and horses. The Revolutionary army was saved.

The Americans fell back to Kip's Bay on Manhattan's
Eastern Shore. On September 15 the forces under the command
of Sir Henry Clinton landed and made an assault, inflicting
heavy casualties on the Americans, particularly in Seth Savage's
company. He and the survivors fell back to American fortifications at Harlem Heights, where another battle occurred the
next day. The assault on Harlem Heights failed; yet the British

were now in possession of New York Harbor and most of Manhattan.

Washington pulled most of his army north to White Plains where on October 28 Howe's army attacked. The battle was fierce. Washington's army fell back. Again, Howe failed to pursue, giving Washington time to escape across the Hudson River and south through New Jersey. On Christmas Day 1776, what was left of Seth Savage's company disbanded, and its members were discharged. Seth returned home to Middletown's Upper Houses and would later reenlist in his cousin Abijah's company.

In Quebec, Abijah Savage was released from prison January 10, 1777, and returned home to Middletown where in March he was appointed a captain in Colonel Sherburne's regiment, Continental Army. The Continental Congress established the regiment as an "additional" regiment in reserve; its members made up of citizens from many colonies. Sherburne's regiment was brigaded with the regiment of Colonel S. B. Webb; Abijah served in Lt. Col. Return Jonathan Meig's company until June 1, 1780.

Serving with Captain Abijah Savage was his young cousin, Seth, who reenlisted in March 1777 as a corporal in Abijah's company. During his three years of duty, much of the time was spent in Rhode Island, where his unit saw action. Corporal Seth Savage was discharged March 24, 1780, from a Continental Army camp in Morristown, New Jersey.

Among Captain Abijah Savage's duties was service as an officer in the guard of the French general, the Marquis de Lafayette. Abijah was later a member of the Society of the Cincinnati, formed in 1783 by officers of the Continental Line. The society was interested in obtaining adequate compensation from the Continental Congress for the service of its members; some in the society also flirted briefly with elevating Washington as the sovereign of the new country. Washington quickly quashed this idea and returned to Mount Vernon in Fairfax, Virginia, permitting the new republic to take root. Decades later, when Lafayette visited America in 1824, Abijah entertained the French general as his guest in Middletown.

In 1782, Seth married **ESTHER PRUDENCE DeWOLF**, born August 31, 1754, in Middletown, a daughter of Simon and Esther (Strickland) DeWolf [#97], and baptized September 8, 1754, at the First Church of Middletown. Both of Esther's parents had died before she reached her eighth birthday. She was raised by family.

Seth, a farmer, also operated a leather tannery and shoemaking shop at the East Berlin Mill behind his home on Savage Hill. In 1817 he was assessed $10 in taxes to help offset the national debt from the War of 1812. Church records describe Esther

Seth Savage recounted his service in pension records

as "a lovely Christian woman, a great reader, but delicate in health." She died October 31, 1815. A widower, Seth married twice more, to widows, Lois Kind of Meriden and Berlin, and to Anna Post, who died November 4, 1836. Seth, who died October 25, 1842, at age 87, and Esther Prudence (DeWolf) Savage, who are both buried at Wilcox Cemetery in East Berlin, had nine children, including a son, Seth, Jr. [#105].

[100]

BENJAMIN MEAD III was born in 1729 in Greenwich, son of Benjamin and Martha (Ferris) Mead, Jr. [#86]. Benjamin married **MARY REYNOLDS**, and they lived with their five children on their Quaker Ridge farm in Greenwich. Mary was a likely descendant of John Reynolds [#27].

During the Revolutionary War, Greenwich and much of lower Fairfield County was a no-man's land. A few miles to the west and south, across the New York border, British forces and their Loyalist and Tory supporters held sway, while in Connecticut's Fairfield County, patriots and their families lived in fear of raids and reprisals from the British or lawless renegades. Though most in Fairfield County opposed crown rule, others believed the Revolution the work of the mob. This division within Fairfield County, together with the fact that

British forces maintained their military stronghold in New York, created a perilous situation for Greenwich patriots.

For Benjamin Mead III, the decision which side to support had been made long before. At the time of the Revolution, he was a member of the Greenwich Committee of Safety, the local militia, and its support operation. His brother, Sylvanus, also had joined the patriot cause. Sylvanus had volunteered in the summer of 1775 at age 38 after Washington's call for more men in Boston. With others from Fairfield, Litchfield and New Haven Counties, Sylvanus was attached to the 7th Connecticut Regiment, Continental Line. Sylvanus was commissioned an ensign in Captain Ebenezer Hill's company. The newly raised troops were stationed along Long Island Sound until September when they were ordered to patriot camps around Boston.

Ensign Sylvanus Mead served in Boston until the spring of 1776 when he volunteered to serve in the coming New York campaign. In May, Ensign Mead was promoted to First Lieutenant of Captain Samuel Keeler's Company, Colonel Phillip B. Bradley's Battalion, Wadsworth's Brigade, which was stationed in Bergen Heights, New Jersey, in the area now called Jersey City.

While Washington's main army was preoccupied with the Battles of Long Island and Manhattan, Lt. Mead and the other colonial troops in New Jersey guarded the Hudson River from a possible British excursion. General Nathaniel Greene, the Quaker from New England in command of Fort Washington in upper Manhattan, in October ordered the patriot forces in Jersey City to reinforce Fort Lee, Fort Washington's companion fortress across the Hudson River. These two forts, General Greene believed, could hold the River.

After the crown forces pushed Washington's army north to White Plains, British General Howe turned his army south to attack the hopelessly undermanned Fort Washington. Frantic, General Greene ordered the troops in Fort Lee across the Hudson River as reinforcements. The siege at Fort Washington was brief. After a battle on November 16, Lt. Mead and 2,800 other patriots were taken prisoner. Though this diversion by British troops enabled Washington's army to flee across the Hudson and through New Jersey, life for the American prisoners turned for the worse.

With the flight of the Washington's army, the British took control of New York. Deserted buildings were turned into prisons, but the quarters soon overflowed with more than 4,000 captured patriots. To accommodate this growing population, the British anchored the prison ship *Whitby* off Manhattan Island in the East River, the first of a dozen ships brought in for the purpose over the course of the war. By war's end in 1783, more than 11,500 patriots had died of smallpox, dysentery, typhoid and yellow fever aboard the 12 prisons ships, 4,000 more than died as a result of combat.

Lt. Mead, like many of the other patriot prisoners, was put on a British prison ship in New York Harbor, where he spent the winter of 1776-77 before his release in a prisoner exchange in the spring. He was ill when he went home to Greenwich.

As the center of the war moved south, a new kind of warfare emerged in Fairfield County.

In April, Major General William Tryon, New York's royal governor, led some 2,000 Redcoats, Hessians and Tories in a raid on Danbury to destroy supplies stored there for the Continental Line Army. In response to this raid, the Connecticut General Assembly in Hartford on May 8 ordered the creation of the Connecticut Rangers. Returned prisoner-of-war Sylvanus Mead, now recuperated, volunteered and was commissioned a captain of the self-defense militia.

The Rangers saw action in February 1779, when Governor Tryon's forces staged another raid, this time on the saltworks in Greenwich. Though the militia drove the invaders back, the property losses were valued at 6,000 pounds. Six months later, Governor Tryon led an assault of 3,000 Redcoats, Hessians and Tories on New Haven, Fairfield and Norwalk. The royalist forces swept through the towns, indiscriminately burning, looting and destroying property and lives. In Norwalk alone, two churches, 40 stores, 130 homes, 100 barns, five ships and flourmills and saltworks were destroyed.

Because of the British assaults, much of the civil order in Fairfield and Westchester Counties had broken down. There were bands of renegades, called "cowboys," whose only allegiance was to themselves. They took advantage of the war to roam the countryside as thieves, murderers and rapists.

Occasionally, the British used these cowboys for their own purposes. One of the men well known to the British in New York was Connecticut Ranger Captain Sylvanus Mead, who had helped organize and lead the defense of Greenwich during Governor Tryon's raids. Tradition holds that one of these ambitious British officers paid a band of cowboys to murder Captain Mead.

Mead rarely spent two nights in a row at one place. Tracking him was hard. Apparently he was hunted for months. Finally, in the early months of 1780, a Tory in Greenwich told the assassins that Captain Mead was staying at the home of Ralph Peck in Mianus, in the eastern section of town. The cowboys approached Peck's home in darkness. One of them knocked on the door. Captain Mead called for the visitors to identify themselves. When he heard no answer, he opened the door to investigate. He stood visibly in the doorway, the light behind him. One of the cowboys leveled his weapon and fired. The ball struck Captain Mead in the chest. The cowboys fled into the darkness. Captain Mead died of the wound the next morning.

The news of Sylvanus' fate plunged his brother, Benjamin III, and the Mead family into sadness. Tragically, the effect of the war would sweep soon into Benjamin's home as well. The Mead home on Quaker Ridge was equipped with a peephole on the second floor through which a family member or member of the Greenwich Committee of Safety could monitor the countryside below. One afternoon, later in 1780, during a Loyalist raid, one of Benjamin's daughters saw a party of Hessian mercenaries and Tories raiding a farmhouse nearby.

Benjamin sent his wife, Mary, and two younger daughters, Mary and Phoebe, to the cold cellar to hide. Benjamin and the older girls, Anna and Theodosia, barricaded the farmhouse doors and prepared for a siege. Obadiah, Benjamin's 18-year-old son, however, was worried about the family's livestock. Obadiah ran outside to put the cattle, geese, chickens, turkeys, and horses into the corral near the barn, apparently believing that if the stock was enclosed on Mead property, the Tories and Hessians would be less inclined to steal it.

As Obadiah was rounding up the livestock, he was seen by a Tory who shouted to a British officer. Obadiah heard the commotion and ran into a neighbor's barn. He'd been seen, however, and soon the Tories and Hessians surrounded the barn. The

Greenwich home of Ralph Peck where Connecticut Ranger Captain Sylvanus Mead [#100] was shot by killers hired by the British in nearby New York in 1780

British officer called for Obadiah to come out or they would set the barn ablaze and he would burn to death.

Obadiah refused to surrender. Instead he leaped from the hayloft at the rear of the building and ran across the orchard behind the barn toward the rocks above Dyspepsia Lane. The Hessians and Tories followed and eventually surrounded the young patriot, who was hiding in a stone hedgerow. Seeing that escape was impossible, Obadiah raised his hands and surrendered. As he walked from his hiding place, the Hessians opened fire. A ball passed through Obadiah's left arm and entered his side, killing him instantly.

Leaving Obadiah's body where it lay, the Hessians and Tories returned to the Mead farmhouse. Benjamin meanwhile had escaped to the woods unseen and was away from the house, unaware of the fate of his only son. Finding only a mother and four daughters at home, the Hessians and Tories killed the Mead's chickens, geese and turkeys, stole a farm horse and carried away the dead livestock in knapsacks.

Benjamin, who died in 1799, and Mary (Reynolds) Mead III had five children, including a daughter, Theodosia [#103].

[101] JOSHUA KNAPP III was born March 17, 1730, in Greenwich, son of Jonathan and Mary (Husted) Knapp [#89]. On April 9, 1754, Joshua married EUNICE PECK, born April 9, 1735 in Greenwich, a daughter of Theophilus and Elizabeth (Mead) Peck [#87].

Israel Knapp, a cousin of Joshua, was the proprietor of Knapp's Tavern, a frequent headquarters for General Israel Putnam during the Revolutionary War. Israel received the license to "keep a public house of entertainment and retail strong drink" in 1754 from the Town of Greenwich. Located on the Boston Post Road and still preserved as an historical site, Knapp's Tavern was a popular "ordinary" and a meeting place for Masons at the time of the revolution. Greenwich, a no man's land in 1779, was known to have ample supplies of food, ammunition and salt. General Israel Putnam, appointed by Washington to supervise New England forces after the flight of the Continental Line Army south in 1776, often used Knapp's Tavern as his headquarters when he toured the southern border of New England to inspect conditions.

During an inspection tour, General Putnam arrived at Knapp's Tavern on February 24, 1779. The next day, a force of Redcoats, Hessians and Tories skirmished with patriot forces commanded by Captain Titus Watson in New Rochelle. Watson's troops were divided, and he was forced to flee through the woods and countryside with 150 troops to Greenwich to warn Putnam. Governor Tryon's forces arrived in Greenwich at 9 a.m. February 26, only a half-hour after Watson had arrived to warn General Putnam of the coming invasion. Putnam, shaving foam still on his cheeks, was ordering his men to points of defense when Governor Tryon's forces arrived. Putnam ordered his men to discharge a volley of musketry and then retreat. The Continentals retreated into a swamp, which proved inaccessible to the British cavalry. Putnam rode to Stamford to obtain reinforcements and returned to Greenwich in time to chase the Redcoats back to New York.

Joshua, who died October 15, 1789, and Eunice (Peck) Knapp III, who died July 8, 1828, had 12 children, including a son, Benjamin [#104].

[102] NATHANIEL HIBBARD, JR., was born in 1750 in Greenwich, son of Jonathan Hibbard [#94]. Nathaniel married ANNA MEAD, born in 1757 in Greenwich, daughter of Peter and Hannah (Mead) Mead [#90]. Nathaniel and Anna (Mead) Hibbard, Jr., had at least three children, including a daughter, Ruth [#106].

[103] EDMOND MEAD was born in 1752 in Greenwich, son of Jonas and Sarah (Ferris) Mead [#91]. In 1776, Edmond married THEODOSIA MEAD, born in 1756 in Greenwich, daughter of Benjamin and Mary (Reynolds) Mead III [#100]. Edmond, who died in 1799, and Theodosia (Mead) Mead, who died in 1827, had several children, including a son, named for Theodosia's slain brother, Obadiah [#106].

[104] BENJAMIN J. KNAPP was born January 1, 1771, in Greenwich, a son of Joshua and Eunice (Peck) Knapp III [#101]. Benjamin married ABIGAIL BRUSH, born in 1780 in Greenwich, daughter of BENJAMIN and REBECCA (FINCH) BRUSH, JR. Benjamin, who died January 14, 1866, and Abigail (Brush) Knapp, who died November 19, 1852, had eight children, including a son, Isaac [#107].

[105]

SETH SAVAGE, JR. was born April 5, 1786, in East Berlin, son of Seth and Esther Prudence (DeWolf) Savage [#99]. On October 30, 1809, Seth married **ESTHER BOARD-MAN**, who was born May 25, 1780, in Westfield Society, Middletown, daughter of Nathaniel and Eunice (Moss) Boardman [#98].

Seth was a farmer like his father and grandfather but found the soil too poor to sustain his family. In 1820, Seth joined his father in working the East Berlin Mill behind his home on Savage Hill. There he tanned leather and made shoes. On the farm, Seth grew flax, which Esther spun into thread used to stitch the tanned leather into shoes. For years, Seth had an annual routine that included hiring a man and taking a wagon and team to Upstate New York's Black River country. There he purchased bark at a sawmill and hauled the load back to East Berlin, where the bark was rendered for its tannic acid and used to tan the leather. Seth and his wife, Esther, spent the summer months making shoes. In the fall, Seth loaded the shoes into a wagon and traveled to Petersburg, Virginia, where he sold the shoes to travelers and peddlers heading west.

Seth Savage, Jr., New Britain

Seth used his earnings to expand his farmland, which eventually totaled more than 100 acres. Esther (Boardman) Savage died in 1850. Shortly thereafter, Spruce Brook flooded and washed the East Berlin Mill house and works away. Seth's business was wiped out. For a time, Seth and his son, Willis Seth, and a nephew, Thomas Savage, worked as tinsmiths in a tin plate business in Berlin. Later Seth opened a shop in Middletown center where he manufactured rules and levels.

On February 17, 1851, Seth Savage Jr., married Phebe C. Tryon, age 40, who was employed as his housekeeper and who would die October 17, 1865.

In 1855, Seth sold his rule and level business to brothers Augustus and Timothy Stanley of New Britain, who consolidated Seth's business with theirs. The Stanley brothers established their new firm on the corner of North and Stanley Streets in New Britain, expanded and on July 1, 1857, brought the various branches of their business into a joint-stock company called Stanley Rule & Level Company, which today is known as Stanley Tool.

Seth, who died October 29, 1868, and Esther (Boardman) Savage, Jr., who died November 17, 1850, had five children, including a son, Willis Seth [#108].

[106]

OBADIAH MEAD was born in 1785 in Greenwich, son of Edmond and Theodosia (Mead) Mead [#103]. In 1809, Obadiah married **RUTH HIBBARD**, who was born in 1789 in Greenwich, a daughter of Nathaniel and Anna (Mead) Hibbard, Jr. [#102]. Obadiah was a farmer and a wit, fond of writing long letters to friends and family.

On October 15, 1856, Obadiah and his brother Solomon signed their names to the following:

THE LIST OF MY ESTATE FOR THE YEAR 1856

1   The first one hundred and forty acres of land
    with two yoke of oxen I now have on hand
    Also twelve cows that I mean to keep
    have wintered and sheared just 38 sheep

2   One horse we have you very well know
    beside an old mare that you prize low
    One yearling colt and two-year-old mare
    to prize very high it would not be fair

3   I give in two poles with my other estate
    And one I think they ought to abate
    I have a steel clock I put with the rest
    Also my carriage which is none of the best

4   As to my cart my barrows, wagons and plows
    you may prize when you see my oxen and cows
    the house hold stuff the poultry and bees
    them you may prize just what you please

5   I think of nothing more excepting my hogs
    Them you may prize with my cats and my dogs
    and when I speak of my dogs and my cats
    I do not forget the mice and the rats

6   I think I have all I now can relate
    of both my real and personal estate
    I had like to forgot my two year old bull
    and now I think I have my list full.

Some of Obadiah's letters were to friends in the western United States territories, including Hawaii, where his cousins, Melicent Knapp and her brother Horton Owen Knapp and Horton's wife, Charlotte Close, another cousin, had gone as missionaries. Obadiah's correspondents had migrated from Greenwich with the New England Protestant missionaries to the Sandwich (Hawaiian) Islands in the early 1800s.

The migration by these New England missionaries to Hawaii has its roots in the Puritan legacy. Hawaii's first recorded contact with Western culture came in 1778 when British Naval Captain James Cook came upon Hawaii, which he called the Sandwich Islands. The natives Cook encountered were the descendants of Polynesian peoples who first came to the islands some 1,300 years before from Marquesas Islands to the southeast, and from Tahiti 400 years later. During the four decades after Cook's discovery, Hawaii underwent profound changes under the influence of American and European traders and explorers.

The first was economic, as American and British traders first exploited the islands' location near the Pacific's whaling hunting grounds and later in their trade of Hawaiian sandalwood to China. This led to the development of Hawaii's plantation and the influx of immigrant labor, who would transform the islands. Another consequence was disease, cholera, measles, bubonic plague, venereal disease and later leprosy from China. The native population, estimated at 300,000 at the time of Cook's discovery, declined more than 75% within a few decades. In addition, exposure to Westerners and their ways brought a social revolution within Hawaiian society, with political power consolidated in one royal family and ancient priests overthrown.

Hawaii's transformation was felt around the globe in New England, home to most of the merchant-ship captains, their crew members and financial backers. At the time, religious zeal in New England combined with the arrival of a few Hawaiians aboard Yankee whalers and trading ships helped stimulate a religious missionary movement dedicated to saving the souls of the people of Hawaii.

A mission school was established in Cornwall, Connecticut to train Hawaiians as missionaries. The American Board of Commissioners for Foreign Missions (ABCFM) in Boston organized the first mission to Hawaii in 1819.

From the first voyage in 1819 to the 12th and final voyage in 1848, a total of 169 people were part of the ABCFM's efforts. They would establish 17 missionary stations and two school sites on the islands, and other less formal preaching stations. Over the years, some of these Yankees would spend their entire lives in Missionary service; others would leave the church to serve the Hawaiian royal family in government services; others returned home; and some resigned and worked in trade.

For the most part, the missionaries formed a mutually supportive community of Americans dedicated to high purpose and righteousness. They would have resisted the modern notion they were America's 19th century version of crusaders as well. But without them, the Hawaiian Islands would never have become part of the United States.

In Boston, as members of the ABCFM Pioneer Company were put aboard the *Thaddeus* in 1819, they were given the following instruction:

> "Your views are not to be limited to a low, narrow scale, but you are to open your hearts wide and set your marks high. You are to aim at nothing short of covering these islands with fruitful fields, and pleasant dwellings and schools and churches, and of raising up the whole people to an elevated state of Christian civilization.
>
> "You are to obtain an adequate knowledge of the language of the people to make them acquainted with letters; to give them the bible, with skill to read it...to introduce and get into extended operation and influence among them, the arts and institutions and usages of civilized life and society, and you are to abstain from all interference with local and political interests of the people to inculcate the duties of justice, moderation, forbearance, truth and universal kindness. Do all in your power to make men of every class, good wise and happy."

Sixteen years after this Pioneer Company left New England, the ABCFM organized the Eighth Company, which, at 32 members, was the largest contingent of Missionaries ever dispatched. The Eighth Company's vessel was the barque *Mary Frazier* and was 108-feet-long, 23-feet-wide, and 288 tons. Captain Charles Sumner sailed *Mary Frazier* from Boston December 14, 1836, arriving in Honolulu 116 days later on April 6, 1837.

Among the couples aboard were Mr. & Mrs. Horton Owen and Charlotte (Close) Knapp, both 23 years old. Horton and Charlotte were Greenwich neighbors and cousins with each other and with Obadiah Mead, who began a life long correspondence, that was later continued by his daughter, Theodosia, and her husband, Isaac Knapp.

Horton Owen Knapp, born March 21, 1813, in Greenwich, was hired by the ABCFM as a teacher. On November 24, 1836, just weeks before the voyage, Knapp married his neighbor and cousin, Charlotte Close, born May 26, 1813, also in Greenwich. One account of the *Mary Frazier*'s 116-day voyage said:

> "Our voyage was of almost uninterrupted happiness
> and prosperity. Our accommodations were excellent,
> the treatment of the Captain was kind, the officers
> were obliging and all the crew highly respectful when
> in our presence. Permission was obtained to have
> morning and evening prayers in the passengers' cabin
> (the Captain taking the lead during the latter part
> of the voyage), and to have public worship on the
> Sabbath. A deeply interesting state of religious feeling
> prevailed among the ship's company and about half
> of them gave encouraging evidence of having entered
> on the Christian life. After their arrival in Honolulu,
> six of the ship's company, including two of the offi-
> cers, made a public profession of religion at the
> mission church."

Horton and Charlotte were stationed for two years at Waimea on Big Island, where a Mission had been established in 1832. In 1838 they were reassigned to Lahainaluna on Maui, where Horton taught school and helped scholars prepare a Concordance to the New Testament as well as mounting maps of the Sandwich Islands. The following year, the Knapps went to Honolulu where Horton was assigned teaching duties. In his diary in 1840, Horton wrote the following account:

> "Sunday Aug 16th—My Sabbath School was much
> larger this morning than usual. I attribute the increase
> to the influence of Mr. Armstrong (a Mission supervi-
> sor) who has taken an interest in it and made efforts
> to bring out children to attend schools. The number
> of children present was about 150, the house nearly
> full. Mr. Armstrong came in near the close of the
> school and made some remarks, then closed with
> singing and prayer, having appointed a meeting for
> the children at Tuesday morning at 1/2 past 8 o'clock,
> at which time he intends to have a feast for them
> consisting of poi and molasses."

In Honolulu, Horton fell ill and died March 28, 1845, at age 32. In a journal entry later that year his widow, Charlotte (Close) Knapp, wrote:

> "Honolulu Nov. 1st—I arrived here a week ago
> yesterday in company with Mr. & Mrs. Whitney and

Dr. Smith after a passage of two days and three nights from Koloa. We had a rough uncomfortable time but felt thankful that it was no worse. Mr. Whitney had been ill for 4 or 5 weeks and suffered much of the voyage. It seemed very pleasant to meet my old friends and neighbors and to be at home again, but there is something wanting—he with whom I once enjoyed them is not here.——"

Charlotte (Close) Knapp, now widowed and 32 years old, lived in Honolulu; she and Horton had no children. Also in Honolulu at the time was a widower, Rev. Daniel Dole, the 37-year-old principal of Punahou School, whose wife had died the previous year giving birth to their second son.

Dole, born September 9, 1808, in Maine, had been married to Emily Hoyt Ballard, born June 11, 1807, in Hallowell, Maine. She was likely a descendant of Simon Hoyt [#51]. Emily Ballard, a teacher, and Dole were married in Gardiner, Maine October 2, 1840, five weeks before the voyage they took with three other Missionary couples in the ABCFM's Ninth Company. After the Doles arrived in Honolulu in 1841, he was assigned to establish and be first principal of the Punahou School, which the ABCFM wished to create to educate the children of the Missionary community.

Charlotte (Close) (Knapp) and her husband, Rev. Daniel Dole, were teachers and missionaries in Hawaii

On June 22, 1846, Dole, now a widower with two young sons, married widow Charlotte (Close) Knapp, whose knowledge, training and availability must have seemed like a act of Providence. Charlotte was a scholar in Hebrew, Greek and Latin and taught with her new husband at the Punahou School. She was also an accomplished homemaker, cook and seamstress that made her a valuable teacher and mission wife.

In a letter to her sister, Sarah Close in Greenwich, Charlotte sent along a daguerreotype taken of herself and Rev. Dole about seven years after their marriage. The photo, she wrote,

> "makes him look older than he does out of the picture, and our hair was do damp with perspiration, that it has a glossy appearance. You have his sober thoughtful expression, when he is speaking or is engaged in conversation he looks quite different...You will hardly think I had on a black silk dress. It is one that has been colored and watered, and somewhat glossy so it does not look as a plain black would, but I had no better suitable. I think black or very dark clothing the best for likenesses. The collar is one Elizabeth Dole sent me and if you will examine close you will see her work. It is run in figures with floss cotton I should think..."

In summer of 1855, the Doles moved to Koloa, Kauai. By that time, Rev. Dole had been principal of Punahou School for 14 years and had been married to Charlotte (Close) (Knapp) for nine years. During his tenure at Punahou, differences had grown up between Rev. Dole and some of the school's trustees. Though some wanted him to say, Dole felt obliged to look elsewhere for work. Since he had not learned Hawaiian sufficiently to preach, many positions at congregations were not open to him. It so happened there was a need for a new school on Kauai, where a Missionary station had been founded at Koloa in 1834. Mission and plantation families there found it expensive to send their children to Punahou on Oahu; they also didn't like sending their young off island to school. The Doles were hired to start and run a school on Kauai.

Among their neighbors in Kauai, were Charlotte's cousin and former sister-in-law, Melicent Knapp, and Melicent's husband, James Wilson Smith, who had lived in Koloa since 1842 and been ordained as a minister for a year. Smith, born July 8, 1810, in Stamford, Connecticut, had become a physician after studies at the New York College of Physicians & Surgeons. He had practiced medicine in New York City for five years before joining the

ABCFM. Smith, at 32, married Melicent Knapp in Greenwich on April 18, 1842. At the time of her marriage Melicent, born in Greenwich October 15, 1816, was 26 years old and her brother Horton, had been teaching in Hawaii for five years.

Three weeks after their marriage, the Smiths sailed with the Tenth Company to Hawaii aboard the brig *Sarah Abigail*. The 210-ton vessel was 96-foot-long, 22-feet-wide, and 11-feet-deep. Captain Doane sailed the brig from Boston May 2, 1842, and arrived in Honolulu 143 days later on September 21, 1842. The Smiths were stationed at Koloa, Kauai. Dr. Smith was the only physician on the island and his duties took him at a moments notice on sudden calls to all parts of the island, from Hanalei 40 miles to the north, to Waimea, 12 miles to the west. In the Koloa Station Report to the ABCFM in 1851, Dr. Smith alluded to the financial problems faced by the Missionaries and how he might be able to earn his keep through other sources. He wrote:

Melicent (Knapp), a teacher, and her husband, Dr. James W. Smith, a physician, served as missionaries in Hawaii

> "As to my salary I explained to one of the officers of the church my relation to the American Board and told him that if the church would raise annually $250 toward my support that with what I should probably receive from foreigners for medical services and from other sources it would be sufficient to justify me in making the experiment of ceasing to draw my support from the Board. This Elder proposed the matter to the church members who all seemed to enter into it cheerfully and the specified sum was soon raised. It remains to be seem whether they will continue to raise the sum year after year.
>
> "Kahookui, whose name has been mentioned in a former Report as well as this, continued to do well as a native preacher & I consider him a useful helper.

He is at present a member of the legislative body now in session.

"On the whole, though there is much worldliness among the people & it is to be feared much impropriety, both in the church & out of it, still there is much encouragement to labor. The people come out to the meetings and seem disposed to hear the truth, the scriptures are in their houses and are read. I have sold for cash during the last 6 months more than 60 Bibles besides testaments. The word of God is among the people."

Dr. Smith was released from the ABCFM in 1851 and ordained to the ministry July 1854 at Koloa. The Smiths had nine children. In 1861, Melicent (Knapp) Smith established the Koloa Boarding School for Girls and maintained the school for a decade. The Smiths lived and worked in Koloa, Kauai for the rest of their lives.

While in Hawaii, Richard H. Dana, Jr. of Boston, wrote a letter published June 5, 1860 in the *New York Tribune*:

"...it is no small thing to say of the Missionaries of the American Board, that in less than 40 years they have taught this whole people to read and to write, to cipher and to sew. They have given them an alphabet, grammar and dictionary; preserved their language from extinction; given it a literature, and translated into it the Bible and works of devotion, science and entertainment, etc., etc. They have established schools, reared up native teachers, and so pressed their work that now the proportion of inhabitants who can read and write is greater than New England; ...and the more elevated of them taking part in conducting the affairs of the constitutional monarchy under which they live, holding seats on the judicial bench and in the legislative chamber, and filling posts in the local magistracies..."

Though Waimea remained the capital of Kauai, Koloa had become its economic center. The Port of Koloa was frequented by whalers, suppliers and travelers of all kinds. Koloa was the center of agriculture. In Koloa, the Doles found friends. In addition to Melicent (Knapp) and Dr. James Smith, the Doles found Lihue plantation manager, William Harrison Rice and his wife, who had worked with the Doles at Punahou. Their daughter, Maria, would be the Dole School's first pupil. A house was built for the Rev. Dole and his family consisting to two rooms and a garret. The cook house was separate. The first Dole school house was a single room, a clapboard building with bare timbers inside under a thatched roof. Rev. Dole, preaching in English, alternated his Sundays between Lihue and Koloa.

Missionary family children, and part Hawaiian children all attended Dole's school. Five of the Smith children attended. Since many parents wanted their children to board at the school, more room was needed. The Dole home became a boarding home for children from Hanalei, Waimea, Lihue, Wailua. Among Dole's students were children of the Rice, Sinclair, Robinson and Gay families, who one day would lead Hawaiian society.

Missionary homes became virtual wayside inns for visitors. The Smith and Dole homes provided lodging for people going to and from Koloa.

The favored ports for whalers since 1825 were Honolulu on Oahu and Lahaina on Maui, which grew to become favored seamen's communities, complete with all the attractions sailors enjoy world round. Since Captain Cook, the Kauai's favored port was Waimea to the south, but Koloa got its share of trade and the trouble caused by the rowdy doings of crew members. In early days, the ships that did visit Koloa tended to those piloted by captains who had more pious ideas. On occasion, Dr. Smith was invited to preach aboard such whaling vessels offshore Koloa. Some captains brought their wives and children with them on their voyages. In January 1857, Dr. Smith noted:

> "Capt. Cox & his wife and daughter came on shore from the Magnolia and stopped with us...Capt. Perse...had his wife and two daughters aboard...Mrs. Jones & child was with him (Captain Jones) & spent several days with us."

In return for this hospitality of this sort, James & Melicent Smith were often given several gallons of whale oil for their trouble. On October 14, 1854, for example, the *Scotland* was at Koloa. Dr. Smith wrote:

> "Capt. S. generously made me a present of 5 gals of Oil—the 2d can full I have received from him the same way—He is homeward bound."

Though Koloa avoided the level of depravity of Honolulu and Lahaina the whalers' trade did caused trouble. Weary of the crews of some ships, Dr. Smith noted in his journal in April 1865: "Three whaleships here at anchor & bad proceedings are expected on shore."

Dr. Smith, who died in Koloa November 30, 1887, at age 77, and his wife, Melicent (Knapp) Smith, who died in Koloa September 24, 1891, at age 74, are buried behind the parsonage of Koloa Union Church. Inscribed on Melicent's headstone are two legends: "Her children rise up and call her blessed," and "Precious in the sight of the Lord is the death of his saints."

Rev. Dole was released from the ABCFM in 1860 but remained a teacher in Koloa of what was known as Rev. Dole's School until his death August 26, 1878, at Kapaa, Kauai. Charlotte Close (Knapp) Dole, who assisted her husband as a teacher, died at age 61 in Koloa, July 5, 1874.

Their son, Sanford Ballard Dole, became a central political figure in the history of Hawaii. Dole was raised in Kauai and studied for two years at Williams College in Massachusetts. He practiced law in Honolulu and was active in politics, being elected often to the Hawaii legislature. An opponent of King Kalakaua, Dole was a leader in the political movement that brought the adoption of a constitution by the legislature in 1887. He was also appointed a justice on the Hawaii Supreme Court that year. In January 1893, Dole led a committee formed to overthrow Queen Liliuokalana (sister of Kalakaua) and seek annexation of the Hawaiian Islands by the United States. The committee deposed Queen Liliuokalana and installed a provisional government with Dole as president. When President Grover Cleveland denounced the overthrow and demanded that Queen Liliuokalana be restored, Dole and his committee declared their independence, creating the Republic of Hawaii in 1894 with Dole as president. Six years later the United States created the Territory of Hawaii and President Cleveland appointed Dole First Territorial Governor, a post he held until his retirement in 1915. Dole died in 1926; by then his nephew, James Dole, had become the principal architect of the agricultural empire in Hawaii and the fruit processing business, and today the name Dole is nearly synonymous with pineapples and canned fruit.

James and Melicent (Knapp) Smith had nine children, all born in Koloa. One was William Owen Smith, born August 4, 1848, whose middle name was for his mother's bother, Horton Owen Knapp. W. O. Smith went to Rev. Dole's school and became a lawyer and politician; he was also a childhood friend and later colleague of Sanford Ballard Dole.

W. O. Smith became a lawyer and served as Sheriff of Kauai in 1870 and later moved to Maui representing that district in the Hawaiian legislature on and off from 1878 to 1912; also serving as the attorney general of the Provisional Government from 1893 to 1899. In 1915, W. O. Smith wrote a reminiscence of his Koloa boyhood for the Kauai Historical Society:

"...my father, Dr. J. W. Smith, succeeded (Dr. Thomas Lafon the missionary physician on Kauai) in 1842. My father was the only physician on the Island and devoted himself to that work although he and my mother, Mrs. M. K. Smith, were engaged in general missionary work. The Island was quite well populated at that time and my father was often away from home. My mother had classes of native women in Bible study and taught them sewing, etc., and later established a boarding school for training Hawaiian girls, in which she was assisted by her sister, Miss Deborah Knapp, and her daughters, Emma and Charlotte. In 1857 my father, at the earnest request of the missionaries, consented to be ordained and become pastor of the Koloa Native Church, which position he held til in the sixties when the American Board adopted the policy of installing native pastors. While pastor he still carried on his medical work.

"During the early days missionary families often had to entertain company. Some of the visitors were acquaintances and friends and many were strangers. There were times the good mothers became weary with the extra work and care of entertainment strangers. The hospitality was given without grudging and the best things were offered to the guests, and many times the appreciation and kindness of the guests fully compensated for the labor; but there were instances of strangers going away and telling of 'the luxury' in which the missionaries lived, little knowing how economies had to be practiced after their departure and of the weariness which they had caused.

"Home life of Koloa was very pleasant. Our Mother, like nearly all of the missionary mothers, was New England born and had training and ingenuity in household matters and making the best of conditions. The children were taught to be helpful and were instructed in the early school branches. The clothing was home made and with a large family this entailed much work and care for the mother.

"As the years passed and the children of these missionaries increased in number and there was no school for them on Kauai, and sending of the young children to Punahou entailed much anxiety and expense, it was decided to establish a school at Koloa, and Rev. Daniel Dole who had been principal of the Punahou School consented to come to Koloa. He came in 1855 with his wife, Mrs. Charlotte C. Dole, and his sons George and

Sanford, and for many years maintained the school; and the mission children from Hanalei, Lihue and Waimea were boarded in his home.

"Father Dole was an excellent instructor and is remembered by his old pupils with great respect and aloha. The reputation of the school was such that some pupils came from the other Islands...Besides maintaining the school Father Dole established a church at Koloa for English speaking people, which he maintained for a number a years."

After Hawaii was annexed by the United States at the end of the 19th century, Sanford Ballard Dole wrote a reflective essay entitled *Hawaii After Annexation*. He wrote in part:

"I do not know that anywhere there is a civilized community whose social life is more natural and unconventional without loss of refinement than that existing in the Hawaiian Islands...

"A charm of Hawaiian society is its cosmopolitan quality. Every large social gathering has representatives from the great world races—Polynesian, Anglo-Saxon, Celt, Scandinavian, Franks, Mongolians...

"What will be the result when the American comes as he is coming now, and faster?...Without doubt the union of little Hawaii with great America lifts the curtain before a future full of great possibilities to Hawaii...

"We shall undoubtedly have our disappointments. There will be some bad mixed with the good. But there will be growth beyond our own precedents. Our local world will be larger and we shall be in touch with the great communities of the rest of the world. We are Americans now, for better or worse."

Shifting continents and historical events, another of Obadiah Mead's relations took part in the settlement of the American frontier.

At the time Obadiah Mead was born in 1785, more than a century and a half had passed since the first English settlers had arrived. Connecticut was a popular colony for immigrants. Between 1730 and 1750, for example, the population had grown from 38,000 to 100,000. The last public land was auctioned off that year. This bursting of population and poor agriculture fed the fever for more land. The relatively static culture of the Puritans, and the tradition of the eldest son inheriting the bulk of the father's estate also stimulated the desire for new horizons. The Mead, Knapp, Ferris, Peck, Brown, Savage, White and Boardman families all saw sons and daughters move west in each successive generation. Over the years, favored destinations were New Jersey in the 17th century, and in the 18th western Massachusetts, Vermont and New Hampshire, as well as upstate New York, eastern Pennsylvania and beyond.

Among the pioneers to head west was Obadiah's distant cousin, David Mead, who was born January 17, 1752, a son of Darius and Ruth (Curtis) Mead. Darius Mead was born in 1728 in Greenwich, a son of Jonathan and Sara (Husted) Mead, Jr., a great-great-grandson of John Mead [#40]. In 1750 Darius married Ruth Curtis of Stamford and moved to Hudson, New York, where Darius purchased farm property. In Hudson, Darius and Ruth had six children, including their eldest, David.

After the last lands were auctioned off in Connecticut in 1750, a number of companies were organized to obtain and settle territory beyond the colony's borders, hoping to repeat the plantation process that had built Connecticut 120 years before. The most famous of these companies was The Susquehanna Company, formed in July 1753 by Eliphalet Dyer, a lawyer from Windham, to claim land along the Susquehanna River in Pennsylvania under Connecticut's 1662 royal charter.

These companies justified their actions because the Charter approved by Charles II granted Connecticut all the land bordered by Narragansett Bay on the east, Massachusetts Bay on the north, Long Island Sound on the south and extending west between the 41st and 42nd degrees north latitude to the South Sea (Pacific Ocean). On March 4, 1681, Charles II gave William Penn all the land bounded on the east by the Delaware River, west to five degrees longitude, and lying between the 40th and 42nd degree north latitude. Thus, both Connecticut and Penn had claims to the upper third of today's Pennsylvania.

For a time common sense prevailed. Connecticut's leaders in the years after the 1662 charter and during negotiations between 1683 and 1725 with New York leaders over their common border, never pressed any claim to territory beyond New York. By 1750, however, with the end of the land auctions, Yankee speculators took great interest in the grants under the 1662 charter.

The Susquehanna Company, set up primarily for land-hungry residents of eastern Connecticut, established in 1753 a "journeying committee" of three men who, in October, went to the Wyoming Valley along the Susquehanna River in Pennsylvania to survey, map and gather information that could be of use to company stockholders who would come later. The company's plans were delayed by the French & Indian War. The land drive resumed on May 19, 1762, when some 109 members of The Susquehanna Company traveled to Wyoming Valley, where they planted crops and cleared land for homes. They went home to Connecticut for the winter. The following spring, some 200 company members returned to the valley and built a blockhouse and log cabins and harvested crops, fully intending to stay. A massacre by Indians that year cost 20 Yankees their lives and sent the survivors fleeing back to Connecticut.

That massacre, part of the conflict today called Pontiac's War, further delayed The Susquehanna Company's plans. With the signing of the Treaty of Fort Stanwix in November 1768, however, 40 Susquehanna settlers were authorized by the company the next month to go to Wyoming and reclaim the land.

This group established what would become known as the "First Forty" fort. Later, they were joined by other Yankees under the command of Major John Durkee who, by May 1769, had built 20 log cabins and a wooden stockade that Durkee named Wilkes-Barre in honor of John Wilkes and Isaac Barre, two members of the British Parliament sympathetic to the American colonials.

The Penn family did not let this Yankee settlement go unchallenged. On several occasions, Pennamite militias were formed to resist the Yankee settlers. Connecticut squatters were occasionally jailed, only to be freed when their captors were overwhelmed by Connecticut militia. Other times, shots were fired, and armed battles occurred. The first so-called Yankee-Pennamite War ended in August 1771. By 1772, more Yankees had arrived, adding to Wilkes-Barre's growth and to the new encampment at Fort Wyoming, later establishing settlements at Charlestown, at the mouth of Muncy Creek, and at Judea, the site of present-day Milton.

By 1772, Pennsylvania had incorporated Wyoming Valley as Northumberland County, with the town of Sunbury, site of Fort Augusta, as the county seat. The Yankees, for their part, incorporated Fort Wyoming as the Township of Westmoreland. In January 1774, the Connecticut General Assembly put Westmoreland under the political jurisdiction of Connecticut's Litchfield County. This conflict would fester for years, with many battles, scores of deaths, and unjust confiscation of land on both sides. Yet the development continued, with many of the settlers coming from Connecticut and elsewhere to join their Yankee kin in pressing Yankee claims in the Wyoming Valley.

One of these pioneers was Darius Mead. In 1773, Darius and Ruth and their six children, including 21-year-old David, moved from Hudson to take title to land in Wyoming County under the Connecticut claim. After clearing the land and farming it for a year, the Mead's claim was ruled invalid by Pennsylvania authorities in 1774. Forced out, the Mead family moved to an area on the western bank of the Susquehanna River's North Branch, six miles north of the town of Northumberland. David Mead, now 22, six-foot-three and reportedly handsome and well built, that year met and married Agnes Wilson, the 19-year-old daughter of John and Janet Wilson of Northumberland.

At the outbreak of the Revolutionary War, David was commissioned an ensign second class in Captain John's Company, Colonel Hunter's Battalion, in the Associated Battalions and Militia of Pennsylvania. The central conflicts of the war were fought to the east and south. However, the Iroquois, urged on by the British, conducted murderous raids in eastern Pennsylvania, believing they would get the land after a British victory.

By the winter of 1777 and 1778, rumors of a joint British-Iroquois attack on the Pennamite and Yankee settlements swept the Susquehanna frontier. By the spring of 1778, the Connecticut settlement in Wyoming Valley was the prosperous home to 3,000 residents, but poorly defended. Raids on outlying farms and settlements by the Iroquois continued. One of the Iroquois victims was David Mead's brother, Asahel, who in the spring of 1778 was caught in an open field by a band of Iroquois warriors and murdered, his body mutilated.

By July 1778, an allied force of some 1,000 British, Tory and Iroquois gathered for an attack on the Susquehanna settlements. More than 400 Americans had gathered to resist. Yet on July 3, the Americans were outmaneuvered. The battle was brief, but the subsequent murder of the wounded and the slaughter of the prisoners left more than 300 Americans dead by the end of the day. The Battle of Wyoming, as it was called, was to be among the bloodiest episodes of the revolution.

That summer, David and Agnes moved with the first of what turned out to be nine children to Sunbury. Their David opened an inn and built a still to make whiskey. In 1779, believing the frontier now secure from Indian attack, and encouraged that his claim in the Wyoming Valley was valid, David and his family returned to the Mead family's original claim settled six years before.

On November 3, 1781, just 15 days after Cornwallis' surrender to Washington at Yorktown, the Supreme Executive Council of Pennsylvania requested a hearing on the Susquehanna land dispute under Article IX of the Articles of Confederation. In August 1782, both Connecticut and Pennsylvania leaders agreed to submit the dispute to a Court of Commissioners to be appointed by the U.S. Congress. In December, the court in Trenton, New Jersey ruled that the land in Wyoming Valley along the Susquehanna River belonged to Pennsylvania and that Connecticut had no jurisdiction. Private ownership of the land was another matter, and that would be decided by a group of commissioners to be named by Pennsylvania. Not surprisingly, the Pennsylvania commissioners rejected the Connecticut settlers' claims to the land, ordered them evicted and granted them land in western Pennsylvania in compensation.

Among those affected was David Mead who in 1782 lost his claim to the family farm in Wyoming Valley. He was forced to return to Sunbury, where he prospered and in 1783 became the justice of the peace for Northumberland County. When the land in Western Pennsylvania became available to him in compensation for his Wyoming claim, David and his brothers, Darius, Jr., John and Joseph accepted the grant in the west and traveled with six other Northumberland men to the frontier.

In 1788, these 10 pioneers traveled more than 100 miles through the wilderness. On May 12, they camped beneath a wild cherry tree on the banks of French Creek. The following day they started building a cabin and planting corn on land between the Cussewago and French Creeks abandoned by Indians. David first built a house on the west side of the creek, calling his claim Cussewago Island. He later built a double log cabin on a bluff above French Creek. To guard against Indian attack, the house was surrounded by a 15-foot-high stockade and protected by a small square blockhouse at the stockade's northwest corner. That fall, David and his brothers brought their parents, wives and families from Northumberland County to their new claims. David and Agnes (Wilson) Mead's daughter, Sarah, was born that fall in David Mead's new home, becoming the first non-Indian child born in today's Crawford County.

The next year, 1789, the area known as Mead's Settlement prospered, drawing other settlers from the east looking for opportunity in the new nation's Northwest Territory. David built a sawmill on the north side of a deep ravine, using waterpower to drive the blades needed to fashion the lumber used for new homes.

In April 1791, Flying Cloud, an Indian friend of David's, warned that Delaware Indians were hostile. Soon 11 Indians were seen in war dress a few miles north of the settlement. The women and children gathered at Mead's house that night and the next day were taken by canoe to Fort Franklin. Several of the men, who followed the next day on foot with their livestock and personal effects, were ambushed and murdered by the hostiles. The terror continued. In the summer, David's father, Darius, now 63, was captured as he worked on a field near Fort Franklin. A Delaware chief, called Captain Bull, took Darius to Conneaut Lake. Days later an armed search party found Darius' body and that of an Indian warrior, with marks indicating they had had a vicious fight. Captain Bull was nowhere to be found.

Mead's Settlement was abandoned in 1791 and 1792 because of the Delaware Uprising. However, a garrison of 15 men from Fort Franklin used Mead's house as an outpost in the winter months of both years.

Despite the hostilities, David Mead continued with his plans to develop his claim. In 1792 and 1793 he went to the claim to lay out plots and the nucleus of his town. By 1793 he had sold a few parcels to interested settlers. With the defeat of the western Indians by General Anthony Wayne, the threat of further Indian attack eased, and the frontier was opened again to new settlement. David Mead surveyed the settlement and in 1795 submitted his plan to the Commonwealth of Pennsylvania. The next year, the Commonwealth granted him a patent, approving his incorporation and plot plan. The town was named Meadville.

David Mead and Meadville prospered. As a militiaman he was appointed major-general of the 14th Division and later of the 16th Division of the Pennsylvania Militia. During the War of 1812, General Mead sent Captain Dobbins of Erie to Washington in the summer of 1812 with dispatches telling the government of the loss of Detroit and Mackinaw. General Mead requested that a naval station be established on Lake Erie and construction of a fleet begun immediately. Command of the lake was given to Lieutenant Oliver Hazard Perry, who arrived in Erie March 27, 1813. Commodore Perry needed men to guard the position. Some men were raised, but more were needed. General Mead obliged with the following broadside:

> CITIZENS TO ARMS
> Your state is invaded. The enemy has arrived at Erie, threatening to destroy our navy and the town. His course, hitherto marked with rapine and fire wherever he touched our shore, must be arrested. The cries of infants and women, of the aged and infirm, the devoted victims of the enemy and his savage allies, call on you for defense and protection. Your honor, your property, your all, require you to march immediately to the scene of action. Arms and ammunition will be furnished to those who have none, at the place of rendezvous near to Erie, and every exertion will be made for your subsistence and accommodation. Your service to be useful must be rendered immediately. The delay of an hour may be fatal to your country, in securing the enemy in his plunder and favoring his escape.
> DAVID MEAD, Maj. Gen.,
> l6th D.P.M.

In August, Commodore Perry successfully launched his fleet. He took time in August and in October to write the following to Mead:

U.S. Sloop of War "Lawrence"
Off Erie, August 7, 1813
    Sir:—
I beg leave to express to you the great obligation I consider myself under for the ready, prompt and efficient service rendered by the militia under your command, in assisting us in getting the squadron over the bar at the mouth of the harbor, and request you will accept, Sir, the assurance that I shall always recollect with pleasure the alacrity with which you repaired, with your division, to the defense of the public property at this place, on the prospect of an invasion.
    With great respect I am, Sir,
    Your obedient Servant,
    O.H. Perry.
    Maj. Gen. David Mead,
    Pennsylvania Militia, Erie.

Erie, October 22, 1813
    Dear Sir:—
It may be some satisfaction to you and your deserving corps, to be informed that you did not leave your harvest fields, in August last, for the defense of this place, without cause. Since the capture of Gen'l Proctor's baggage by Gen'l Harrison, it is ascertained beyond doubt that an attack was at that time meditated on Erie; and the design was frustrated by the failure of Gen'l Vincent to furnish the number of troops promised and deemed necessary. I have the honor to be, dear sir,
    Your obedient Servant,
    O. H. Perry.
    Maj. Gen. David Mead
    Meadville

Though there is no record whether Obadiah Mead corresponded with his cousin, David, in Meadville, Obadiah's letters spanned the globe, from New England to Hawaii.

Obadiah, who died in 1878, and Ruth (Hibbard) Mead, who died in 1825, had five children, including a daughter, Theodosia Caroline [#107].

[107] **ISAAC KNAPP** was born February 20, 1811, in Greenwich, son of Benjamin J. and Abigail (Brush) Knapp [#104]. On November 25, 1838, Isaac married **THEODOSIA CAROLINE MEAD**, born March 22, 1819, daughter of Obadiah and Ruth (Hibbard) Mead [#106]. Isaac, who died April 1, 1891, and Theodosia Caroline (Mead) Knapp, who died April 18, 1899, had five children, including a daughter, Theodosia Caroline [#109].

Isaac Knapp, New Haven

Theodosia Caroline (Mead) Knapp, New Haven

[108] **WILLIS SETH SAVAGE** was born March 14, 1818, on Savage Hill, East Berlin, son of Seth and Esther (Boardman) Savage, Jr. [#105]. Willis Seth was admitted to the Berlin Congregation Church on August 2, 1835. On March 20, 1839, Willis Seth married **ULYSSA LOIS MOSS**, who was born in Cheshire March 10, 1820, a daughter of Leverett and Lois (Tuttle) Moss. It is certain that, but unclear how, Ulyssa was

related to the descendants of John Moss [#21], John Moss, Jr. [#63], or Benjamin Moss [#88].

A farmer, Willis Seth worked with his father in the leather tanning and shoemaking business, in the rule and level business, and in Berlin with his cousin, Thomas Savage, at T. Savage & Company, manufacturers of tin ladles, brass candlesticks, raised

Willis Seth Savage, Hartford

Ulyssa (Moss) Savage, Hartford

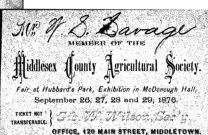

A business card for the family smith works, and a membership card in the local agricultural society were among Willis Seth Savage's possessions.

tea kettle bottoms and tin tops. Willis Seth later operated the Wood Scott Mill Company in Berlin. Willis Seth, who died September 6, 1885, and Ulyssa (Moss) Savage, who died July 28, 1902, and who both were buried at Wilcox Cemetery, East Berlin, had three children, including a son, Henry Elliot [#109].

Willis Seth Savage's ledger book
noted every cent earned and spent

PART THREE

Builders of the New Union 1840-1960

[109] **HENRY ELLIOT SAVAGE** was born February 9, 1840, on Savage Hill, East Berlin, son of Willis Seth and Ulyssa (Moss) Savage [#108]. In 1860, **THEODOSIA CARO-LINE KNAPP**, born in 1842 in Greenwich, daughter of Isaac and Theodosia Caroline (Mead) Knapp [#107], moved to Berlin to become the village schoolteacher. Henry and Theodosia met and began a courtship that was interrupted by the Civil War.

By 1862, the Union's yearlong effort to subdue the Confederacy had not worked. General George McClellan's campaign on the Virginia Peninsula had failed, and his Army of the Potomac had been recalled to Washington. President Abraham Lincoln issued another call for volunteers from the states. In Connecticut, Republican Governor William A. Buckingham responded.

Connecticut had long been in the Union camp. Yankee farmers and tradesmen, raised in the Puritan tradition, believed that the Union was more than just a political arrangement. It was a vehicle by which Americans would create a new Zion in the Wilderness, free of the Old World's corruption, a land ordained

Theodosia Caroline (Knapp)
Savage (Hartford)

Sgt. Henry Elliot Savage

Theodosia Caroline (Knapp)
Savage

Henry Elliot Savage

Henry Elliot Savage (7th from right) with other Civil War veterans at Grand Army of the Republic (GAR) gathering in Middletown, Connecticut cemetery.

by Providence for the fulfillment of Divine Will. The Union was a sacred trust, and the Constitution the ultimate symbol of earthly authority. Connecticut's Congregationalists, the descendants of Puritans, accustomed to obedience to higher authority, found the Confederacy's secession not only treasonous but also bordering on a violation of Divine Law.

Aside from this abhorrence of secession, Connecticut was no friend to slavery. By 1848, when slavery was banned by state law, only 20 blacks remained in servitude in the state. During the political turmoil over the slave issue in the 1840s and 1850s, Connecticut was a haven for abolitionists and anti-slave societies. Many residents were active in the Underground Railroad, smuggling runaway slaves north to Canada and hiding them in safe houses in Deep River, Hartford, Killingly, Middletown, Guilford and Willimantic along the way. Connecticuters were "free soil" supporters during the days of Bloody Kansas, and among the most active in the formation of the new Republican Party. At the outbreak of the war, Connecticut's manufacturers and tinkers factories turned to producing war materiel. Thousands volunteered to serve in the army. Eventually, Connecticut would raise 33 regiments and provide more than

50,000 residents for federal service, the largest percentage of a state's population in the Union.

When the federal forces in August 1862 languished around Washington, Governor Buckingham had already anticipated Lincoln's call for volunteers. The previous month Buckingham had authorized Col. Frank Beach of the U.S. Army to go to Middletown and raise the 16th Connecticut Volunteers. More than 900 farmers, tradesmen, artisans, merchants and others volunteered. Among them was Henry E. Savage, whose family in East Berlin had long supported the Union. Among the publications kept in the Savage home was a newspaper called *The Emancipator*. Henry volunteered in Middletown July 30 and was mustered into U.S. service August 24 by Lt. Watson Webb.

Private Henry Savage, of Company G, was sent by train with the 16th Connecticut Volunteer Regiment August 29 to Washington. The 16th went into a camp in Arlington, Virginia, near today's Bailey's Crossroads, joining the Army of the Potomac under the command of General McClellan. The recruits were green. Lt. B. G. Blakeslee, the 16th's regimental historian, said the unit had

> "...no drill, no discipline, few instructions even in marching. It was little more than a crowd of earnest Connecticut boys..."

As the Union forces regrouped near Washington, General Robert E. Lee understood that after a year of war, the Union was now on the defensive. Its continued ability to wage war depended on defeating Southern forces in the South. Lee knew an invasion of the North by the Southern Army would, if successful, produce tremendous political benefits. A vocal peace movement was growing in the North, calling on the federal government to sue for a cease-fire and let the Confederacy go its own way. The will of some Northerners to maintain the Union was weakening. Lee made a strategic decision to invade Union territory. Lee knew that if he could inflict a wound on Union armies in the North the peace movement's momentum would grow and the war might end. Lee also hoped that a Southern victory would cause European governments to recognize the Confederacy and deny materiel, money or trade to the North, or increase such to the South.

Lee's 55,000-man Army of Northern Virginia crossed the Potomac River near Leesburg, Virginia September 5, 1862, and entered Maryland intent on marching to Pennsylvania. McClellan, with a newly reorganized and fortified Army of the Potomac, marched his 95,000-man force northwest from

Washington along today's Leesburg Pike to find Lee.

Lee, whose goal was Pennsylvania, took a risk and split his forces into four parts. Major General D. H. Hill was sent to Turner's Gap in South Mountain to make sure no federal troops got through. The other divisions of Lee's army were placed in three wings under the command of General "Stonewall" Jackson, who was dispatched to capture Harper's Ferry, where 12,000 federal troops were garrisoned. Lee ordered the capture of the garrison to secure a supply and communications base for his troops when they reached Pennsylvania.

Lee remained with 19,000 troops in his immediate command. As fate would have it, he faced mortal peril. Lee's Special Orders No. 191, dated September 9 and issued to his generals regarding the deployment of his army, fell into Union hands. A copy of the orders, wrapped around three cigars and addressed to General D. H. Hill, were found in a field by Union soldiers. The orders were forwarded to McClellan's headquarters where on September 13 one of McClellan's staff officers recognized the writing as authentic. The Army of the Potomac, now near Frederick, Maryland, and its commander, General McClellan, had been given the opportunity of the war.

McClellan ordered his army toward Turner's Gap, where his men met some rebel resistance. Lee, knowing his plans had been discovered, ordered his far-flung divisions to regroup near the town of Sharpsburg near Antietam Creek. Stonewall Jackson sent word that the 12,000 federal troops at Harper's Ferry had surrendered. Jackson said he would leave immediately and meet Lee at Sharpsburg 17 miles away. Left behind to secure the arsenal was General A. P. Hill, whose forces would join Lee as soon as possible.

McClellan, whose troops were approaching Antietam Creek and facing only Lee's force of 19,000, could have attacked September 15. Ever cautious, McClellan chose to wait and gather the entire Army of the Potomac to prepare for an engagement.

Private Savage and the 16th Connecticut had made the march and, on September 16, brigaded near Antietam Creek with the 8th and 11th Connecticut Volunteers and 4th Rhode Island Volunteers under the command of General Edward Harland. Together these four regiments constituted the Second Brigade in the 3rd Division, 9th Army Corps, commanded by Major General Ambrose Burnside.

That same day, Lee was joined by Stonewall Jackson, whose wing arrived after a hard march from Harper's Ferry. Three other rebel divisions arrived that day, and two more would arrive the morning of September 17. McClellan's advantage was lost.

At dawn on September 17, Lee's right flank was behind Antietam Creek, and his left was in the woods north of Sharpsburg on Hagerstown Road. As rebel artillery rained upon the Union troops across Antietam Creek, the first in a series of Union assaults began from the Union's right to its left. The names of the engagements live on: Dunkard Church, Bloody Lane, the Cornfield. The charges, countercharges, the missed opportunities, lost orders, the heroism and incompetence, and the death. Seldom in history have fellow countrymen inflicted such ferocious violence on each other in so short a time.

On the Union's left flank, Burnside's 9th Army had orders to keep the pressure on the enemy all day. The orders weren't specific. Did pressure mean an attack outright, or simply to create a diversion to assist in other assaults by other Corps?

Burnside, who had been an army commander, preferred to keep a wing headquarters for himself and leave moment-to-moment command of the 9th Army to Brigadier General Jacob Cox, commander of the Kanawha Division, one of the 9th Army's three divisions. At 10 a.m., Cox ordered his Kanawha Division to attack across a bridge that spanned Antietam Creek. For hours, some 14,000 Union soldiers repeatedly stormed the bridge under fierce artillery shelling and musketry fired by some 500-rebel troops secreted across the creek in the trees and scrub along a high ridge. Time after time the rebels were able to repel the Union advance toward the span, dubbed Burnside's Bridge. Other brigades in the Kanawha Division were sent downstream to locate other likely crossings. The 3rd Division, which included Henry Savage and the 16th Connecticut, was ordered by Brigadier General Isaac Rodman downstream to Snavely's Ford to bring additional pressure on the defending rebels. Another brigade of Union troops went upstream to do the same thing.

Meanwhile, the 2nd Division of the 9th Army stormed the bridge in successive bayonet charges and finally was able to clear the area. Yet it could not establish a firm hold on the opposite bank. New York and Pennsylvania regiments finally crossed the bridge and established a hold. Regiments from the Kanawha and 3rd Divisions, including the 16th Connecticut, crossed and by 1 p.m. Burnside's Bridge was in Union hands. Yet as Private Savage and the others on the opposite bank waited, more than 10,000 soldiers of the 1st Division under Brigadier General Orlando Willcox took two hours marching eight abreast to cross the span. Lee used this time to shift several rebel brigades to reinforce the Confederate line above the ridge and beyond.

Finally at about 3 p.m., six brigades of the 9th Army Corps advanced up the steep ridge and, under artillery fire and musketry, moved across the cornfields toward the town of Sharpsburg and the Confederate line. The inexperienced men of the 9th Army, like those in the 16th Connecticut, failed to move in unison. Some took cover in nearby stone fences, or in trees; others ran recklessly toward the town, opening large gaps in the advancing Union line.

The regiment on the extreme left flank of the Union advance was the 16th Connecticut. Exposed and ahead of the main advance, Private Savage and others in the 16th saw a long column of blue-coated infantry approaching up the road from Shepardstown Ford. The men of the 16th, not recognizing the troops and fooled by the Union colors and blue uniforms, did not realize they were watching the 3,000 men of Confederate General A. P. Hill's Light Division, who were just completing a 17-mile forced march after successfully looting the federal arsenal at Harper's Ferry. Among the rebels' booty were the blue uniforms and Union colors now flying.

The 16th Connecticut continued its advance to within a few score yards of the Confederate soldiers. Suddenly, the rebels shouldered arms and opened fire. In his diary, Lt. Blakeslee wrote that the 16th had just been ordered to keep moving when a

> "terrible volley was fired into us from behind a stone wall about five rods in front of us...In a moment we were riddled with shot...orders were given which were not understood. Neither the line-officers nor the men had any knowledge of regimental movements."

Private Savage dropped to the ground. Others broke and ran. As they ran toward their own line, the fleeing members of the 16th were met by the fire of others in the 9th Army Corps, who had been ordered to fire on Hill's rebels. Caught in the crossfire, the slaughter of the men of the 16th was appalling. Soon the Connecticut soldiers, joined by members of the 4th Rhode Island, attempted a counterattack. But the green recruits had had virtually no drilling "and hardly knew how to form in line of battle," Lt. Blakeslee wrote.

The Union's assault on Sharpsburg soon crumbled. Private Savage, seeing many of his boyhood friends slain around him, gathered himself up and made his way back to safety. With the rest of the 9th Army, he retreated to just below the ridge above Antietam Creek, where the Union line stayed. That evening both sides rested, cared for their wounded and tended to their dead. Union losses were put at 12,000, Confederate losses at 10,000. September 17, 1862, would remain the single bloodiest day of the

Civil War. As for the 900 men of the 16th Connecticut who marched to Antietam Creek, only 250 were able to fight again. The losses of the 16th were the greatest suffered by any regiment, North or South, that day. That evening Henry Savage was given sergeant's chevrons.

The evening of the next day, Lee ordered his men to retreat, slipping the Army of Northern Virginia back south. Lincoln used this opportunity to claim victory and announce the Emancipation Proclamation, which, in banning slavery, gave the North the unifying cause that would carry the Union through in prosecuting the war. Lee's mission in the North was an utter failure. After the battle, Henry sat down and wrote his family about his experience.

Henry Elliot Savage earned his sergeant's stripes at Antietam.

Near Sharpsburg, Sunday, Sept 21/62

Dear Parents

I should like to have written before, but this is the first time I have had a chance and felt as if I could. Last Monday we left Frederick City early in the morning; at night we came up within the place where they fought the day before (that night we put up our tents as usual I went in with Ed & Wad since then until last night we had had no chance to use tents).

Tuesday morning we started as usual, and about noon we joined one brigade; we were marched into a piece of woods, ordered to load our pieces and rest for a while; about 3 o'clock we started again and kept moving slowly until dark when we were marched up near and under a reb. battery and ordered to keep as still as possible but were permitted to lie down on our arms; don't think I slept very well that night; in the morning we could not see but when everything was all right some of the men got up on the fences and were looking around; pretty soon over came, some shells near, so pretty soon one struck among the 8th Co. killing three of them; they kept coming thicker and nearer and soon our commander thought best to move us out of range and were kept moving from one place to another so as to get some advantage of the rebels, & were kept under the fire of these batterys a good deal of the time till about four o'clock in the afternoon when the battle commenced in earnest.

We were so worried out with our marching that we could scarcely stand up (& by the way on our march from Washington we were obliged to walk till most of our men fell & then we were halted for the night) we were bought up near a large corn field and formed in line of battle the corn was this large southern kind, and the field was very large; after we got into the field we were marched over a very high rail fence giving the rebs a chance to see and know where we were coming, we did not know they were in the corn, that of our company we received a volley, one of our men fell dead; we were then marched around to another place and ordered to lay down; we then, some of us, fired when were ordered to fix bayonets and change; by that time we received the awfullest volley that ever was; the rebs were not more than three rods from us; our Col. then rode into the field and ordered us out; just before we were ordered out the word was given not to fire because we were killing our own men so that I did not so much as fire off my gun and it was the same with several of the rest of them;

Where we retreated the bullets kept coming faster than you ever saw hail stones and it is the greatest wonder that I or any of the rest of us got off alive (you will probably hear about the killed and wounded long before you get this so I shall not be very particular about it).

I did not stay long to see the fight but get out of the way as best I could. One reason the fight was so hard for us our artillery got out of ammunition and were drawn off the field; the rebs had batterys so they could play on us from two ways; some time after dark the rebs planted a battery where ours was but we were said to take it, guns and all, but I do not know whether its best to believe it or not; at any rate the rebs kept these pickets on the corn field till Friday morning and our dead and wounded had to lay on field —

Thursday we were marched up a hillside and had to lay on our arms all day and part of the night til the morning we were drawn up in line when Burnside rode past and said we might have an hour to rest and get our breakfast, a very encouraging thing when one had but one cracker in his haversack.

After that came the worst and most sorrowful days work I ever did. After we got on the battlefield the first body we can to that we knew was Ed's. It was on a plowed field under a black walnut tree after that we entered the corn. Word came that they had found the orderly's body then right in a row we found about six others and several of the wounded had been supplied with water by the rebs.

Our first business was to gather the wounded we found; I found much as ten who had lain on the field and Charly amongst them, he is wounded in the thigh.

After the wounded were gathered we got the dead we found some of our company and the next morning (one more making ten in all of our boys, we buried thirty-four in one grave) and it was near 10 at night before we had the funeral. The grave is near and under a locust tree; yesterday and today it has been dreadful solemn in camp. Today is the first day of rest I have had since we enlisted.

Last night the mail came in and I was much disappointed not to get anything; you might write as often as you can for you can not tell how much good it does one to get a letter or paper from home think I have had as much soldiers experience in three weeks as I wish to have could write much more but am tired send me the (Hartford) Courant that gives an account of this battle.

from your affectionate son
Henry

Sgt. Savage returned with the 16th to the outskirts of Washington, D.C. President Lincoln soon replaced McClellan with Burnside, who led the 115,000-man Army of the Potomac

south toward Richmond in pursuit of Lee's Army. The Union
army, which included the 16th Connecticut, arrived at
Fredericksburg November 17 where a small rebel force stopped
the Union advance on the banks of the Rappahannock River.
Delayed by supply problems, the Army of the Potomac was further bogged down when Lee's Confederate forces came north and
held the high ground behind Fredericksburg.

Finally, Burnside ordered an assault on Fredericksburg
December 11. The Army of the Potomac crossed the river on
pontoon bridges in the face of Confederate snipers hidden in
buildings along the riverfront. After the Confederates withdrew,
the Union forces took the town, which had been abandoned by
its inhabitants, leaving behind the buildings and contents to the
Union soldiers who ransacked and looted the town. Two days
later, Burnside ordered his army to remove Confederates from
well-fortified hills outside of town. The assaults were failures,
costing the Army of the Potomac 13,000 casualties. After the battle, the Union retreated across the river and repaired. Sgt. Savage
wrote his family the following letter.

> Tuesday, Dec, 16, Camp opposite
> City Fredericksburg
>
> Dear Parents brother and sister
> Last night we returned to camp after being out
> four days we went out Friday morning
> We got up Thursday morning at 4 o'clock and
> ordered to have our haversacks packed with three
> days rations and woolen blankets. Thursday we did
> not move out of camp until after dark and then were
> marched about a half mile when our order for march-
> ing was countermanded and we were marched back
> to camp and staid there that night but were ordered
> to be ready the next morning
> Started about 8 o'clock; marched down to the
> river, lay there til about 4 o'clock in the afternoon
> when a few shells came over killing one man and
> wounding three more of the 15 reg; we were then
> marched back to a safe position, waited till after dark
> when we were marched back to the bridge and over
> into the city.
> The city the day before was completely riddled
> with shot and shell; and our men went in and tore the
> houses to pieces for firewood to make camp fires that
> night. I made my coffee in a fire place; did not have
> to go out of the room for the wood from a shell burst
> in the room and made plenty of kindlers, we drew

out some boards and fixed a place to lie down; were ordered not to use our guns but did to cook our meals. At midnight our rations came across and we had to turn out and draw them; did not sleep very warm that night, it froze quite hard.

At sunrise we were marched to the south end of the city and lay there in mud up to one's ankles all day and until nearly night; we were between the shots, from our guns and the enemy's that is. There came several shell bursts near us from our guns and killed several men, wounded two or three of the 15, that was Saturday.

At night we were again set a moving, marched out back of the city, formed in line of battle and marched within bullet range of the enemy, while our first brigade went up and engaged the enemy. We were expecting to go into it every minute but had the privilege of lying on our blankets and sleeping on our guns, a very comfortable way of sleeping as you may imagine.

The enemy are fortified in the strongest way imaginable, having breast works on a steep hill and any quantity of cannon. Then a little beyond that is a another hill fixed in the same way, as we have no chance to take these works by storm. Saturday the brigade made three charges on the works, losing nearly all there men in the first place; they charged on the works but lost most of their officers except Meagher; that made them mad. They then made two charges with great loss but gaining nothing; through the fight there has been but little gained and great loss of life.

At sunrise Sunday we were marched back to the city and staid there till night. Sunday the boys spent the day in going around and getting books, pictures and most everything you could think of; there was lots of flour got and any quantity of griddle cakes made. We spent the sabbath there quite comfortably. I did not wander about any, rather stay near the gun.

According to orders, after dark we were marched out and placed on picket; then were marched and posted in groups of three, except nine of us were placed in a block house. At the outpost were out beyond the first parts the house had 36 holes for shooting rifles through. We were posted about 8 o'clock; through the night Sam Woodruff and me stood guard with the 2nd Lt. Lt watched with us or stood in readiness for us to call on him if it was

necessary to give an alarm. We were ordered not to
fire our guns from the place, except to give an alarm
but all was quiet through the night near us.

But in the morning the reb pickets began to tap
away at our men outside. From our post holes we
could see the whole rebel picket line, counted 18
heads pocking up at one time; after a while they got
to firing at our house. But it being made of logs a
foot thick but it scared our men.

Some should had quite a pleasant time if it had
not been we were in danger of shell from the rebel
guns but it happened that we did not get any had
some of the rebs come within 5 rods of us. There
picket line was about 20 rods from where the outpost
through the night. But in the day time had the 8th reg
and two hundred braden sharpshooders were posted
beyond us

We stood and watched the rebs through the day
and until about 8 o'clock at night when we were
relieved; some time a dozen bullets would plug the
old house at a time. After we were relieved we were
marched into the city, around one side formed in
time; staid there about an hour when we were started
again with orders not to speak a loud word; did not
know but were going into battle; but when we came
to march, fetched around down to the pontoon
bridge marched across and back to our old camp got
there about 12 o'clock.

After being out 4 days and 3 nights we tired as
you ever got; used to think I got tired at home but I
find that I never knew what it was to get tired; to
thank kind Providence that I came out of it without
getting shot and with no other injury except a slight
cold.

It seems that Burnside has tried the strength of
the enemy and turned around and retreated. The loss
to our side estimated at some seven thousand; don't
know anything about the loss on the other side.

My other box has not come yet; perhaps you better see Mr. Down and see what he thinks about it. I
own the boot I got and wore it through the battle; it
happened to come on the foot that had the leaky
boot, but I note to lost the glasses. Send me the wrap-
per as soon as you can and a pair of draws should be
it. Wonder if we staid here some time now; don't
know as you can figure out this letter, had been two

days writing it and have written down lines at a time.
Out of eleven days rations we had had one of fresh
beef and the rest salt pork; had to eat it raw mostly
while out. The Berlin boys are all right; there was no
loss in our reg. So I might as well close this from
your son and brother
Henry.

PS I have a sabbath school that came out of
Fredericks; a few kernells of corn that got me in the
block house. Sam has some popcorn he is going to
give me.

The Army of the Potomac remained outside Fredericksburg.
In January 1863 became bogged down in a quagmire of mud
when Burnside ordered it in the dead of winter to move upstream
and cross the Rapponhonock. The elements doomed the maneu-
ver. Lincoln, exasperated with Burnside, removed him from command of the Army of the Potomac. Burnside, who remained head
of the 9th Army, which included the 16th Connecticut, moved his
corps to Newport News, Virginia.

The 16th later was sent to Suffolk and placed under General
Harland's command. The 16th saw action in Suffolk during the
siege by Longstreet's Corps, first at Edenton Road April 24,
1863, and then at Providence Church Road, May 3. On June 16,
the 16th moved to Portsmouth, where it later met with General
Dix and went up the Peninsula in an effort to destroy the links
between Lee's army and Richmond. An engagement called the
Blackberry Raid failed, dooming the attempt. In a forced march,
the 16th and the rest of the Union Corps returned to Portsmouth,
where it remained for the rest of the summer.

In September, five companies of the 16th were sent to South
Mills, Virginia for two weeks of picket duty. Their return trip
through swamps was hazardous, with many of the Yankees
picked off by snipers.

While on duty in Virginia, Sgt. Savage obtained a 10-day
leave to go home to East Berlin. The leave papers give a vivid
description of his physical appearance and the particulars of his
enlistment and record.

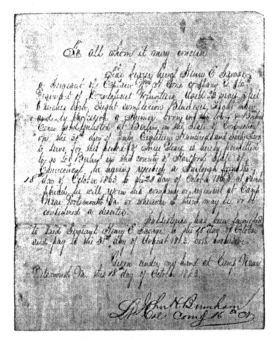

Sgt. Savage was granted a 10-day furlough in October 1863

To all whom it may concern

The bearer hereof Henry E. Savage, a Sergeant of Captain Wm H. Cone company G, 16th Regiment of Connecticut Volunteers. Aged 22 years 5 feet 6 inches high. Light complexsion. Blue eyes. Light hair and by profession a Farmer, born in the town of Berlin Conn. and enlisted at Berlin in the State of Connecticut on the 30th day of July Eighteen Hundred and Sixty Two to serve for the period of three years is hereby permitted to go to Berlin in the county of Hartford State of Connecticut he having received a Furlough from the 18th day of October 1863 to the 28th day of October 1863 at which period he will rejoin his company or regiment at Camp near Portsmouth Va or whereever it then may be or be considered a deserter.

Subsistence has been furnished to said Sergearnt Henry E. Savage to the 18th day of October and pay to the 31st day of August 1863 both inclusive.

Given under my hand at Camp Near Portsmouth Va., this 18th day of October 1863.

John H. Burnham
Lt. Col Company of 16th CV

On the outside fold, the pass was signed and counter-signed by Lt. Col. Burnham, and by Col. Hand and finally noted that "this 10 day furlough had been granted by command of Brig Gen. E. Harland, and signed by Hazard Stevens, Capt. AAG." Sgt. Savage's attendance record was noted.

Absent with leave		0
" " out "		0
" detached		5
" sick		13
present		32
Present & Absent		50

In January 1864, the 16th was sent to Plymouth, North Carolina where it joined a garrison January 24. By that time, the Union forces had occupied Plymouth for more than a year. After the loss at First Bull Run in 1861, the Union had turned its attention to the coast of North Carolina. Control of these coastal waters and the navigable rivers flowing into them, would eliminate the threat of rebel pirates, enable command and control of the eastern third of North Carolina and threaten Wilmington & Weldon Railroad, one of the main lines connecting Richmond with the south.

After battles to take Fort Hatteras in August 1961, and the subsequent surrender of Ocracoke and other coastal defense points to the Albemarle and Pamlico sounds, the Union established bases of operation against Eastern North Carolina. A garrison at Plymouth was established by the summer of 1862, a little town strategically situated on the south bank of the Roanoke River, where near its mouth the Union established a key supply depot for the land forces in Eastern North Carolina.

By 1864, more than 2,834 manned a garrison under command of Brig. Gen. H. E. Wessells, who commanded a series of forts that ringed the town on its land side. Forts named Williams and Wessells, were connected by strong redoubts, breastworks and formidable obstructions. Up the river nearly three miles was Fort Gray, and on the east side of town, Fort Comfort and two redoubts protected the Columbia Road. In the river were the gunboats, *Miami* and *Southfield*, plus two smaller vessels, the *Whitehead* and the *Ceres*.

In 1864, from the garrison, the 16th Connecticut would make several raids into the North Carolina interior, breaking up Confederate cavalry camps, capturing or burning cotton and tobacco stores and taking prisoners. This activity continued for weeks. Finally, Sgt. Savage and Company G were ordered March 3 to Fort Stevenson to relieve a company from the 21st

Connecticut. Their return trip March 20 was a near disaster. The men of Company G were returning to Plymouth aboard the *Thomas Collyer* when a storm off Roanoke Island nearly caused the vessel to wreck on some shoals. The vessel swamped, and the men had to be rescued by the steamer *General Berry*, after having spent hours in the icy rain on the deck of their swamped ship.

The men of Company G returned to the garrison at Plymouth only to have their days on active duty end less than a month later when the garrison was overrun by a force of 12,000 Confederate soldiers under the command of General R. D. Hoke. To take Plymouth, the Confederate Gen. Hoke devised a land and sea assault. The Confederate Navy had constructed an iron-clad ship named *Albemarle,* which was 152 feet long, 45 foot at the beam, with two engines were 200 HP each, drawing eight feet of water. The ship's frame was made of yellow pine timbers, 8 x 10 inches thick, dovetailed together and fastened with iron and treenails, sheathed in four-inch thick yellow pine. The ship's 60-foot octagonal shield was covered with two courses of iron plating 2-inches thick. The 18-foot prow built of oak and covered with iron plates was used as a ram.

The siege on Plymouth began April 17, when the Rebel army moved to within five miles of town. Frantic women, children, Negroes and non-combatants fled by the steamer *Massasoit* to Roanoke Island. Shelling from Confederate ships began pounding Fort Gray at daybreak April 18. *Albemarle* arrived the night of April 18 and by the next day was engaged in battle.

The evening of April 19, a sergeant from the 85th New York, wrote:

> "...I went out on the line of works and delivered the
> men their rations. The men seemed in good spirits
> and said the rebs could never take their works in
> front, but we all knew it was only a question of time
> for we were completely surrounded on the land and
> the ram had command of the river and could hold it
> against any force..."

The next morning, General Wessells lost hope. He later explained:

> "I was now completely enveloped on every side, Fort
> Williams, an enclosed work in the center of the line
> being my only hope. This was well understood by the
> enemy and in less than an hour of cannonade of shot

and shell was opened up it from four different directions. The terrible fire had to be endured without reply, as no man could live at the guns. The breast-height was struck by solid shot on every side, fragments of shells sought almost every interior angle of the work, the whole extent of the parapet was swept by musketry and men were killed and wounded even on the banquette slope. A covered excavation had been previously constructed, to which the wounded were conveyed, where they received sufficient medical attention. This condition of affairs could not be long endured without reckless sacrifice of life; no relief could be expected, and in compliance with the earnest desire of every officer, I consented to hoist a white flag at 1 a.m. of April 20. I had the mortification of surrendering my post of the enemy with all it contained."

Included were approximately 2,500 men from four full regiments, parts of three others, 28 pieces of artillery, 500 horses, 5,000 stands of small arms, 700 barrels of flour, with other commissary and quarter supplies, immense ordnance stores and importantly, the town itself, which would now enable the *Albemarle* to drive Union gunboats from both Albemarle and Pamlico sounds. Fearing capture, North Carolina natives who had been part of the Union army, deserters from Confederate ranks mostly, had fled from Plymouth in canoes and were rescued by Union boats in the sound. Less lucky where the Negroes who were captured and shot later that afternoon. Union forces later recaptured Plymouth and sunk the *Albemarle* in the fall of 1864.

For now, however, the 16th Connecticut had lost 436, killed or captured. Among those captured was Sgt. Savage, who, with the other prisoners, was sent to Andersonville Prison in Georgia. Sgt. Savage's diary of that period remains. The description of his siege at Plymouth and his capture follows.

April 17—A fine quiet morning attended Church— About four in evening Rebs attacked Plymouth by driving in pickets and shelling Fort at Warneck on Roanoake River—

April 18—Rebs opened on same Fort this morning at five—we were kept behind breast works thorugh the day—Had quite an engagement in evening pickets all drove inside the works. The gunboats silence the Rebs

Batterys and make them move back to a safe distance.
The Bomb shell was sunk by land battery.

April 19th—At three o'clock this morning the Rebel
Ram Albemarle came down the river sinking one our
best gunboats and driving the rest out of the river. At
ten o'clock evening Co. G was send out on skirmish
line near Colombia coast -

April 20—Were drove into small redoubt at five in
morning and captured soon after. The whole town
was captured before noon are treated very well by
our captors.

April 21—Were all herded together and kept near
picket post on Washington road last night. Got four
days ration this morning of hard tack and pork and
started on our march at noon did not halt till nine
evening made about twelve mile —

April 22—Were started this morning at sunrise
marched till about five in evening—marched very
slow made about fifteen mile.

April 23rd—Commenced marching soon after sun
rise halted near Hamiton at ten; marched about six
miles. Halted in small grove.

April 24—Commenced marching again about noon;
marched about twelve mile and stopped for nine in
some fine woods.

April 25—Were started about six this morning and
reached Foxboro about noon. Drawed our first
Confederate rations this evening; they consisted of
about a pint of black beans and pound and quarter of
bacon.

April 26—Stay on banks of Fox River—The Officers
and part of the men take cars for Georgia—rations
corn meal and beans.

April 28—Were kept on bank of River some same
rations

April 19th—Left our camp on banks of river at about
nine, got aboard cars near Foxboro at eleven, the
only place of any importance was Goldsboro, arrived

at Wilmington about ten, were kept aboard cars till
three o'clock next morning —

April 30th—Crossed Cape Fear river about five this
morning on ferryboat and went a board cars for
Charleston. cars move very slowly train stopped for
the night at Marion Court House.

May 1—Cars started this morning about five.
Reached Florence at noon and Charleston at eleven at
night. Were two hours getting off the cars when we
were marched off ... and then spent the remainder of
the night.

May 2—Drew rations today of two hard tack and
quarter pound meal a big thing after fasting all day
yesterday. Took cars at five this evening.

May 3—At day light this morning found ourselves
near or in the outskirts of Savanah. Left Savanah
about seven and passed through Macon about eight
in evening and arrived at Andersonville Georgia at
midnight —

Andersonville was at the virtual limits of civilization, an
obscure locale 60 miles south of Macon, 300 miles from the
Gulf of Mexico and 400 miles from Chattanooga. The first
Confederate work gangs arrived at the future prison site to begin
construction in January 1864. The site they picked was in a pine
forest about a quarter-mile from the small railroad station. The
work gang and its military leaders cleared a 16-acre site. The soil
was an arid yellow sand. The pines of the forest had no limbs
except at the top. One could see clearly through the trees. Only
in a few swamps nearby could you see low-slung trees, vegetation
and moss, where vermin, snakes and mosquitoes dwelled. Pine
logs, each 25-feet long and two to three feet in diameter, were
cut down, shaved clean, cut flat into posts, and planted five feet
deep into the sandy soil so close together that light could not be
seen between the posts.

The rectangle stockade was 1,000 feet north to south, and
about 800 feet east to west. The sandhills inside the compound
sloped from the north and from the south down toward the center where a creek bed a yard wide and 10 inches deep ran west to
east. Two massive wooden gates, with heavy iron hinges and
bolts, were placed at the east and west walls. Outside each door
was another, smaller stockade so that anyone going in had to go

through a locked door, enter the stockade, have the door locked behind him and have the other door unlocked before he could penetrate the compound.

Along the top of the stockade wall, a platform was constructed so that guards from the 26th Alabama and 55th Georgia Regiments, standing at intervals, had a full view of the camp. The guards, mostly farmers and sharecroppers from interior South Carolina, Georgia and Alabama, were called goober-grabbers, clay-eaters and crackers by their Yankee prisoners.

The first prisoners arrived at Andersonville in early February 1864. The prisoners had been taken by train from Raleigh through Charlotte, Columbia, Augusta and Macon and let off at Andersonville. The trip took six days; men were kept aboard the train cars, cramped and ill fed. When prisoners first arrived, the camp warden, Captain Henri Wirz, organized them into squads of 90 men each, with three squads to a detachment. The prison was designed to hold a few thousand men and the detachments were lined up in an orderly way from gate to gate. The first prisoners were each given meals after roll call, which required each prisoner to remain at attention in his squad and detachment until he was accounted for. If, for some reason, a prisoner tried to disrupt this process, the entire contingent of prisoners was forced to stand at attention until the job was completed. Often, on a whim, Wirz would refuse food after roll call.

Each day in the first weeks, a prisoner was issued a quart of meal, a sweet potato, some meat and a spoonful of salt. First the salt disappeared; then the potato; then the meat. Later the prison guards distributed peas, a quart to each detachment. Since each detachment had about 270 men, a squad of 90 men got a third of a quart, a few spoonfuls to each of four messes in the squad, with each man eventually counting in one hand the number of peas that were his daily ration.

The jailers never issued cooking utensils, and the prisoners improvised by using tin sheets from tobacco packing boxes as pans in which to cook hoecakes, or fried dough. Boots were common water carriers, and men used carved pine knots as cups. Much of the day's work consisted of gathering fuel for the squad's fire. Fuel was obtained by paying peas to other prisoners, or buttons, pencils, rings or trinkets to the guards. Cowpeas were used as poker chips, and skilled players from a squad were heroes to their mess and detachment. A prisoner with many trinkets and other small personal possessions was rich.

The months of February and March that year were cold. Prisoners were weakened by lack of food, stress and the disease that bred in the fetid creek that ran through the center of the camp. Warm fires were hard to come by. The sooty flames and turpentine gases from the fires turned the prisoners' faces and necks black with grime, and gummed up their unkempt hair.

The rainfall in that part of Georgia is about 60 inches a year. The cold nights, constant rain for days at a time, lack of proper food, occasional heat and constant exposure brought on a wave of sickness. Prisoners fell victim to lung ailments and diarrhea. Though the prison stockade was suited for only a few thousand men, prisoners continued to arrive by the trainload, 500 to 600 at a time, so that by the end of March more than 5,000 Union soldiers were imprisoned at Andersonville. By the end of March, more than 300 had died.

Then in April the camp changed with the arrival of the prisoners from Plymouth. The men who were now prisoners had considered duty in the Carolina pretty good for about a year. Local militia and rebel forces had been expelled in March 1862, and the garrisons at the Union forts had not been involved in any active campaigns for 16 months. Regiments of Carolina forces had taken the Plymouth prisoners to the railhead at Rocky Mount, five days away, where cattle cars scooped them up for a 4-day journey to Andersonville. First group of 600 prisoners arrived at 2:30 pm April 30, sore from the bumpy ride and hungry from the light provisions supplied. At the time there were 12,000-15,000 men in the 16-acre stockade.

Prisoner John McElroy, a private from Company L, 16th Illinois Cavalry, who had been in Andersonville since early February, later wrote that in late April he and his fellow prisoners awoke one morning to find newly arrived prisoners from the Plymouth garrison lying asleep in the main streets near the gates. Among them were Sgt. Henry E. Savage and the 16th Connecticut, and men from the 101st and 103rd Pennsylvania, 85th New York, 24th New York Battery, and two companies of Massachusetts heavy artillery and a company of New York cavalry. Wrote McElroy:

> "...They were attired in stylish new uniforms, with fancy hats and shoes; the sergeants and corporals wore patent leather or silk chevrons, and each man had a large well-filled knapsack of the kind new recruits usually carried on coming first to the front. They were the snuggest, nattiest lot of soldiers we had ever seen.
> "One of my companions surveyed them and said, 'Hulloa! I'm blanked if the Johnnies haven't caught a regiment of brigadier generals, somewhere...
> "They were as a rule intelligent and fairly educat-

ed. Their horror at the appearance of their place of incarceration was beyond expression. At one moment they could not comprehend that these dirty haggard tatterdemalions had once been clean, self-respecting, well-fed soldiers like themselves..."

Four days of cars arrived with the men from Plymouth. Because of the details of their enlistments, the prisoners has been paid $1 million in bounties, and regular pay. One of the conditions of the surrender at Plymouth was that the men could keep their possessions and pay. Later estimates were that the Plymouth prisoners collectively had brought a half a million dollars with them into the stockade. This came in handy in prison, though it attracted the jealousy of the other inmates and drew thieves. These prosperous prisoners from Plymouth were dubbed "Pilgrims" by their fellow inmates. Sgt. Savage's diary, describing his first days in Anderson prison, continued:

> *May 4*—Entered Andersonville Prison about noon. The stockade is of shaved logs set on end about fifteen feet high; within this fence is a dead line made of slats nailed to a post about three feet high, which if we cross we will be shot. The Prison is the most offensive place I ever saw. Our rations are meal and bacon and no facilities for cooking.

> *May 5*—Last night was awful damp and cold. Some men slept out last night. Brought a piece of tent so that we had a very respectable shelter. Have Jacob Bower, William Bidwell & Nelson Ritechie in tent with me. There is about eleven thousand men inside; this prison forty or fifty die per day.

> *May 7*—They commenced giving us cooked rations. Bread made of course unaltered meal—eggs are sold for ten dollars for dozen.

> *May 8*—Sunday, every day seems like the Sabbath for that matter as there is nothing to do here. Last night a Raider stole a blanket from a poor sick man—there is an organized band of robbers here.

> *May 11*—Rained last night and continues this morning; wind great around northwest making it quite cold. Weather seems more changeable than at the north; about a dozen new prisoners came in today.

May 13—Thirty seven new men came in today. We have a new Sergeant at roll call, every man has to be present or the Co goes without there ration. Drawed cooked rice today; paid one dollar for a piece of soap an inch square and three long—

May 14—Upwards of a hundred new Prisoners came in today; were taken near Newbern and some near Dalton. Made a salt of daminaes.

May 15—An old one-legged man crossed the dead line and was shot. He was crazy or thought guard wouldn't shoot him.

May 17th—Last night some men escaped. At roll call today we were kept in line upwards of three hours; there was upwards of four times the usual guard put on. Eight men that had escaped were brought in had been marched all day with a thirty two pound ball attached to one leg with a chain.

May 18th—Two hundred new prisoners came in; had an order read to us that any rushing towards the gate in a body the artillery would open on us; and that all tunnels would remain open; and the detachments from which men escaped would be reduced to four days rations a week until the men were caught.

May 19—Received rations of boiled beans so today they were boiled without being picked over at all.

May 20—Ten prisoners came in—received rations of salt soup and vinegar a spoonful of each. Had one of the hospital nurses say that twenty men had died of consumption (?) and that was more than had died of small pox.

May 21—Nearly a thousand prisoners came today; part are Danville Prison and the remainder recently captured in Wilderness battle.

May 22—Five hundred new prisoners came to day; were captured in Wilderness and equal many of Pa Reserves. Have a new Sergeant at roll call.

May 23—Seven hundred new prisoners came today among them Charly Brandegee & Andrew Bacon— The Capt. Commanding the Prison gave orders for a detachment to go out and enlarge the stockade but part objected so that they not any of them go.

May 24—Seven hundred more prisoners today; all from the Potomac army. A plot has been laid for breaking out the Prison -

May 26. Six or seven hundred more prisoners. The plot for getting out has been discovered. The Dutch Capt. says if Sherman sends down any force to release us he will turn the guns on the camp. Our rations are getting reduced.

That was the last entry in Sgt. Savage's diary. It is likely the prisoner shot at the dead line referred to in the diary entry May 15 was George Albert, who had arrived from Germany, and whose name was probably Albrecht. This man, who spoke no English upon his arrival to New York City, had been swept into the 52nd New York Regiment by substitute brokers in New York seeking replacements for the rich who were permitted to pay another to take their army enlistment ordered by the draft. Albert had been in uniform only a few weeks before he was taken prisoner and brought to Belle Isle in the middle of the James River in Richmond, where he became sick. He was among the first transported to Andersonville when it opened in February. Some said he'd gone crazy, more likely no one could understand his German. Suffering from diarrhea, he ventured from his tent at the hospital, reached for some bread that lay across the dead line and was shot. His killing stood as a lesson to the nearly 3,000 new prisoners.

In May, the number of prisoners taken from the Battle in the Wilderness mentioned in Sgt. Savage's diary imprisoned at Andersonville was 7,450. In June and July another 16,000 arrived. By the end of July, prisoners were crowded 1,500 to an acre. Crowding and hot tempers caused trouble. The food became scarcer, the guards surlier. Filth covered everything. White maggots, lice and mosquitoes were everywhere, into food, clothing and soil, everything. The creek that ran through the camp had become a festering swamp of human waste and disease. Cranky guards were ever eager to shoot those found too near the deadline. By May, some 20 a day were dying in Andersonville. By August 12, the population at Andersonville had grown to reach some 33,000, with some 680 prisoners dying that week.

The prison had taken on a reality of its own. Among the prisoners were bounty jumpers from the 7th New Hampshire, men who had signed up for money in regiment after regiment only to desert each time and sign up in another state. Their final stop was the 7th New Hampshire, where they had to choose between surrender to the Confederacy or a firing squad. Others in the 48th New York were little more than thugs, who cared little for the war or the Union, and who had only signed up for the bounty and the promise of new clothing and regular meals.

These prisoners started to rule the camp through terror. They murdered prisoners for their buttons, trinkets, blankets or possessions that could be used to trade with the guards for food, clothing, tobacco and fuel. Called "Raiders," they set up their own area on the south side of the creek against one of the walls, declaring that there territory. At night they raided other areas of the camp, and murdered and stole from sickened prisoners too weak to resist.

Finally, in early July, some of the healthier prisoners decided they had had enough. One evening a group of these so-called "Regulators" organized an attack on the Raiders camp. The rebel guards were notified not to interfere. At darkness, a gang of Regulators crossed the swamp in the center of the camp and waged hand-to-hand battle with the Raiders, eventually overcoming the group and taking their leaders back for justice.

A trial of the ringleaders was held July 4. Their sentence was death. With the permission of Captain Wirz, the Raiders were held in the north gate enclosure while a scaffold was constructed. On July 11, six ringleaders of the Raiders were hanged. Thereafter, the internal order of the camp was maintained by a squad of "police" appointed by the Regulators to keep peace and prevent further theft, assault or murder.

Throughout the spring, summer and fall the death toll of the prisoners mounted. By the end of July another 1,200 of the 26,367 prisoners had died. That month another 7,128 prisoners captured in Petersburg, Shenandoah and Tennessee were put into the camp. By the end of August another 1,800 had died.

Every morning, the mess would take the dead among its members to either the south or north gate. There messmates would strip the prisoner of his clothing and any valuables for use in trading. Other prisoners lined up every morning to look into the faces of the dead to see if friends were among them. Once at the gate, the dead were carried outside the compound to the deadhouse. While outside the stockade walls, the prisoners would scavenge for fuel, or a trinket that might save a life of other members of the mess inside. This was the life for Sgt. Savage and the others in Andersonville from July through November, during which some 12,000 more died.

Meanwhile, Andersonville had become notorious. General Winder, the Confederate Prison Administrator, boasted to friends in Richmond that he didn't care about conditions. "I am killing more Yankees than 20 regiments in Lee's Army," said he. It wasn't until November that President Jefferson Davis agreed to trim the prison population in Andersonville by accepting the conditions of a prisoner exchange. After the war, when tallies were made, it turned out that between February 1864 and April 1865, more than 41,000 prisoners were taken to Andersonville, where some 13,000—about a third—would perish.

Among those released in an exchange in early December was Sgt. Savage, who was taken by rail to Savannah, where the group was picked up by a Union vessel under a flag of truce, sailed to Annapolis, and hospitalized. The men were a sight. Clad in rags, vermin ridden, emaciated, some looked like living skeletons, most barely able to walk. One prisoner from Connecticut, Albert Hyde of Greenwich, later wrote that he, like most of the others, was so sick "I did not know where I was. Christmas and New Year passed without my knowing it."

Henry Savage was still in the Annapolis Hospital in April 1865 when he heard the news of President Lincoln's murder. A few days later, he wrote, he heard the cannons firing during the memorial procession for the President. Henry Savage recuperated and on June 24 was mustered out of federal service with the rest of the surviving 16th Connecticut Volunteers. He returned home to his family farm on Savage Hill in East Berlin.

On December 28, 1865, Henry Savage married Theodosia Caroline Knapp at the North Greenwich Congregational Church. Theodosia's family and friends considered her a prime catch, perhaps better educated and more refined than her new husband, who was a farmer from the uncertain confines of East Berlin, a modest community near Middletown. Their honeymoon consisted of their journey by wagon back to Henry's home on Savage Hill. On the way, they passed a large dam with water spilling over the flume. Theodosia saw the water and said: "Isn't that dam pretty?" To the end of his days, Henry teased that his wife swore on her honeymoon.

It would be several years before Theodosia's brother, Obadiah Mead Knapp, returned from service. Obadiah volunteered in New Haven on September 29, 1861, and was mustered into Company I of the 10th Connecticut Volunteers as a corporal October 2. The 10th Connecticut served in North Carolina, where Obadiah was wounded in the summer of 1862. He was given a disability discharge from the 10th Connecticut on August 5, and hospitalized in Washington. On November 13, 1863,

Obadiah, now recovered, volunteered to be a "hospital steward" in the Army Medical & Hospital Department. He was given the rank of sergeant of ordnance.

Later, Obadiah served in the Reconstruction Army. In Natchez, Mississippi, February 18, 1865, Obadiah was named a captain of the 121st Regiment of Colored Troops. The next month, in Louisville, Kentucky, Obadiah was assigned to the 125th Regiment of Colored Troops. On October 25, Obadiah was given the rank of captain of the 125th, and on April 22, 1866, the rank of Major. Obadiah returned home to Connecticut in 1867.

Henry, unlike his father and grandfather, concentrated on farming and specialized in dairy cattle, poultry and orchards. He did well; purchasing adjoining parcels of land over the years until his property totaled more than 100 acres. Henry was a member of the Grange, a deacon of the Berlin Congregational Church, and from 1894 to 1903 a trustee of the Berlin Savings Bank.

Obadiah Mead Knapp, Major of 125th Colored Troops, Louisville, Kentucky 1865

Henry didn't talk much about his experiences in the Civil War, though he was a member of the Grand Army of the Republic, and participated in memorial services and parades. Many times when the war came up in conversation later in life, Henry would simply stare into the distance and weep.

The Thursday January 10, 1907, edition of *The Berlin News*, contained the news report that Henry E. Savage had died at home on Savage Hill at 10 a.m. Friday, January 4, and was buried at Wilcox Cemetery on Monday, January 7. The paper said Henry had suffered a stroke in 1903 and been bedridden for four years. The cause of death was a "severe attack of the grip."

The news account described Henry Savage as "a man of recognized influence in the community for the past 40 years." He was a worker and faithful member of Berlin Grange, of the Berlin Agricultural Society, of which he was president, and of the Connecticut Dairymens Association. The funeral service was attended by prominent town citizens and Civil War veterans, including surviving members of the 16th Connecticut Volunteers, and from the Connecticut GAR (Grand Army of the Republic).

His casket bearers were Henry L. Porter, Huber Bushnell, Edwin I. Clark and Walter E. Penfield, all Civil War veterans, and F. A. Shaw of the Grange and Deacon Francis Deming of the Berlin Congregational Church. He was survived by his wife, three sons, one daughter, and brother, Willis M. Savage. Henry's wife, Theodosia Caroline, and daughter, Caroline Knapp Savage, were overcome with grief, ill at home and unable to attend the funeral service.

"A beloved, kind hearted citizen passes to his last rest," the paper reported, "a most valuable citizen of his native town, exemplifying in every act of his life the truest traits of Christian manhood and brotherly love."

Henry Elliot, who died January 4, 1907, and Theodosia Caroline (Knapp) Savage, who died in May 6, 1925, had five children, including a son, Willis Isaac [#115].

[110] SINON COLLINS was born in 1812 in Kilrush, County Clare, Ireland, son of JAMES and CATHERINE (BRIAN) COLLINS. In September 1840, Sinon married MARY LANGAN, born in 1822 in Kilrush, a daughter of JAMES and MARY (GORMAN) LANGAN. Sinon, like all his family and most of his neighbors, was a Catholic, the heir of both a religious tradition and a tragic legacy that shaped his life and that of all Ireland.

Home of the Celtic Gaels since the time of Christ, Ireland was first evangelized by Patrick, who came to the island from England in 432 A.D. With Patrick came the Roman alphabet and Latin. Learning spread in a way unique to Ireland. Unlike the British, who favored the Roman system of bishops, dioceses and parishes, religious life for the Irish centered around the monastery, where religious leaders held forth in a manner suited to Celtic society, which distrusted any authority outside the clan.

Irish monks built monasteries throughout the island that became centers of learning and religion. For four centuries Irish monasteries served as centers of Western scholarship during the barbarian conquests of Europe and the collapse of the Roman Empire. Irish monks traveled widely, to France, Germany and Switzerland, keeping the teachings of Ancient Rome alive. Western civilization's Middle Ages began when Irish monks arrived at Charlemagne's Court.

In the ninth century, Ireland was invaded by Viking bands that looted and burned monasteries. For two centuries the Norsemen from Sweden, Norway and Denmark came, first as pirates and later as settlers, and traders built the towns of Dublin, Wicklow, Arklow, Wexford, Cork and Limerick. In time, the Viking invaders intermarried, and their descendants merged into the Celtic tradition.

Irish clan warfare between MacMurrough and O'Rourke brought about the first invasion of English forces in the 12th century. MacMurrough, defeated in battle, escaped to England, where he asked King Henry II for troops to aid in MacMurrough's efforts to become Ri, or king, of Ireland. Henry II was concerned about the Norman forces in Wales under Richard Fitzgilbert de Clare, and approved an expedition by de Clare to Ireland to assist MacMurrough. Pope Adrian IV, who was English, also approved of the expedition because the conduct of Irish churchmen had declined. In 1170, the Norman, Richard Fitzgilbert de Clare led an invasion of Norman legions into Ireland. They deftly vanquished MacMurrough's enemy. O'Rourke's forces, Gaels and Vikings, were no match for de Clare's well organized Norman legions armed with iron mail suits, swords and lances. Following de Clare's victory, Henry II was proclaimed King of England and Ireland.

Norman rule spread. Normans formed counties and encouraged the growth of villages and farms, churches and abbeys. By the 14th century the Normans controlled most of the island. In time the Normans intermarried with the Gaels and, like the Vikings before them, became as Irish as the Irish themselves, causing consternation in England.

The experience of the Norman, William de Savage, illustrates what happened. William was the grandson of Thomas le Sauvage, a Norman who came to England with the 5,000 soldiers of William the Conqueror in 1066. This Norman was the ancestor of John Savage [#35]. In 1177, King Henry II granted to John de Courcey the land de Courcey and his Norman legions had conquered in Ulster. In de Courcey's train was William de Savage who settled in County Down. In 1186, Pope Urban III, at the request of de Courcey and Bishop Malachy, endowed the abbey at Downpatrick and sent a nuncio to translate the sacred reliques there. A history of County Down describes the fate of the Anglo-Norman Savage this way:

> "The Savages, and other English (Anglo-Norman) families settled here under de Courcey, the conqueror of Ulidia (Ulster), in the 12th Century, who maintained themselves in a flourishing condition for a considerable time. But in the reign of Edward III, the sept (clan) of Hugh Boye O'Neill, of Tyrone, drove the Savages out of the greater part of it, and confined them to the south of the peninsula, the Little Ards."

Another English writer later said of the Anglo-Norman families such as the Savages:

> "...were often in rebellion against the Crown of England. They were also engaged in broils and disputes against each other, which in the event, much diminished their strength and power."

The problem of the Norman integration into Irish culture haunted the English. In the 14th century, Parliament in London passed a law requiring every Englishman in Ireland to use the English language and possess an English, not a Gaelic, name. Later, in 1465, the English Parliament tried to prevent even the use of Irish surnames. Parliament said:

> "Every Irishman that dwells betweix or among Englishmen in the County of Dublin, Myeth, Vriell, and Kildare...shall take him the English surname of one town such as Sutton, Chester, Trym, Skryne, Corke, Kinsale, or color as white, black, browne, or arte or science as smith, or carpenter, or office as cooke, butler, and he and his issue shall use the name under payne of fortifying of his goods yearly til the premises be done."

Collins, Sinon's name, is an English version of the Gaelic O'Coileain, which in West Munster was commonly pronounced: O Quill Awn. One authoritative modern account holds that the name O'Coileain means young dog, and that the O'Coileains were closely related to the O'Donovans and were originally from Ui Connaill Gabhra, which is now Conello in County Limerick. In 1178, the O'Coileain were expelled from their lands in Limerick by Normans and fled to West Cork, where they settled.

In time the name returned, with subsequent family migrants heading north to become heard again in Limerick, Cork and across the Shannon River to County Clare, where Collins and O'Collins became common. The name Sinon is a typically West Clare name, derived from St. Senan, the area's most noted religious leader.

In 1537, Lord Leonard Grey, during an invasion of Ulster to put down a rebellion, entered Lecale and the Ards peninsula and moved against the Norman Savages of Ulster. His scribe, Cox, described the Savage clan as "degenerate Englishmen."

Grey and other agents of the English crown came to Ireland to end what England perceived to be a threat. The Reformation in Europe had swept away 1,500 years of Christian unity within a generation. The year before Grey's invasion, England's King Henry VIII established the Church of England. Wishing to banish Roman Catholicism from Ireland, he ordered monasteries there closed and confiscated church properties. To Catholic Ireland, the Protestant Reformation was English domination by another name. The rebellion in Ireland continued.

In 1541, Henry VIII declared himself King of Ireland and ordered English law established there. He further divided the land among those Norman lords who had sided with him. Yet the resistance never stopped. In the next decade, Henry's daughter, Queen Mary I, tried to end the rebellion by establishing plantations of loyal Englishmen in Ireland.

The English plantation program in Ireland was similar to that in North America. The difference was that Ireland had a large native population of similar blood and culture actively resisting the English settlement and with no illusions about English intent. The divisive issue of how to worship Christ embroiled Ireland in England's expansionary influence on the world stage. Protestant England was competing with Catholic Spain for influence, trade, markets and maritime domination. When Spain attempted to aid the Catholic Irish against Protestant England, the reaction in London was swift and permanent. In the late 16th century, Queen Elizabeth accelerated the Irish plantation program. After the defeat Christmas Day 1601 of the O'Neill and O'Donnell clans at Kinsale, Elizabeth gave considerable amounts of the confiscated lands in Ulster to Scottish Presbyterians.

The plantation of Ireland continued under the Stuart kings, James I and Charles I. Yet the continued rebellion by Irish patriots brought Ireland into the English Civil War. After an Ulster uprising in 1641 led by Sir Phelim O'Neill, who claimed he was acting on behalf of Anglican King Charles I, the Puritan leaders of Parliament in London knew that both Anglican sympathizers in Ireland and their Catholic supporters would have to be dealt with. In 1649, the year in which Charles I lost his head to Oliver Cromwell's Puritans, Cromwell and the army arrived in Ireland to subdue supporters of the crown, Catholic and Anglican alike. Cromwell and his military successors, Ireton and Ludlow, massacred tens of thousands; the worst slaughter was at Droghed and Wexford, where none was spared.

After subjugating all Ireland by 1652, Cromwell decided to clear all Irish from the good land and grant the land to loyal Protestants. Over the next 50 years, 12 million of Ireland's 15 million acres were taken from Catholic owners and given to loyal Protestants. By 1704, Catholics, who made up 80% of the population, were left with only 14% of the land; by 1798, only 5%.

The succession of the English crown brought Ireland again back into the English wars when James II, the Duke of York and the Catholic son of Charles II, inherited the English throne in 1685. The Protestant nobility, ever distrustful of James II, called on William of Orange in the Netherlands to assume the English crown. The deciding conflict between James and William in the "Cogdh an Da Ri," or War of the Two Kings, occurred July 1, 1690, at Ireland's Boyne River. William's 35,000-man force of English, Dutch, Danish, German and Huguenot mercenaries beat James' force of 25,000 French and Irish. After William's victory, the Protestants of Ulster, Dublin and London insisted that William treat Irish Catholics as a conquered people who could not be trusted. The purpose was to preserve the victory of the Battle of the Boyne, but the result was to extend a bitter legacy between Catholics and Protestants in Ireland for generations.

The anti-Catholic laws and practices, adopted in the late 17th century and codified by Parliament in London in the early 18th century as the Penal Laws, were harsh in the extreme, establishing a religious apartheid.

Priests were required to register themselves and their parishes, or be branded with an iron or castrated. Priests were required to swear allegiance to the English crown or be banished. Friars, monks and bishops were banished from Ireland in 1719; those caught were hanged, drawn and quartered. Public crosses were destroyed and banished. Religious articles, such as rosary beads, were forbidden. Catholic chapels were not permitted to have belfries, towers or steeples. Catholic pilgrimages to shrines were banned, and pilgrims discovered were flogged. Registered priests were forbidden to travel outside their parishes. Catholics were forbidden from being barristers, solicitors, magistrates or judges. Catholics could not serve in the army or navy, or bear arms, and could not be members of municipal corporations. Catholics could not be elected to the Irish Parliament in Dublin, could not vote for a member of that parliament, and could not be members of grand juries, local governing bodies. Catholics were prohibited from sending their children abroad to school or to have Catholic schools. A bounty was paid to anyone turning in a Catholic schoolmaster.

Only marriages performed in the Protestant Church of Ireland were legal. Catholics were forbidden from marrying Protestants, and any priest performing such a marriage would be put to death. A Protestant heiress who married a Catholic forfeited her inheritance. A Catholic wife who became a Protestant could live apart from her husband and force him to support her.

Catholics were forced to pay tithes to the Protestant church. In County Clare, for example, though inhabitants had to pay the tithe to the Established church, 62 of the 67 Protestant parishes in 1753 had no churches, and most had no ministers. Yet the taxes were levied and paid.

Protestant artisans could take no Catholics as apprentices. Catholics were forbidden to make or sell books or newspapers. Catholics could not hold a lease longer than 30 years. Catholics could not buy land from Protestants. If they owned land, they could not grant mortgages, nor deed their estates as a whole. A Catholic son who became a Protestant could inherit his father's estate whole. In short, the Penal Laws declared war on Catholics.

For Irish Catholics, the result of the laws was to make them a kind of underclass bound to their land in a de facto slavery, unable to improve themselves economically, get an education or develop trades without extreme effort, guile or luck. To keep their faith and culture alive, Catholics devised open-air hedge schools away from towns and villages. Secret masses were held in fields or caves. Pubs became places for talk of rebellion. Irish Catholics grew to distrust all government and authority as that of outsiders, trusting instead priests, storytellers and poets, the spiritual descendants of the Gaelic Brehons, who maintained community standards and kept the past alive.

In time, the antagonism between Catholics and Protestants in Ireland eased; the Penal Laws were not strictly or often enforced. Protestants in both England and Ireland had little stomach for the tyranny, particularly in the face of a people who refused to yield. The principles of the Enlightenment were spreading. Furthermore anti-Irish trade laws passed in London discriminated equally against Protestant and Catholic. These laws galvanized Dublin Protestants and Ulster Presbyterians against London. The American Revolution enabled Dublin and Ulster Protestants to bargain more autonomy for Ireland. Some results were the 1770 relaxation of the Penal Laws and a 1780 act by Parliament permitting Irish woolen products to enter English markets.

Yet these changes were not enough. Irish patriots led sporadic rebellions, Wolfe Tone's United Irishmen the most successful. Tone's rebellion in 1798 brought the animosity between England and Ireland to a head. London and Dublin parliaments decided that effective January 1, 1801, the two countries henceforth would be known as the United Kingdom of Great Britain and Ireland.

Dreams of Catholic emancipation that came with Union waned, however, particularly in the face of the Orange Order in Ulster, whose members were descendants of 17th century Scottish Presbyterian settlers who remained loyal to the British crown and fervently suspicious of those they called Papists. The Orange Order—named for William of Orange who, ironically, was sympathetic to Catholics in Ireland—effectively blocked Catholic emancipation.

Change came slowly. New tactics were devised. Tone's dream of a United Ireland, a republic apart from Great Britain, was alive. Catholics and sympathetic Protestants felt the way to freedom was home rule, repeal of the 1801 Union, and Sinn Fein (Gaelic for "Ourselves Alone"). The task now was to get a voice in the London Parliament. Daniel O'Connell, an educated Catholic from southwest Ireland enamored of the principles of Thomas Jefferson and the French Revolution, helped create a mass political movement called the Catholic Association. From 1824 on, members of the association were assessed a penny a month for membership, the so-called "Catholic rent." In 1828, O'Connell was elected to the London Parliament from County Clare, yet because of his religion he was refused permission to sit in the House of Commons. O'Connell's challenge so dramatized the Catholics' position in Ireland, the following year Catholic emancipation became reality.

With Irish Catholic members now in Parliament in London, O'Connell and the Catholic Association called for repeal of the Union. But before the movement could gain the kind of acceptance it required, events were about to play on another stage that would dwarf all other acts in Irish history: the Great Famine of 1845-48.

The Great Famine's impact can be shown in these grim facts: In 1841, Ireland had a population of eight million; in 1850, the population was four million. Two million had died of starvation, and another two million had fled the island—half for Great Britain, Canada, Australia, and New Zealand, and half to the United States.

Sinon Collins and his family were among the lucky ones. Sinon, like his father, was a blacksmith. To be a worker of iron was to have station and respect, commanding an art harking back in Irish mythology to the Druid's forge of fire and stone. He, who possessed the Druid's knowledge of alchemy and technique, commanded the ability to produce swords and conquest. The Collins forge was in Kilrush, located on the northern bank on the Shannon River estuary in the territory known from ancient times as Corca Baiscinn, or West Clare.

The name Kilrush derives from the Celtic "Cill Rois," which means church of the wood or promontory. Kilrush's earliest claim on history occurs as a result of its proximity to a 179-acre island two miles away in the Shannon that once was a religious center in western Ireland. Called Inis Cathaigh, or Scattery Island, St. Senan established a monastery there in 540 A.D.

Inis Cathaigh was a major religious center in Ireland for centuries. Raiders often attacked the island and it often was the focus of conflict between Norsemen and Irish, or between Norsemen and other Norsemen. In 950 A.D. the Norsemen of Limerick made the island a stronghold, but in 974 they were attacked by a tribe of kinsmen. Finbar, the lord of the Limerick Danes, was carried off the island by his enemies. By 977 A.D. the Irish leader Brian Boru invaded Inis Cathaigh and massacred the Norsemen and their chief, Maghnus. Boru's success was short-lived, as he was killed during his forces' triumph at Clontarf.

New upheavals occurred with the arrival of Normans in 1169. The Limerick Norsemen reasserted Norman authority and took over Scattery in 1176. Three years later the Anglo-Norman knight, William Hoel, laid waste to Scattery Island and destroyed Viking resistance forever.

After Norman invasions, ecclesiastical affairs were reorganized in 1188 and the island became attached to the see at Killaloe. As the Celtic monasteries declined in influence, so did the influence of Inis Cathaigh. In 1578, Elizabeth I made a grant of the island to the mayor and citizens of Limerick, making the once holy island a mere administrative district of Limerick.

All that remains of the monastery is the Round Tower, the highest such structure in Ireland. Standing 120 feet tall, the tower has walls four feet six inches thick and has a circumference at its base of 52 feet four inches. Of the 11 active churches that once occupied the island, the ruins of seven remain.

The village of Kilrush was about 1,500 acres, one tenth of the parish area that bears the name. Its earliest times are unchronicled except in legend, but events begin to focus toward the end of the 16th century, when ships from the Spanish

Armada anchored off Scattery Island near Kilrush, which by that time was a settlement of 80 permanent residents.

The Armada had sailed in August 1588 and was defeated by winds and Elizabeth's navy in the English Channel. Storms tossed the surviving Spanish ships, which sailed around Britain to the west coast of Ireland. Many were wrecked, but on September 5, 1588, seven of the surviving ships lined up in the Shannon estuary and anchored off Carrigahold. Two of the ships were 2,000 tons each, two were 400 tons, and the remaining three were smaller craft.

The Spaniards came ashore at Kilrush hoping to trade wine for water. English authorities had warned locals to refuse. Any Spanish captured should be killed. Those cooperating with Spanish were traitors to Elizabeth. What actually happened is the subject of tales. Perhaps a few Irish welcomed the Spanish and gave them water. Or some simply tried to keep from being bombarded by the Spanish and didn't care to murder a vanquished English foe. Either way, the Spanish didn't stay long, though one boat, the 700-ton *Annunciada* was leaking beyond repair and apparently was torched by the Spanish as they departed. Of the 130 ships of the Armada who sailed to England, only 76 returned to Spain. England lost eight ships. Some 10,000 Spanish sailors died, 10 times the English casualties; the Armada's destruction set the stage for England's subsequent domination of the New World.

By the end of 1600, the war by the Ulster chiefs O'Neill and O'Donnell to drive the English from Ireland was failing. A blockade by English forces of rebel Irish ports, led by Lord Mountjoy and Sir George Carew, was working. Having defeated Connacht, Carew had his sights on Munster to the south. Kilrush became his base of operations for the invasion. On July 24, 1600, Carew came to Kilrush with 1,050 infantry and 75 cavalry and stayed in town for three to four days. He then crossed the Shannon for a landing at Carrigfoyle to begin the conquest of Munster.

The four provinces of today's Ireland—Ulster, Leinster, Munster and Connaugh—take their names form the ancient Celtic Kingdoms of Ulakh, Laighean, Mumha and Connacht. England's King John created the first 12 counties of Ireland, with Mary I and Elizabeth I adding others. There are today 32 counties in Ireland, of which six are in Northern Ireland, and thus part of the United Kingdom of Great Britain and Northern Ireland, with the remaining within the Republic of Ireland.

With the end of the war in 1601, and the consolidation of English authority over the four Irish provinces, Kilrush was turned over by the crown to Sir Daniel O'Brian, the Earl of Thomond. By the earl's confirmation in the Acts of 1661 and 1667, the population of the parish was some 270, with some 90 residing in the town itself. Kilrush had commercial trading relations with Europe, as did Galway, Limerick and Kerry.

In 1688, Rev. John Vanderleur, a Protestant minister, came to Kilrush and began his family's relationship with the village that would have a tremendous impact on both. The Dutch Vandeleur family had originally settled in Sixmilebridge in 1630. Eleven years later, James Vanderleur claimed his estate was harmed in the 1641 rebellion. In 1642 he told the crown his loss was valued at 1,836 pounds. Vanderleur property losses included two water mills, a malt house, a tanyard, and other tenements together with four quarters of lands. Cromwell's plantation program restored Vanderleur's lands, which was reconfirmed under the Charles II.

Giles Vanderleur, James' son, became High Sheriff of County Clare, and his descendent, the Rev. John Vanderleur, became the leading Kilrush resident when he rented a home and land from the Earl of Thomond. In 1691, Vanderleur, like many of his fellow Dutchmen, fought in the Battle of Aughrim, one of the many victories of the Dutch sovereign, William of Orange, who also triumphed at Athlone, Limerick and, of course, at the Boyne. Subsequently, the Rev. John Vanderleur, and later his son, John, and grandson, Crofton, consolidated their holdings either in leaseholds or purchases from the Earl of Thomond and the crown so that by 1749 the Crofton Vanderleur held title to Kilrush and much of the surrounding area.

In 1797, Right Hon. John Ormsby Vanderleur succeeded his father, Crofton, as head of the Vanderleur household and estates. He acquired wealth by negotiating a pocket borough vote in favor of the Act of Union of Great Britain and Ireland of 1801. His subsequent marriage to Lady Frances, daughter of the Marquess of Drogheda, helped as well.

Vanderleur holdings were considerably improved by the arrival in 1802 of a Scots businessman, Sir James Paterson, who settled in Kilrush and went into the oats trade. Paterson later began trading with Shannon River ships, purchasing directly in Kilrush rather than dealing through Limerick.

With the Napoleonic wars in Europe, farm prices rose and Paterson's business and Kilrush prospered. By 1805 there were 30 liquor and grocery establishments, 10 cloth shops and shopkeepers and tradesmen of all descriptions in the village, many doing regular and prosperous business with Dublin and other trading centers.

Vanderleur in 1806 decided to develop Kilrush as a port for export, under the direction of the collector of Limerick. A Customs house was established and substantial private residents were built. In 1808, Hely Dutton, in his survey of County Clare, wrote:

> "Kilrush is rising fast into some consequence and if capital did not prevent it would export many articles of agricultural produce that are now bought on commission for the Limerick merchants. A good quantity of corn and butter is brought by Mr. Paterson, a very active and intelligent inhabitant, who had been of utmost benefit to Kilrush and the adjoining counties."

The year Paterson began his oat market business in Kilrush— 1802—the market sold 12,000 barrels of oats at 6,666 pounds; five years later, the Kilrush market sold 26,000 barrels at 18,795 pounds; by 1812, more than 34,000 barrels for more than 25,000 pounds.

In 1810, Paterson exported butter, and in 1812 went into the shipping business and set up a ferry service between Kilrush and Limerick; Kilrush became a market for families bound for holiday in Kilkee to the west. By 1835 wharf traffic, trade and ferry work in Kilrush was so prosperous, two banks were established in town and branch offices of the National Bank and the Agricultural & Commercial Bank were opened.

By 1831, Kilrush had 712 houses, as well as establishments making flannels, stockings, storm sheeting and bandle cloth and other forms of linen. The town also had a tanning yard, a soap manufacturing plant, a mail factory and a rock salt refinery. The wharves were loaded with corn, cattle, butter and pigs for export. Vanderleur expanded downtown and by the mid 1850s much of his town plan was finished.

But as these improvements were made, other problems away from Kilrush were set to undermine everything. First disease and then the potato famine devastated hundreds of thousands of lives and wrecked the economy.

The first outbreak of disease was a cholera epidemic in 1832. Western Ireland and particularly Clare were devastated. Tenant farmers, fishermen and poorer townspeople were most susceptible. Dr. Charles Lever, a young doctor sent to Clare by the Dublin Board of Heath, came to Kilrush in May 1832. "On his (Dr. Lever's) arrival he found the town sunk in gloom and despondency, owing to the ravages of the fearful disease," wrote

Francis Keane of Ennis. Dr. Lever himself wrote:

> "Of the fearful raves in the West, in the wilds of
> Clare, and that lovely promontory that stretched at
> the mouth of the Shannon into the Atlantic, I have
> been the daily witness, and even to recall some of
> these incidents passingly was an effort of great pain."

Until 1838, Catholic tenants were still required to pay tithes to support Protestant clergy. With reforms in 1838, the Poor Law Union divided the country into districts, or unions, in which local taxpayers were made financially responsible for the care of the poor and starving in their area. The Poor Law Union covered an average area of 10 miles' radius from the poor house, which was usually located in the market town.

In 1841, the Kilrush Workhouse was completed on a six-acre site on the north side of town. It was built to accommodate 800 people, and the first poverty-striken people took up residence in July 1842. After the famine struck, the workhouse was renovated to hold another 500. Smaller auxiliaries were set up in nearby buildings and in neighboring villages. With the famine, economic collapse and related failures, tenant farmers couldn't pay the rents. Evictions mounted. Between August 1848 and January 1849, more than 7,000 people were evicted in the Kilrush area. In 1849, 150 tenants a week were evicted. Under the Poor Law it often was cheaper to pay a person's boat passage out of the country than to supply food indefinitely to a needy family.

A British M.P., the Hon. Paullette-Scrope, who toured the area that year, said 20,000 people were evicted in 1847-49. Logs of the Workhouse note that during that time, 3,900 died. This does not count those who died in the fields, in abandoned hovels or by the roadside.

While not all of these people were from the Vanderleur estates, most were. Most were evicted for nonpayment of rent, but some were for "clearances" so the landlord could use the tenant plots for pastureland for cattle. By 1850 the workhouse was looking after more than 5,000 people. Between March and September of that year, 1,014 died.

Rev. S. Godolphin Osborne, a Protestant cleric who inspected the area, laid most of the blame for the misery and starvation rampant in the Kilrush area on the Board of Guardians, which was chaired by Crofton Moore Vanderleur. Inmates at the workhouse had insufficient food, and conditions for the evicted were inhumane. Noting the contrast between Ireland and England, where in 1850 preparations were under way for the Great Exhibition of Industry to be housed in the Crystal Palace, in London's Hyde Park, Rev. Osborne wrote:

> "When, the other day, I looked on the Crystal Palace, and thought of the Kilrush Workhouse as I have seen it and now know it to be I confess I felt as a Christian and the subject of a Christian government, utter disgust."

In 1860 and 1861, Henry Coulter toured Ireland and wrote "The West of Ireland: Existing Conditions 1862." Coulter found a strong farmer class emerging, as hostile to the small farmers and laborers as the Vanderleurs and other landowners. Demand for land was intense. Farmers were eager to expand, and this was done at the expense of weaker tenants. Wrote Coulter:

> "The town is a remarkable instance of the improvement which has taken place in so many country towns throughout Ireland since 1846. ...the shops in Kilrush have doubled in number and greatly increased in size...
>
> "For example, in 1846 there was scarcely a shop in town more than 24 feet in length, and there was not one having a plate-glass window; whereas now there are 12 shops with plate-glass windows, some 30 feet in front and over 80 feet from front to rear."

Yet many people who borrowed money or lived on credit had trouble paying their bills. Before the famine, Coulter said, people paid their loans promptly.

> "Now it is almost impossible to obtain money from them except by legal process, and in numerous instances the traders who endorsed their bills to the Banks, have been obliged to meet them to their serious embarrassment."

Bad weather, poor harvests, loss of the potato crop in 1859 and 1860 had taken their toll.

> "The land for several miles around Kilrush is very poor, having a light surface and a very retentive sub-soil; to use the expression in common use among the people it is 'cold, spewy land.' The wetness of the Spring and Summer therefore peculiarly unfavourable

to tillage in this locality; the loss fell almost entirely on the small farmer and the labouring man...

"With regard to the large labouring population who live in and about the outskirts of the town, the want of employment has reduced them already to a miserable condition, and they are now living on the money raised at the pawn offices, which are the only establishments at present flourishing in Kilrush."

But the small tenant farms were failing, and their livestock and goods sold off. Tradesmen in town suffered. Coulter said the emigration that had drained off the population immediately after the famine had dwindled to a trickle by 1862. However, Coulter said that the poor harvests of 1859-61 would cause a new wave of emigrants.

"If landlords do not act with judicious forbearance and if some assistance be not given to enable people to struggle through their present difficulties."

Throughout this period, Sinon Collins and his family made their way. Blacksmiths by trade, Sinon and his sons could read and write and were among the more fortunate Kilrush artisans.

Sinon's parents were originally from the nearby village of Ballykit. When he was age 28, Sinon married 18-year-old Mary Langan, daughter of James and Mary (Gorman) Langan. Mary's mother had died about two months after her birth and she was raised by and resided with her father until her marriage. Mary's father, James Langan, was a foreman ship carpenter in the Kilrush shipyard and lived to be 102 years old.

Sinon and Mary had at least four children, including a son James, twin sons Eamon and Andrew, and a daughter Catherine. James' birth November 28, 1841, is recorded as #4775 on the Kilrush register for the years 1827-62. The twins' births January 4, 1844, are listed as #5644 and #5645, and Catherine's birth April 5, 1845, is noted only as "C". Collins was a common name in the Kilrush register until 1860, after which the name all but disappears, with local historians saying the last Collins left Kilrush in 1910.

Together Sinon and his father and sons worked in a blacksmith shop in Kilrush, where they fashioned cleats, sail loops, hinges and other iron parts used in the Kilrush shipyard. Kilrush was a western port on the Shannon River and active in trade throughout Great Britain, Ireland and Europe.

Mary (Langan) Collins died in March 1859, and Sinon

remarried. Records indicate that Sinon's second wife was named Honora. Sinon and his family were able to make a living until the farm and economic crisis in 1862-63.

In April 1863, Sinon Collins, Honora, their young daughter, also named Honora, and Sinon's 22-year-old son, James walked down Frances Street—a thoroughfare 100 feet wide and named for Lady Frances, the wife of John Ormsby Vanderleur—which connected Kilrush's Lower Moore Street to the Merchants Quay of the wharf and the shipyard that could no longer support them. There at the Merchants Quay, the Collins family boarded a vessel bound for Liverpool, England. They would be joined by James's sister Catherine and twin brothers, Eamon and Andrew, who would all eventually make the crossing to New York.

On April 25, 1863, in Liverpool, Sinon, Honora, their baby and James boarded the *American Union* bound for America. Their berths were on the lower deck. Sinon and James, listed as passengers #514 and #520, though blacksmiths were identified as labourers. The 181-foot sloop arrived at South Street Seaport in New York City May 25, 1863.

Sinon and his sons worked at odd jobs in New York until September 1864, when he and James moved to Jersey City, New Jersey where they found work as blacksmiths in the yards of the Erie Railroad. Sinon worked continuously for the Erie until his death October 21, 1886, after a few days' illness. He was buried at Bergenhill, Jersey City. Sinon and his wife Mary (Langan) Collins had at least four children, including a son, James [#113].

[111] PATRICK HOWARD was born February 9, 1832, in Dublin, Ireland, a son of THOMAS and NELLIE (WELSH) HOWARD. Patrick married SUSANNAH LUNNEY, who was also born in Dublin. Patrick and Susannah immigrated to the United States in the 1850s eventually settling in Stanwich, a village on the North Stamford/Greenwich border. On October 30, 1860, Patrick became an American citizen after raising his hand before a magistrate in Fairfield County Superior Court in Bridgeport and swearing that it was his intention to be a citizen of the United States and "to renounce forever all allegiance to every foreign prince, potentate, State or sovereignty whatsoever, and particularly the Queen of Great Britain and Ireland..."

Patrick worked at odd jobs and was able to purchase a small piece of land, which he farmed. Patrick, who died on January 2, 1909, and Susannah (Lunney) Howard, who died September 30,

1886, and who were both buried in North Greenwich Cemetery, had at least one son, James Reynolds [#114].

[112] THOMAS FRANCIS O'CONNELL was born in Ireland, at the height of the Great Famine. At the time of Thomas' birth, Ireland had already suffered from two successive years of potato crop failures.

The blight that spoiled the potato crop turned Ireland into one of the saddest islands on earth, a place of death and despair, changing the land and its people forever. The potato was the staple crop for Irish tenant farmers, who depended on the root for their survival. The crop failed first in 1845, then in 1846, 1847 and 1848. Few events compare with the famine. Some two million died, often amid such incredible horror that the survivors never really recovered. Entire villages were wiped out, families torn apart and destroyed.

Despite this devastation, tenants who could do so continued to produce grains throughout the famine for landowners who, incredibly, shipped the food to England. Between 1845 and 1850, more than two million quarters of wheat grown in Ireland were shipped to England. British policy seemed reluctant to recognize the necessity for the relief of the peasants, but did see the need to ease the financial burden on the landlords. The Poor Law Act of 1847, for example, decreed that no peasant with a holding of a quarter acre or more was eligible for public assistance, thus forcing peasants to give up their land for a pittance so they could receive whatever charity might provide, casting them forever onto the road, homeless and jobless.

The blight shattered a tenant's ability to pay his taxes. Since landlords were obliged to pay taxes on productive land, the landlords were given an incentive to clear tenants off the land so taxes weren't required. This meant that tens of thousands of tenants were forcibly evicted from their huts, driven to wander.

It was from such an Ireland that Thomas O'Connell came to America. Passage on the "famine" or "coffin" ships was hard. One such ship, the *Elizabeth & Sarah*, was a 330-ton vessel with only 36 berths. Only 32 were made available to the 276 passengers. Kegs containing 12,000 gallons of water leaked, making only 8,000 gallons available for the month-long journey. Each passenger was to have received seven pounds of food a week, but it was never distributed. There were no privies. Passengers remained in the hold below decks for days on end, without food or water, lying in their soil. Disease spread. One passenger in five died on that voyage.

Thomas O'Connell, with whatever family accompanied him and who are now lost to memory, landed in New York City and migrated west to Ohio, where Irish laborers were in demand in the construction of the Ohio Canal, which stretched from Cleveland south to the Ohio River town of Portsmouth, where Thomas lived.

The Ohio Canal was only one of scores of such works opening up the country and giving refugees like Thomas O'Connell jobs and hope. Between 1800 and 1820, more than 4,000 miles of canals were dug across the country. Over the next 20 years, the states, eager for development, invested $200 million in canals, tying the nation together in a network of small ditches, which were not more than four feet deep, and 40 feet wide at the top and 28 feet wide at the bottom. The canals became the life streams for the new nation. Roads and turnpikes were few. The inland rivers, often impassable because of rapids, waterfalls or shallows, provided limited access to the interior lands of the Northwest Territory. Canals solved many of these problems and permitted farmers to settle and establish the Midwest states of Ohio, Indiana, Michigan, Illinois and Wisconsin. They could produce their crops with the reasonable assurance that they would reach markets in time for profit. Manufacturers, for their part, used the canals to transport their works to the farmers.

Canal towns like Portsmouth, Ohio, were prosperous at first. Soon however, railroads became the favored method of transport and the canal towns began to languish. Thomas, who had learned to work iron, moved to Middletown, Ohio, where he obtained a job in one of the buggy manufacturing companies there.

Thomas married and had two children. His wife later drowned in the Middletown canal. To make ends meet, Thomas often worked at odd jobs in town. He had skill making iron rims for carriage wheels. While repairing a carriage wheel for a family in Middletown, Thomas met the family seamstress, CATHERINE SHEEDY.

Catherine was born in 1847, daughter of JOHN and ELLEN SHEEDY, who resided at 5 Peter Street in the village of Clonmel, County Tipperary, Ireland. Catherine had sisters, Alice and Ellen, and a brother, Michael. Michael learned the craft of stonecutting and masonry in Tipperary. On September 24, 1862, Catherine was maid of honor at the wedding of her brother Michael to Ellen Elizabeth Halley at Clonmel's St. Mary's Cathedral, a noted Norman structure that had once been the scene of a violent battle between Cromwell's army and Irish warriors.

Thomas Francis O'Connell   Catherine (Sheedy) O'Connell

   In December 1862, Michael set sail for the United States
intending to settle and send for his wife and sister. Michael settled in Middletown, Connecticut where he was hired as a stone-
mason during the construction of the Connecticut Hospital for
the Insane. In the spring of 1863, Catherine Sheedy and her sister-in-law, who was pregnant, boarded a ship for the United
States. The crossing was miserable. Ellen lost her child. Catherine
swore the crossing would be her last. By the time the women
arrived, Michael had moved to Hartford, where he was working
in construction. Catherine stayed in a rooming house with a
family on Capital Avenue, but after a year decided to go to
Middletown, Ohio, to visit a relative.
   Found among family papers are two letters from Catherine's
father, John Sheedy. In a letter written in Clonmel to Catherine
November 12, 1871, John Sheedy writes of the death of her
brother, Will.

      "dear Cathy I would wright to you before now to
      returne you thanks for your gift that you sent us
      September last may God spare ye all a long life and a
      happy death as I hope some our family got a few
      weeks ago dear Cathy when you wrote to Will to
      know if mi letters about your poor mother were true

he never told me one word of it or since dear Cathy i
am sorry to tell you that when you wright to him
again you will have to change his address from
Cashel St. to Abbey Church yard for Will is no more
he is gone may the Lord have mercy on his soul
Amen dear Cathy Will lived only from Sunday night
until Thursday at ten o'clock he was out in marl field
with Jane and Wm. Kennedy that Sunday Evening
October the 11 he took a pine in his side in Abbey he
came home went to bed when Jane went up to bed
she found him speechless and dead of one side he
never opened his eyes until he died he had a most
grand funeral and much regretted by rich and poor

"dear Cathy we are now left lonesome we have
neither son or daughter to call on when we have need
of them the grave and America left us a lone couple
in our old days thank God."

John Sheedy points out that Will's death seemed to have little
effect on Will's widowed wife, Jane, or their son, Tom ("...they
seem in no way fretted about him, all true."). Her father asked
Cathy to send a copy of his letter to her sisters, Ellen and Alice,
and brother Mike and his wife, Ellen. He extended greetings to all.

"..we hope they are all in good health may they be
always be so dear Cathy we now close for this time as
I can't bare up in writing much more now my feelings
are much touched at present but will send you a long
letter next time dear Cathy I hope you will excuse this
writing you know that is time that my hand should go
stiff and my sight get weak and my never shook...dear
Cathy your poor mother and I join in sending our
hearts love to you and Alice and not forgetting Poor
Ellen may ye live a long and happy life amen may ye
spend a hapey Christmas we remain your father and
mother John and Ellen Sheedy... adue"

In May 1874, John Sheedy wrote Catherine's sister, Ellen, in
America, a letter artfully rich in a lyrical prose and colorful
phrases containing the wounded feelings and anxieties of parents
left behind and alone in Ireland with little but memories, pain
and death to look forward to. (Catherine is alternately called
Kaete, and Kate).

"...dear and loveing daughter Ellen it is time that I
should wright to you hopeing this will find you in

good health and also your sisters Kaete and Alice may the greate and Almighty God grant ye a long and happey life in this world and a happey death here-after...this is our prayer night and day for ye dear Ellen we received your kind and loveing letter with your fine and grand picture and I am happey to tell you that every one that see it admired it you may be sure your poor old mother showed it many with tears in her eyes.

"dear Ellen you say that ye got no letter from us since January the first for that was the day your poor mother got your letter with two pounds and she got Mr. John Butler to wright a letter to you on the fourth that was 3 days after getting yours for I was in hospital ten days up to that time and twice since but with the help of God to go there no more would sooner die in a ditch than go there agine.

"dear Ellen I always said that you were gifted with sound and good sense but I see now that I was not mistaken in you and it is for the answer you send to that ill natured ruffin Mike when he thought to dupe ye and rob ye of your hard earnings and to send it here to Jane and Mary Jane the former a drunkard and for Mary Jane she was in three or four nice places minding children but she got too fond of com-pany that leaves her now, a cad going about, may God help us all.

"dear Ellen I think that Mike would have as good wright to think of your mother and me as ye do but he has children like Will to do for but let him take are that God would have them orphins like Will's and have another widow in the family which I hope to hear from before I die to make it short we have no friends on this earth but our blessed Lord and his Blessed Mother and ye three may Almighty God spare ye to us.

"dear Ellen your poor mother is holding her old grip still she says if I died she would face the sea live or die sink or swim to see ye all once more...

"dear Ellen I must close with you now and say something to poor Cathy tho she is keeping a great silence with us this time back but perhaps she can't help it she may have but little time to spare but God help us we have all our time is spent in idlness and little do which leaves us often to think of ye

"dear Kaete your mother wonders much that you would forget her in so short a time but often says that is our own fault but dear Kaete if we are in the fault you must forgive us for we have many bills to meet with here in Clonmel which you often see before now but God was kind and good to ye and brought you to the land of promises and he left us old sinners to die with the druids.

"dear Kaete, Ellen, Allice your mother and me are struggling together with the good day and the bad day waiting for the last day may that day be a happey day to all Amen dear girls you mother has pretty good health at present thanks to Almighty God but I cannot say that this two years but this winter since October I suffered much and up to this I am suffering with a cough and shortness of breath the same as poor Stephen Scanlon for all the Sheedys died with the same complaints I could not escape it but God's will be done now dear girls we close with ye for the present may the Blessing of God and our ten thousand blessings and your hearts love be with ours forever and the blessing of the Holy Mother of God be with ye now and forever amen dear girls we close for the present adue... we remain your affectionate Father and Mother John and Ellen Sheedy, Peter Street No. 5, adue..."

These letters were circulated among the Sheedy children in America. Catherine decided to stay in Ohio and moved in with a Middletown family. It was there that she met Thomas O'Connell.

In 1880, Catherine's employer was moving to France and asked Catherine to go with the family to Paris. Thomas O'Connell, the widower with two children, knowing Catherine had no wish to make a second Atlantic crossing, asked her to marry him. Catherine and Thomas were married and for the next 13 years they lived in Middletown, where they had three children. For a time, Thomas was employed as a night watchman and resided at 78 First Street.

In 1893, the nationwide depression forced the shutdown of many of the buggy manufacturers in Middletown. Thomas lost his job. That year, Catherine's brother, Michael Sheedy, invited the O'Connells to move to Hartford, where Thomas could get work in Michael's construction business. In the 30 years since his arrival from Ireland, Michael had prospered. He had worked as a mason in the construction of the Hartford Theological Seminary, the Church of the Good Shepard and many homes along Farmington Avenue. Later, he formed his own company, purchased land along Franklin Avenue and built homes for the town's growing middle class. Michael and his wife had settled in a home he built at 165 Franklin Avenue.

In Hartford, the newly arrived O'Connell family lived in an apartment near Hungerford Street, and Thomas worked in his brother-in-law's construction business. By 1905, Catherine had saved enough to purchase a three-family brick home built by her brother at 193 Jefferson Street, where she and her family lived on the first floor and rented out the other two.

The O'Connell children, all daughters, attended Catholic schools in Hartford and became dressmakers. The oldest, Frances, married William J. Rankin, who was active in Democratic Party politics in Hartford. Thomas O'Connell obtained a job in the Hartford Municipal Water Department through his son-in-law.

Thomas Francis O'Connell on porch of family three-flat at 193 Jefferson Street, Hartford

Rankin was a political ally of Thomas J. Spellacy, the political leader who helped build the Democratic Party in Connecticut. Rankin served one two-year term as Mayor of Hartford in 1931-33 and was later Fire Commissioner and Postmaster. One of Mayor Rankin's secretaries and aides was John M. Bailey, another ally of Spellacy's, who would later serve as chairman of the state Democratic Party from 1945 to 1975. Bailey was an early supporter of John F. Kennedy's bid for the Democratic nomination for president in 1960 and later served as chairman of the National Democratic Party.

Catherine was a good storyteller and often told of her life in Middletown, Ohio when Civil War officers visited her employer. She retained her brogue and liked to dance if coaxed. However, she was a taskmaster, ran the family finances and kept a sharp eye out, protecting her family's welfare. Thomas, a quiet man, never learned to read or write. In the evenings he would sing as his daughters played the piano, listen to his wife read the newspaper, and liked to relax by tending his flower garden.

Thomas worked on municipal road crews installing and repairing waterlines until a week before his death in 1923 at age 76. Catherine (Sheedy) O'Connell died in 1928 at age 81. Both were buried at Mt. St. Benedict's Cemetary, Bloomfield. Thomas and Catherine had three daughters, including their youngest, Alice [#116].

[113] JAMES COLLINS was born November 29, 1841, in Kilrush, County Clare, Ireland, son of Sinon and Mary (Langan) Collins [#110], and came to America with his father, arriving in New York City in May 1863. On July 16, 1864, James married **MARY KEARNEY**, born in 1846 in Kilrush, daughter of **JOHN** and **MARGARET (MANGAN) KEARNEY**, who also made the Atlantic crossing from Ireland that year. The wedding took place at St. Andrew's Catholic Church at Centre and Duane Streets, New York City, with the Rev. Father Curran officiating. In September 1864, James and his wife moved to Jersey City, New Jersey where James and his father obtained jobs as blacksmiths in the yards of the Erie Railroad.

The Erie and scores of other railroads were reshaping the nation, providing employment for immigrants as well as binding the industrial and agricultural economies of the growing nation together. In 1830, there were only 22 miles of railways in the U.S., by 1840–2,818 miles, by 1850–9,000 miles. By the time the Collins family arrived during the Civil War, more than 30,000 miles of rail linked the nation.

The Erie Railroad was chartered by the New York legislature in 1832 to establish a rail along New York State's Southern Tier and to compete with the successful Erie Canal between Albany and Buffalo to the north. The Erie Railroad was to establish a rail link between New York Harbor and the Midwest markets, and to provide prosperity along the way. After several financial panics, and spending $15 million, five times the original estimate, the Erie was completed in 1851. Stretching nearly 448 miles from Piermont on the Hudson River to Dunkirk on Lake Erie, the Erie passed through and stimulated the growth of many New York towns: Middletown, Port Jervis, Hancock, Susquehanna, Binghamton, Owego, Elmira, Corning, Hornell, Wellsville, Olean and Salamanca.

The year of the Erie's inauguration, the line was taken over by financier Daniel Drew, who in time proved more interested in manipulating Erie stock than railroading. The Erie faced strong competition from the New York Central to the north, and the Pennsylvania Railroad and Baltimore & Ohio Railroad to the south. The Erie launched a rapid expansion program. By the Civil War, Erie lines were in Buffalo, Niagara Falls, Rochester and Newburgh in the north, and in the New Jersey towns of Paterson, Passaic and Jersey City, where the Collins father and son found work.

James Collins worked in the Erie yards in Jersey City for four years. However, there was trouble. Details are unclear, but the continuing turmoil in Ireland found its way into the Erie yards in New Jersey, work place and home to thousands of Irish immigrants. In 1864, the same year James and his father went to Jersey City, the United States was visited by James Stephens, founder of the Irish Republican Brotherhood. In Dublin, several years before, Stephens and his co-conspirators had taken a blood oath:

James Collins

"...in the presence of God, to renounce all allegiance to the Queen of England, and to take arms and fight at a moment's warning to make Ireland an Independent Democratic

Republic, and to yield implicit obedience to the commanders and superiors of this secret society..."

In America, Stephens' comrade, John O'Mahony, had founded a companion organization, known as the Fenian Brotherhood of America. The task of the American Fenians was to raise money and arms for the secret society in Ireland. Support for this came from the Irish neighborhoods, saloons, gathering and work places, such as the Erie yards in Jersey City. Stephens thought the Fenians in America weren't generous enough. He complained:

> "...of bayonets, gala days and jolly nights, banners
> and sashes, bunkum and filibustering, responding in
> glowing language to glowing toasts on Irish National
> Independence over beakers of fizzing champagne..."

The pressure for money and loyalty was intense. Not all Irish immigrants cared to remember Ireland, let alone give money for a war against England. T. J. Kelly, who commanded an Irish-American brigade in the Union Army during the Civil War, had deposed Stephens for leadership of the Irish Republican Brotherhood and returned to the United States in late 1866, again working the Fenian Brotherhood in America to build support. In early 1867, Kelly returned to England where he set up a London headquarters to conduct guerrilla war in Ireland. By the end of the year there were enough incidents for Irish nationalists to claim new martyrs to the cause. It would be another 70 years before the Irish Free State was declared, largely through the efforts of an Irish patriot from County Cork named Michael Collins, a distant cousin from the ancient clan O'Coileain. But in 1867 the conflict over how to secure Ireland's future apparently split the Collins family in Jersey City.

James, his wife, Mary, twin brothers Eamon and Andrew and sister Catherine all lived with Sinon, the head of the family. Within months of the visit to New York of the Fenians to raise money, twin brothers Eamon and Andrew went west to the Indian territories beyond the Mississippi River, Catherine married and moved to Chicago, and James and his wife moved to western Pennsylvania. Catherine remained in Chicago, where she raised a large family. Eamon married an Indian in the Montana Territory and was later murdered. Andrew returned years later to Jersey City, where he died. As for James, who followed the Catholic Church's teaching in opposition to "secret societies," his home thereafter was Meadville, Pennsylvania.

James in December 1867 got a job in Meadville as a blacksmith in the maintenance shops of the Atlantic & Great Western Railway, an affiliate line of the Erie. The job lasted for 11 months, and James and his wife returned to Jersey City for a short time. From November 1869 on, James never worked anywhere else but Meadville, where he was a foreman in the A&GW shops.

The Atlantic & Great Western Railway was typical of the hundreds of smaller railroads that grew in the country before and after the Civil War. In 1853, local business leaders established the Meadville Railroad Company. Like many such local ventures with high hopes and low accounts, the Meadville Railroad had financial trouble. Meanwhile, in Ohio, the Franklin & Warren Railroad, founded in 1851, also was in financial straits. The Meadville and Franklin & Warren railroads merged, becoming the Atlantic & Great Western Railway, which by 1861 had built a connection to Salamanca, New York, that extended south to the New York-Pennsylvania line. The Civil War complicated final construction, though by 1863, the A&GW had a line that led from Salamanca to Corry, Meadville, Greenville and Sharon in Pennsylvania. By 1864, the A&GW had an extension from Sharon through 12 Ohio towns, including Kent, Akron, and Marion and ending in Dayton. The entire Atlantic & Great Western line was 388 miles.

The Atlantic & Great Western affiliated with the Erie, which was seeking its own line to the west to compete with the New York Central, Baltimore & Ohio and Pennsylvania railroads. The relationship between the A&GW and Erie was rocky and one-

Birthday party for James Collins 1914, Meadville, Pennsylvania, seated center with family.

sided, with the Erie and its financial troubles dominating the smaller A&GW in the years ahead.

One of the largest maintenance shops along the A&GW was in Meadville. The maintenance shops were in a huge depot, 327 feet long and 127 feet wide, and containing some 41,520 square feet of floor space, and large machine shops, where the rolling stock of the A&GW and Erie was maintained. Nearby tenements housed many railroad employees. West of the depot was McHenry House, a large hotel featuring a dining hall with black walnut paneling and stained glass windows. Outdoors were lavish ornamental evergreens, trees, shrubs and flowers. On January 19, 1864, New York editor Horace Greeley, after a visit to McHenry House, wrote:

> "Meadville is a great hotel and dining hall of the road...the dining hall is among the best in America...here also are the machine shops, etc. for the Eastern Division of the road. Meadville, formerly one of the most secluded and out of the way county seats in the West, is henceforth as accessible and eligibly located as any town in Pennsylvania west of Pittsburgh. It was always a beautiful spot, situated in a fertile and delightful region. Henceforth its trade must be large and its growth rapid and sure..."

After James' arrival, he and Mary settled in a small wooden cabin he built a half mile from work on the banks of French Creek, the waterway that went through Meadville. James and Mary had 10 children, of whom four survived. Four others died of disease as infants, one daughter drowned in French Creek and another perished when her dress caught fire.

There was plenty of work. The post-Civil War traffic on the Erie and the A&GW was intense, stemming from the movement west of newly arrived immigrants and pioneers, as well as from the boom set off by the discovery of oil in western Pennsylvania. The promised boom for Meadville, however, never occurred. The Standard Oil Trust monopolized oil traffic on other lines, and the A&GW and Erie had to convert from six-foot to standard gauge rails by 1880, slowing the line's growth and losing any chance to dominate traffic west.

Throughout James continued to work. At home he was the boss, permitting little dissent and nonsense. He was a devout Catholic, active in parish affairs, spending hours to get a new church and school constructed. James also provided a home for Margaret (Mangan) Kearney, his wife's mother, who came to live in Meadville after her husband, John, died in New York City.

The French Creek home never worked out. The waterway periodically flooded, inundating the Collins home. A wooden rowboat was kept by the side of the house for emergencies. In time, James moved his family to a home on Mead Avenue.

In 1886, Mary (Kearney) Collins died. The following year, James married his late wife's good friend, Susan Keating, at St. Bridget's Church. James continued to work at the A&GW shops as foreman until an injury forced his retirement in 1897. His second wife, Susan, died in the spring of 1916. Thereafter, James lived with his daughter, Ellen (Nel), and her husband, Charles Bertram, a railroad conductor, at their home on Park Avenue. James attended church every Sunday until 1924, when failing health and weak legs prevented this.

James, who died in August 1928, and his wife, Mary (Kearney) Collins, who died in 1886, had 10 children, including a son, James Michael [#116].

[114] JAMES REYNOLDS HOWARD was born November 11, 1856, in Greenwich, son of Patrick and Susannah (Lunney) Howard [#111]. James married MARY ANN MAGEE, who was born in April 1858 in Connecticut.

Little is known about the origins of Mary Ann MaGee, except that she was born in Connecticut and that her family name originates from County Antrim in Northern Ireland. A clue was found next to Mary Ann's name in a family Bible, where there is the notation "Eire." Family tradition holds that her family came to the U.S. from Canada. Nothing is certain. One of her sons, Arthur, explained: "We were raised in the era when children were to be seen and not heard."

At the time she met and married James Howard, Mary Ann was a housekeeper for a family in Stanwich. In nearby Stamford, a section south of the New York, New Haven & Hartford Railroad tracks had become so populated with Irish immigrants who had fled the Great Famine it was known as "Dublin." Could Mary Ann or her family have lived there, perhaps near what is today called MaGee Street?

James and Mary Ann's children considered themselves Scotch-Irish. The label Scotch-Irish is more a term of art than a description of any precise ethnic identity. In 18th century, Americans used the term to distinguish the Scot, Northern Irish and Northern English settlers from earlier English immigrants— Puritans from East Anglia, Anglicans from South England,

Quakers and Methodists from the English Midlands—and from Germans, Dutch and Swedes.

Later in the 19th century, the term Scotch-Irish was used as a way to distinguish these immigrants, their ancestors and descendants from the Irish Catholics who were arriving during the potato famine in the 1840s and 1850s. The famine Irish were more often ignorant and poor, in contrast to the earlier emigrants from Ireland, be they English, Irish or Scots. The famine Irish were predominantly Catholic and once in America were quickly relegated to society's lower orders and treated accordingly.

Mary Ann (MaGee) and James Reynolds Howard, Stamford

The Scotch-Irish, in fact, were any combination of Anglo-Irish, Anglo-Scots, Angle, Scot, Irish or English from Northern Ireland or that section of Scotland and England called the Borders. Some of these Scotch-Irish in America were English settlers in Ireland who had never been in Scotland. Others were from Northern England near the Scot border and had never set foot in either Ireland or Scotland. What the Scotch-Irish Borderers shared was a cultural link. If you look at the map of England, Scotland and Ireland you will see around the Irish Sea between the islands a very tightly bound set of coastal land in all three countries. In fact, these peoples no matter what part of that geography they came from, shared a common culture. For more than 1,000 years they shared a common history of political turmoil, violence, continuing threat of war, remote political authority and migration, war and marriage with each other.

The earliest Scots were in fact Celtic tribesmen from Ireland who migrated the short distance—at points as close as 12 miles—between the north of Ireland and Scotland across the Irish Sea and conquered the indigenous peoples of the area now called Scotland. Their culture evolved into the Scots' Celtic Highland culture, which was closer in behavior, folkways and life patterns to Ireland than to the Normans, Saxons and Angles to the south. As the northern peoples evolved into Scots and the southern peoples into English, the border between the two was the focus of continuing dispute.

Mary Ann (MaGee) and James Reynolds Howard

The name MaGee, for example, is a Celtic name for a clan
Kee, Gee or Ghee; in Scotland the spelling is MacGee, MacGhee,
McGee, McKee, or MacKee. All were bound by blood and cul-
ture for centuries across the islands of the waters between
Northern Ireland and Scotland. The MacGees and McGees were
closely allied in Scot history with the MacDonalds, who were
among the last clans to stop resisting English domination of
Scotland and who were finally destroyed at Culloden in 1745.

Along the English-Scot border, there were continuing invasions, war and destruction. From 1040 to 1745, every English
monarch except three faced a Scot invasion or invaded Scotland.
History records a story of centuries of greed, pride, betrayal,
cruelty and butchery. The English-Scot wars make a grim tale.

North of the border the land swept from a lowland plain into
hills and mountains called Highlands. In these Highlands and
glens between, the distinctive Celtic culture remained. Apart from
the border culture, the lasting division between the Scots people
was between Highlanders of the upper hills and mountains and
the Lowlanders of the valleys below leading to the coastal plain
along the North Sea. Highlanders were people most closely related to the Celts of Ireland with whom they shared blood and a
clan culture. Lowlanders, through continuing invasion by
Norman, Angles, Saxons and English ways, evolved into a more
feudal society, like England.

As for the Scot and English peoples, their kings could never
agree on a border. As a result the Borderers region of each country became a bloody battleground for centuries, ensuring that the

James Reynolds Howard raised dogs on his Stanwich farm

culture that survived there was violent, rootless, anti-authoritarian and extremely suspicious of outsiders. The Scotch-Irish Borderers were reduced by history and habits to a people of impatience, simplicity and directness.

Highland culture was destroyed following the Uprising of 1745, when the Highland Clan forces of Prince Charles dedicated to restoring a Scot Stuart to the British throne were destroyed at Culloden and the clan chiefs wiped out. After the English crushed the rebellion, the subsequent Highland clearances removed the people from the lands, replacing them with sheep.

The surviving clan chiefs found it lucrative to raise sheep for money rather than maintain clans with people his English rulers preferred to transplant to Ireland or North America. Clan ties and sentiment were broken, the bitter seeds of resentment by Scots of their English rulers sown, no matter where they eventually found homes.

English sovereigns, in the conquest of Catholic and Celtic Ireland, often used the population from the Scots and English border as the weapons of domination in subjugating the Irish. Confiscated Catholic lands in Ireland were awarded to loyal Scots and English who migrated to Ireland as part of England's plantation policies. The peoples of the region eventually bound together by commerce and trade, as well as the normal intercourse of humankind. Dublin and other cities in Ireland became frequent migration points for ambitious Scots and English who wished to pursue their future in a place far from home.

The name MaGee is known to have come from County Antrim, Ulster where off the coast road leading to Larne, there is an island seven miles long and a half mile wide called Island MaGee. The little island has sad stories told of it. Island MaGee was the site of a massacre by Presbyterian Scots in 1642 in retaliation for an Irish massacre of Scots nearby. Islanders were thrown off the cliff, 210 feet into the sea, from a place called Druid's Altar. Island MaGee later was known as a theater of sorcery when eight families were tried for witchcraft in 1711.

One possibility possessing the most likely clues about Mary Ann's family origins, are the couple William and Agnes MaGee of Edinburgh, Scotland, who came to America with their children in the mid-19th Century, apparently stopping in Canada and upstate New York before several adult children settled in Connecticut. Other MaGees from this family would migrate south to Virginia and Tennessee. One daughter, Agnes Jane, born in Edinburgh in 1838, married John McCoy in Middletown, Connecticut in 1860. Another daughter, Martha Jane, born in 1845, married Truman Cowles in Hartford in 1869. In considering ancestor Mary Ann's origins, one wonders if Agnes Jane and Martha Jane may have had a married brother who named a daughter Mary Ann. Ancestor Mary Ann MaGee was born in Connecticut in April 1858 and would name a daughter Agnes, perhaps after an aunt? Whatever the facts of the MaGees' origins in Connecticut, or whatever motivated the parents of James Howard to emigrate from Dublin to Connecticut, it is mostly now educated guesses. Hundreds of thousands of Irish and Scots who made the crossing remain anonymous; their history, heritage and individual stories, like themselves, tossed out by the consequences of war, famine or poverty. What are left for us today are whispers of a Canadian connection, the memory of a Scotch-Irish legacy, and the word—Erin—penciled next to Mary Ann MaGee's name in a family Bible written by an unknown author in years past.

Mary Ann and James had eight children. They lived at the Howard family farm in Stanwich, near today's Howard Avenue. The Howards were a large prosperous family. James was a kindly, quiet man with a large white handlebar mustache. Mary Ann was stern, with definite opinions. As the years went by, James and Mary Ann lived in separate houses, though amicably.

James, who died in 1933, and Mary Ann (MaGee) Howard would be buried in North Greenwich Cemetery. They had eight children, including a daughter, Louisa Close [#115].

[115] WILLIS ISAAC SAVAGE was born March 27, 1880, on Savage Hill, East Berlin, a son of Henry Elliot and Theodosia Caroline (Knapp) Savage [#109]. Willis attended Berlin and Middletown schools and the State Agricultural College

in Storrs before returning to Savage Hill to run his family's farm.

About 1910, Willis met **LOUISA CLOSE HOWARD**, born March 23, 1884, in Stanwich, daughter of James Reynolds and Mary Ann (MaGee) Howard [#114]. Louisa had moved to Middletown with the Rev. Frank C. Potter and his wife, Mary Olivia (Close) Potter. The Potters had been a next-door neighbors of Louisa's parents in Stanwich, where Rev. Potter was the minister at the Stanwich Congregational Church. Louisa was one of the Howards' eight children. Rev. Potter and his wife, Mary Olivia (Close), had no children of their own, and, fond of Louisa, wanted to care for her. As a girl, Louisa moved next door to live with the Potters, who treated her as their own. By all accounts, Louisa's "placing out" worked out well, as Louisa was able to take part in the affairs of both families and came to consider the Potters as close to her as her parents.

Willis Isaac Savage

When Rev. Potter retired, he was obliged to leave the Stanwich area, in custom with the practice of Congregationalist ministers. Rev. Potter and his wife, Olivia, moved to Middletown where they purchased a home on Lawn Avenue. With the Howards' permission, Louisa went with them. Louisa enrolled in Middletown High School, where she graduated. Louisa later attended Mt. Holyoke College. In retirement, Rev. Potter filled in for Congregational ministers in the area from time to time, and served as a chaplin at Long Lane Farm Girls Reform School.

Willis graduated from Middletown High School and enrolled in the agricultural college in Storrs, which is now the University of Connecticut. He had to leave school to support his parents after his father suffered a stroke and could no longer work. This ailment also caused Willis' sister, Caroline Knapp Savage, to abandon her plans to attend Mt. Holyoke College and forever give up her dream of going to China as a missionary.

In March 22, 1913, Willis and Louisa married in Rev. Potter's home in Middletown. Before their marriage, Willis and

Louisa purchased the home at the eastern foot of Savage Hill on Ledge Road, which had been built in the early 18th century by Solomon Sage, Jr., and through the years had been the dwelling of Eli Barnes, Benjamin Wilcox, Allen Flagg and Titus Penfield. The home was known as "the Penfield House." It adjoined the farm of Willis' father, which had become a fruit, dairy and poultry enterprise. The great farms of the Midwest had eclipsed the farms of New England, which by the mid-19th century had turned to specialty farming to survive. Willis and Louisa had three children: Mary Close, Agnes Howard and Charles Wilfred.

Willis was elected a corporator of the Berlin Savings Bank in 1915, taking a seat on the bank board as a trustee two years later, a position held by his father, Henry Elliot, from 1894 to 1903. Willis served as a trustee for 40 years.

In 1924, for the 50th anniversary celebration of the Berlin Savings Bank, the trustees wrote a statement on their vision of their role:

> "The prosperity of the present is based on the thrift and the savings of the past. The prosperity of the present and future can only be continued by the same practices.
>
> The mutual Savings Bank is the special friend of persons of moderate means; it receives their surplus moneys in such small sums and at such times as they may choose for depositing it, and invests it solely for their profit, not its own; the investments are made with great caution, and with a single eye to safety; there is no temptation on the part of the Trustees to make loans at high rates of interest on doubtful securities, for they receive no part of the profits; and experience proves that a multitude of persons, each with a little money, can make no more safe or profitable, or convenient investment of their means than by bringing them together in a Savings Bank.
>
> The mutual Savings Bank is the proof of community life as its owners are those who become depositors, and the Banks exists solely for their welfare. Its Officers act as Trustees, and the State of Connecticut, by constant supervision, holds them responsible for an efficient and safe administration of the funds entrusted to them.
>
> A Savings Bank's influence is all pervasive in a community and affects the best quality of character of its people. The Savings Bank is not only an institution, it is also an inspiration to character building and prosperity."

In addition to his farm work and bank duties, Willis also was elected Assessor of Berlin, served on the East Berlin Fire District Committee and was its treasurer. He was a deacon of the Berlin Congregational Church and a member of the Grange for 50 years. During World War I, the draft board considered Willis' duties as a farmer more important than military service. Willis volunteered to serve in the Connecticut Home Guard, where he was a private in Company B, First Separate Battalion. Louisa's brothers, Ralph and Arthur, were drafted in 1917 and sent to France, where they were wounded in a mustard gas attack in 1918.

Louisa was active in the Berlin Congregational Church, the Berlin Visiting Nurse Association, the New Britain Girl Scout Council and the Newington Garden Club. Willis and Louisa were unpretentious, thrifty and a portrait of constancy. They were generous to widows, widowers and unmarried adults in the Berlin community, who often enjoyed Savage hospitality. Later, as Rev. Potter grew ill and needed nursing care, he and his wife sold their Middletown home to Wesleyan University and moved in with Louisa and Willis until he died. Both Rev. Potter and his wife, Mary, were buried at Wilcox Cemetery in East Berlin.

Willis and Louisa were modest and unassuming. I learned this lesson from Louisa during one of the many outings she took us on as children. On these luncheon excursions, we frequently went to parks and out-of-the-way places near the farm. One day we passed a stone tower, where we picnicked. On the base, some teenage vandals had painted their names and class years. Said Louisa: "Fools' names and fools' faces are often found in public places." I hope she can forgive her loving grandson this narrative.

One story about Willis illustrates his character and dry humor. It occurred one Christmas at the Savage Hill farmhouse, where grandchildren, aunts, uncles, in-laws and friends were gathered for the holiday dinner. The men were in the living room near the fireplace, enjoying what Louisa would call "a libation" before dinner, and the conversation was robust and friendly. Willis sat with the men, who included bankers, businessmen, teachers, doctors, yet few farmers. Willis stayed quiet by-and-large as others expounded on the events of the day. At one point, the conversation turned to farming. One of the men held forth on government farm policies, while another talked of the latest in farm technology, crop chemicals and pesticides. Another voiced his views on the techniques of managing an orchard. At this point, my father realized that the only person there who really knew the subject was Willis, who was saying nothing. After one of the men had given his opinion about the most suitable time to prune apple trees, my father turned to his father-in-law and said:

Louisa (Howard) raised produce in the garden behind the East Berlin farm house, 1941

"Father Savage, what do you think? When is the best time to prune the orchard?"

Willis glanced about the group. "Well," he said with a wry smile, "I prune when my saw is sharp."

For more than a half century, Willis' daily chores began well before dawn when he arose to tend to the livestock in the barn and chickens in the coop 150 yards behind the house. Some 200

Willis Isaac Savage displays the goods of the family farm

Louisa Close Howard,
Middletown, 1903

Rev. Frank C. Potter,
minister of North Greenwich
Congregational Church, and
his wife Mary Olivia (Close)
"took in" Louisa Close
Howard as their own.

laying chickens were cared for, as were, at times, cows, pigs and
the occasional work horse. There was a vegetable garden near the
house where beans, squash, and other produce were grown, and
surrounding the barn some 40 acres of apple orchards. Morning
chores ended about 8 a.m., when it was time for breakfast. After
breakfast came whatever chores needed finishing, or town work,
if any. Every afternoon at about 2 p.m. it was time for a nap,
taken on a well-worn couch on Louisa's sun porch where her
plants and greenery demonstrated to all who saw that Louisa's
art was her ability with plants and flowers. In season, Willis
would tend his stand on the Middletown Road, where he sold his
produce and eggs to passers by and townspeople.

Willis Isaac Savage died in August 7, 1960, and was buried at
Wilcox Cemetery in East Berlin. Within a few months Louisa,
unable to manage the farm herself and no longer interested in the
daily rigors of farming, sold the Savage farm and moved into a
small apartment in Berlin across the street from the

Congregational Church. Louisa turned down offers from her three children to live with them and their families.

At the time, son Charles Wilfred, born September 25, 1918, lived with his family in California. Charles had graduated from Yale University and the University of Chicago Medical School. An M.D., Charles studied psychiatry at Yale and later at the U.S. Naval Hospital in Bethesda, Maryland. Charles married Ethel Maurine Truss in 1940. They had two children, Charles Wilfred III, and Elma Louise. Charles worked at the Stanford University Medical Center in Palo Alto, California; at the Johns Hopkins Medical Center in Baltimore, Maryland; and with the U.S. Veterans Administration. Charles and Ethel retired in 1980 and divided their time between their homes in suburban Maryland and St. John, U.S. Virgin Islands. Ethel died in 1990 and was buried at Wilcox Cemetery in East Berlin.

Charles, perhaps ruled by the same instincts that inspired his missionary ancestors, often found himself in medical "missionary" service. In the early 1960's, Charles spent six months in Nigeria, where he worked with physicians in rural areas near Lagos. In retirement, Charles worked with the St. John Public Health Service. He also taught himself Spanish and ventured regularly to Guatemala, where he worked with Anglican missionaries giving medical treatment to Indians.

Louisa's daughter, Agnes Howard, graduated from Connecticut College and in 1950 married Paul Griswold, a native of Guilford, Connecticut, and a descendant of Matthew Griswold [#58]. Agnes, a teacher and artist, and her husband, Paul, an engineer retired from Hamilton Standard, a division of United Technologies, lived in retirement in Lakehurst, New Jersey, until Paul's death in 1997. He was buried in Guilford and Agnes

The farm house of Willis & Louisa as seen from atop Savage Hill

retired to Wallingford.

Louisa lived in the Berlin apartment for five years before entering Jerome Home, a retirement home in New Britain where many of her friends and former neighbors lived. Willis Isaac and Louisa Close (Howard) Savage, who died in March 8, 1975 and was buried at Wilcox Cemetery in East Berlin, had three children, including a daughter, Mary Close [#117].

Louisa Close (Howard) Savage

[116] JAMES MICHAEL COLLINS was born
September 27, 1871, in Meadville, son of James and Mary (Kearney) Collins [#113]. As a boy, James attended Catholic schools in Meadville and earned money selling sandwiches and fruit to rail passengers, many of whom were immigrants who stopped at Meadville's McHenry House on their way west.

After graduating from high school, James went to work with his father in the A&GW shops, where he learned to be a machinist. James, as a young man, met Gustine Twain of nearby Frenchtown. On December 13, 1893, Gustine gave birth to their son, Earl C. Collins. A day later Gustine died of complications. Without a wife to take care of young Earl, and because Earl had been born out of wedlock, James was persuaded by his stepmother, Susan (Keating) Collins, that the wisest course was to place Earl with a nearby family that wanted a child, relocate and start anew. The parting was amicable; James' father and stepmother looked after Earl, who was placed with a family named Snyder in Sagertown.

A written canvassing of friends and associates in railroads throughout the northeast resulted in an invitation from a friend of James' father who worked in Hartford at the New York, New Haven & Hartford Railroad yards. The man, whose name was Wilder, was a general foreman in the NY/NH&H shops, then located near today's Armory. On October 3, 1897, James began work as a machinist in Hartford, sending money home every month to his stepmother to help pay for Earl's upkeep. James did well. After starting at a wage of 35 cents an hour, he had risen by May 1, 1902, to be general foreman at a salary of $26 a week.

By the time James joined the NY/NH&H railroad, nearly all of the line's 1,794 miles had been completed, a task begun by predecessor companies in 1838. The railroad industry was mature. Steel had replaced the original iron rails, the Pullman sleeping car was in use, the Westinghouse air brake had given way to the automatic air brake, the automatic coupler had been adopted and most lines had been converted to the standard-gauge track. Railroad construction and operation dominated the U. S. economy. Indeed, the NY/NY&H Railroad was among the most successful firms in the nation. At the time James joined, shares of stock in the NY/NH&H, under the control of banker J. P. Morgan, were selling for $200 a share and paying a steady 10 percent dividend. Its revenues were three times those of the State of Connecticut, and it was the dominant firm of its day. In 1911, the NY/NH&H employed 34,767 men and carried more than 84 million passengers in Connecticut alone.

Government, at all levels, had been eager to stimulate railroad growth. The rail-roads were the technological engine building and binding the country. The federal government over the course of a few decades had made 72 grants totaling 130 million acres to various companies,

James Michael Collins, railroad master mechanic, 1922

Alice (O'Connell) Collins

land equal in size to the combined areas of Michigan, Indiana, Illinois, Wisconsin and half of Ohio. The rail companies sold much of this land to raise money to pay for construction, and held other parcels for their increase in value as development came. Other companies used the land grants to raise mortgage and other funds. The total value of the federal grants was $1.2 billion. The states gave away an additional 48 million acres to various rail companies in inducements to construction, and authorities in towns and counties issued more than $91 million in subscription stock to raise funds for construction. By 1890, some 163,597 miles of track had been laid, the transcontinental line between the Union Pacific and Central Pacific was two decades old, and the New York Central, Pennsylvania, Erie, Baltimore & Ohio, and Grand Trunk were the major arteries for the nation's commerce.

James worked in New Haven for a few months in 1904 and returned to Hartford in December to be named master mechanic of the NY/NH&H Railroad shops in East Hartford. By that time, the railroad was moving its shops from Hartford across the Connecticut River to East Hartford and also elevating the downtown rail line leading to Union Station above Asylum Avenue. The move across the river was in deference to the insurance companies, real estate developers and other firms in Hartford who wished to rid the downtown of factories, industrial plants and tenement slums, such as "Frog Hollow."

James worked continually for the NY/NH&H Railroad, moving from assignments in Boston, East Hartford, New Haven and New York, where he worked in the Harlem Yards and in the conversion of the New Haven line from steam to electric power.

Throughout, James continued to support his son, Earl, in Meadville, and visited him and his family several times a year.

In Hartford, James made friends with Pat and Tom Sheedy, who were handy about the railyards and as saloon operators. Their cousin, Michael Sheedy, was a prosperous contractor, and his sister, Catherine (Sheedy) O'Connell [#112] lived nearby with her husband, Thomas, and their three daughters. Pat and Tom suggested that James meet their niece, ALICE O'CONNELL.

Alice, born in 1882 in Middletown, Ohio moved with her parents, Thomas and Catherine (Sheedy) O'Connell [#112] to Hartford in 1894. Alice attended Catholic schools and was graduated from high school. She became a dressmaker. With her sister, Frances, Alice designed and made dresses, which they sold to clothing stores in town. Unlike her sisters, Frances and Edith, who had a gift for easy socializing, Alice was shy and seemed somewhat aloof. She preferred to play the piano, sing and sew. Her sisters often had men callers but Alice did not. Her family feared she might never marry. However, her uncles took an active interest in finding her a suitable mate. Alice often went to New York to visit the Fifth Avenue dress shops and see the latest designs. On one of those trips her relations, Pat and Tom Sheedy, arranged for her to meet James Collins, who was assigned to the railroad's New York operations. Alice was in her mid-20s when she met James, who was 12 years older, well-dressed in derby, starched collar and tailor made suits. James seemed worldly and confident and displayed an independent spirit that sparked her imagination. Their courtship lasted four years. James' job took him to East Hartford, New Haven and New York during the week, but on weekends he visited Alice at her Jefferson Street home. Alice and James were married in June 1909, two months after James was assigned to the East Hartford yards.

James and Alice lived in an apartment on Burnside Avenue in East Hartford for three years. Their first son, Robert Thomas Collins, was born there May 14, 1910. In 1912, they purchased a new wood-frame home at 157 Ashley Street in Hartford, built by Alice's uncle, Michael Sheedy. Soon, James was transferred by the railroad to New Haven. Alice was reluctant to leave Hartford and her family, so James took a room in New Haven and came home on weekends.

In 1916, James' stepmother, Susan (Keating) Collins, died in Meadville. At the funeral, James introduced his 20-year-old son, Earl, to Alice and Robert. Alice insisted that Earl come to Hartford to live. Earl came a few months later and got a job with the Austin Organ Company, and later as a fireman on a switching engine in the NY/NH&H railroad yards in East Hartford.

War was raging in Europe. The United States was no longer able to stay free of entanglements. America's sympathies for Great Britain, the nation's tremendous capacity to produce massive necessary goods, and Germany's U-boat warfare brought the U.S. into the war in the spring of 1917. On May 18, 1917, Congress passed the Selective Service Act, causing the registration of 24 million young men. By the fall, some two million had been drafted or had volunteered. One of the draftees was Earl, who was inducted into the Army October 31 in Hartford.

Earl was sent to Camp Devens in Ayer, Massachusetts, for basic training and was assigned to the 301st Field Hospital, which was part of the 301st Sanitary Train of the 76th Division (National Army). Earl, one of 10,977 Connecticut men assigned to the New England division, was trained as a medic. On May 1, 1918, Earl was assigned to the 303rd Infantry Regiment, which was part of the 76th Division's 152nd Infantry Brigade in the command of Brigadier General Frederic D. Evans.

On June 8, Earl was made a private first class and a month later was one of 22,000 men in the 76th Division who sailed from Boston, Brooklyn, Halifax, New York and Montreal to Europe. After a brief stay in rest camps in England, the men of the 76th crossed the English Channel to Bordeaux, Cherbourg and Le Havre in France. By July 19, the 76th Division had established its headquarters in the St. Amand-Mont-Rond area in Cherbourg.

The transport of the American forces across the Atlantic was a strategic masterstroke. The German high command never believed the Americans could bring so many men to Europe in such a short time. However, the U.S. Navy had developed the convoy system of ocean travel, where vessels were grouped into fleets and escorted by warships. U-boats were reluctant to attack such a heavily guarded array of arms at sea. Consequently, the U.S. Navy was able to move 2.5 million American soldiers across the Atlantic with a loss of only a few hundred lives, a monumental military achievement that helped win the war.

The first Americans to arrive in France in early 1918 were poorly supported. The U.S. Army had a lot of learn about overseas duty. Supporting a force with food, medical supplies, clothing, footwear, ammunition, weapons and the like was a tactical nightmare. Mistakes were made. Fortunately, General John J. Pershing, commander of the American Expeditionary Force in France (AEF), refused to permit the French and English commanders to use the American relief forces in their trench warfare assaults. Pershing had been shocked to see the losses his European counterparts were willing to accept.

Alice (O'Connell) Collins with stepson, Earl C. Collins (left), and son, Robert T, before Earl went to France with US Army in 1918.

By the time the 76th Divsion arrived, the AEF had experienced nearly 10 months of war. Men from the 26th and 42nd Divisions, and the 1st, 2nd and 3rd Divisions already had suffered great losses and had been victimized by mustard gas attacks. The Central Powers had launched what turned out to be their last offensive in April through July, and Pershing was poised for a counter attack to check the German advance.

Some 26 American divisions were in France at the time. Seven of them were at the front, 15 were in training, two were in reserve, and two more, including the 76th, were just arriving. The last of the 76th arrived in Cherbourg August 8. Two days later, General Pershing was given sole control over the American forces, which were combined into the 1st American Army/Europe. A short time later, a 2nd American Army was created. In the weeks that followed, the 76th Division acted as a depot division, training, equipping and forwarding to the front some 19,971 men to infantry, machine gun, ammunition and supply train units. In the final weeks of the war, PFC Earl Collins moved with the 152nd Infantry Brigade to the St. Aignan-Noyers area, where his unit was used as a skeleton brigade as men were sent elsewhere.

The records of Earl Collins' service were destroyed in a fire at the Army Records Center in St. Louis years later. Telling exactly where he was at what time is impossible. But sometime in the late summer or early fall, Earl and the 303rd Infantry Brigade were in a forward positon, where they had established a base camp; tents were erected for the officers, medics and communications and mess units.

The German army was decimated. Nearly four years of war with the Allies had claimed the lives of millions. Too many of the Germans now in uniform were either too young or too old. Their commanders were desperate, knowing that after the failure of their offensive in the spring and early summer, combined with the arrival of more than two million Americans to reinforce the exhausted French and English armies, it was only a matter of time before the fate of the German army would be sealed. Consequently, many German officers, hoping for a miracle, took huge risks with their new recruits, boys and older men. One such officer ordered a night attack on the 303rd Infantry's camp.

Later, Earl would tell the story only twice—once to his father and once to his stepmother, without enthusiasm—and he refused encouragement later to discuss the war or his experiences in France. But the night of the German patrol's attack on the 303rd, Earl was in the medical tent. Cots had been set up, and a table with a kerosene lamp and medical supplies laid out. Earl was armed, a .45 caliber pistol in the holster at his waist. Suddenly there were shots, screams and officers issuing orders in the night. Earl heard a sound behind him, turned and saw a bayonet blade pierce the canvas wall of his tent, slicing down in a quick motion. Earl drew his pistol and watched as a German soldier peeked through the hole he had torn. The enemy shouldered his weapon to chest level and charged, screaming like a madman. Earl fired. The soldier fell backward, the force of the .45 shot slamming him onto his back. He heaved a few breaths, moaned and said something in German. Earl went to the soldier's side and bent over. There was nothing to do. The soldier's face burned into Earl's memory, the small blemishes around his nose and mouth, the soft boyish growth on his cheeks and lip, the blond hair. In a few minutes the soldier was dead. The face of that German soldier haunted Earl's nights for the rest of his life.

The 303rd Infantry was one of the first units ordered to return home after the armistice November 11, 1918. On November 25, the regiment went to St. Nazaire. Over the next weeks, the 303rd and other regiments in the 152nd Infantry would leave France. By February, the 303rd was demobilizing at Camp Devens, and on July 18, 1919 Earl was honorably discharged from the Army.

Earl returned to Hartford, where he took a job with the Phoenix Fire Insurance Company. On July 19, 1923, Earl married Lillian Borndt, born July 22, 1900, in Meadville. They lived at 30 Colonial Street in Hartford. Earl died of stomach cancer in May 1935 and was buried at Northwood Cemetery in Windsor. Lillian worked at the Phoenix for several years and then moved to New York City, where she lived until her death in August 1982.

Throughout the war, Earl's father, James, worked under the direction of the War Industries Board as a scheduler and expedited rail movements on the NY/NH&H lines, reporting to the

Railroad Administration, which controlled rates, wages and rail operators. For James, this was the most exciting time in his career, yet also the most frustrating. He saw many men of lesser ability promoted to management positions, while he, who did not have a college degree, had to be content with supervisory posts. James developed ulcers and a dependence on alcohol, which led to his hospitalization for nearly six months at Stamford Hall, a convalescent facility. There his ulcers were treated and his lifelong vow to abstain from alcohol taken. James also developed a renewed commitment to the faith, which sustained him the rest of his life. He carried a small prayer book, worn from much use, in his coat pocket every day.

In September 1919, James and Alice had a second son, James Francis. Within a short time, Alice's health began to fail. As a child, she had suffered from rheumatic fever, which damaged her heart. On October 31, 1924, Alice died. She was buried at Mt. St. Benedict's Cemetery, Bloomfield. James, whose job kept him away from Hartford for days at a time, placed his second son, James Francis, in the care of Alice's sister, Frances (O'Connell) Rankin. His son, Robert Thomas, remained in military school on Long Island.

James kept in touch with his sons, sending them money for spending and expenses, and demanding weekly letters in return. James insisted they excel in school, swearing that they would never fail to advance for want of academic degrees. For himself, James had an engineer's approach to problems, rejecting theories and rhetoric. If he thought his son, Robert, was not focusing on the central point of a situation, he would demand: "What do you mean maybe, perhaps, ought? What are the likelihoods? Put on a number on it! A 10% chance, a 90% chance, what...? How does it measure up?..."

James also had a practical view about jobs. If a particular job wasn't pleasing, James insisted his sons stay put and work to improve the situation. Never quit in a huff. His advice: "You're on the train now. Stay on the train and work your way up to a better seat. Don't get off the train or you won't have any seat at all."

James retired from the NY//NH&H Railroad in 1935, and lived in the Ashley Street home with his son, Robert, until Robert and his wife, Mary, purchased a home at 49 High Farms Road in West Hartford. James lived with them until his death in 1946. He was buried at Mt. St. Benedict's Cemetery, Bloomfield. Among his survivors was a son, Robert Thomas [#117].

[117] ROBERT THOMAS COLLINS was born
May 14, 1910, in Hartford, son of James Michael and Alice
(O'Connell) Collins [#116], and lived with his parents on
Burnside Avenue, East Hartford, until 1912, when the family
moved to 157 Ashley Street, Hartford. Robert attended local
schools in Hartford until 1923 when he enrolled in Clason
Military Academy, Bronx, New York, a parochial school run by
the Christian Brothers, which a few years later relocated to
Oakdale, Long Island, and was renamed LaSalle Military
Academy.

On October 31, 1924, Robert's mother, Alice (O'Connell)
Collins, died of heart disease. Thereafter, his father rented much
of the Ashley Street home to tenants and reserved only a small
attic room for Robert's use on holidays. For the rest of Robert's
childhood, LaSalle and subsequent schools were his home.

Robert's brother, James Francis, who was born September 6,
1919, was placed by his father in 1924 with his mother's sister,
Frances (O'Connell) Rankin, whose husband, William Rankin, a
Democratic Party official in Hartford, was elected Mayor of
Hartford in 1931 and served a two-year term. John R. Case, in a
letter to the editor of the Hartford *Courant* November 7, 1984,
wrote of Rankin's visit with presidential candidate Franklin D.
Roosevelt in 1932:

> "I wrote the Hartford Times account of Franklin D.
> Roosevelt's first campaign visit to Hartford in 1932.
> At the time, I was a reporter for the Times and also
> co-secretary to Hartford Mayor William J. Rankin.
> The other co-secretary was John M. Bailey, the
> renowned Democratic leader who died in 1975.
> Rankin and I met the Roosevelt car on the Buckeley
> Bridge and the mayor told FDR that I was a strong
> Roosevelt supporter...Bailey and Rankin were Al
> Smith Democrats and had backed him (FDR) for the
> 1932 nomination."

Mayor Rankin later became fire commissioner and postmaster. James Francis was raised with his cousins, William Jr., Alice
and Catherine, in the Rankin household. James Francis attended
local schools, was graduated from Trinity College in Hartford,
and Harvard University Graduate School of Education. During
World War II, he served in the U.S. Army as a personnel officer
in India. After the war, James Francis was graduated from
Harvard Law School. On January 22, 1949, James Francis
married Constance Virginia Sullivan of West Springfield,
Massachusetts, a graduate of Boston University's Sargent

College. They had four children: James, Elizabeth, Patricia and Mary. James Francis practiced law in Hartford for 22 years and was active in Republican Party affairs. During his career in Hartford, James Francis served as a police court prosecutor, assistant corporation counsel, regional counsel for the U.S. Small Business Administration, and legal counsel to the Republican Party in the state House of Representatives. In 1962 and 1964, James Francis ran as the Republican candidate for the U.S. Congress from Connecticut's First Congressional District (Hartford), both times unsuccessfully. During the 1964 race, James Francis became close with another GOP congressional candidate, Thomas Meskill, mayor of New Britain. In 1970, Meskill ran successfully as the Republican candidate for governor with James Francis as a political adviser. In 1972 Governor Meskill appointed James Francis as Judge of the Court of Common Pleas, and in 1974 as a State Superior Court Judge. James Francis died of cancer in November 1975.

After graduating from LaSalle Military Academy in 1928, Robert attended Roxbury Preparatory School (now Cheshire Academy) in Cheshire, Connecticut. His father, whose job kept him moving between New York, New Haven and Hartford, wanted Robert to have some family supervision during college. Robert entered Allegheny College in Meadville, Pennsylvania, where James's brother Sinon and his wife, Rose (Woodring), lived with their sons. Robert could count on family support and weekend meals at his Uncle Si and Aunt Rose's, with whom he became close.

In his sophomore year Robert enrolled in a joint-curriculum program with the University of Pennsylvania in Philadelphia, through which he received his B.A. from Allegheny and C.E. (bachelor's degree in civil engineering) from the University of Pennsylvania. Throughout Robert's academic years, both in prep school and college, he competed in track & field athletics, primarily in the 440 yard run. Robert competed at track meets in Boston, Hartford, New Haven, New York and Philadelphia, frequently with record breaking performances. His running career ended when he fell during Olympic Trials held at the Penn Relays in Philadelphia in 1932. Robert's schoolmate and 440 rival, named Carr, won the heat and went on to win the Gold Medal in the Los Angeles games later that year. Robert carried small track cinders in a healed-over scar on his knee for the rest of his life as a reminder of the fall.

After graduation, Robert returned to Hartford to live with his father at the Ashley Street home. There was a Depression, with one person in three without work. However, Robert held two jobs, a delivery truck driver by night and by day a clerk, first with the Connecticut Trust Company and later with the National Fire Insurance Company. In 1935, Robert began a six-year teaching career at Sedgwick Junior High School in West Hartford, Windsor Locks High School, Canterbury Preparatory School in New Milford and Wethersfield High School. There he taught science and business and acted as guidance director.

Robert's father's emphasis on education encouraged Robert to obtain further credentials. Throughout his teaching career, Robert attended Boston University's Graduate School of Education on weekends; he received his master's degree in education and completed the course work for his doctorate. Robert also attended night classes at Trinity College in Hartford.

In a psychology class at Trinity in 1935, Robert met another student, **MARY CLOSE SAVAGE**, born November 26, 1914, daughter of Willis Isaac and Louisa Close (Howard) Savage [#115]. Mary Savage was raised on her parents' East Berlin farm and was graduated with honors from Middletown High School. She obtained a scholarship to Connecticut College in New London. After graduating in 1935, Mary obtained a job in the state Department of Education, editing and preparing education materials for publication. In the evenings, Mary took graduate courses at Trinity College, where she met fellow graduate student Robert Collins.

Robert and Mary dated for several years and were married in September 1942 at St. Joseph's Cathedral in Hartford. Though Mary was raised a deacon's daughter, her parents did not object to her marrying a Catholic. Mary's mother, Louisa (Howard), told Robert: "I might have been Catholic. Only a priest never came to serve Mass in Stanwich and we lived next door to the Congregational minister."

Mary continued to work with the Education Department until her first child was born in 1945. Robert continued his teaching career until 1940 when, through mutual acquaintanc-

Mary Close Savage

es, he was offered a position in industrial relations with General Motors Corporation's New Departure Division's Bristol plant.

Only a few years before, GM had agreed to bargain with the trade unions. New Departure's general manager felt that Robert's experience in education and as a guidance counselor meshed well with GM's need in industrial and personnel relations. Robert was hired to write job descriptions, standardize wage scales, upgrade labor and management systems for settling disputes and otherwise help maintain labor peace.

By that time New Departure was a manufacturer of ball bearings, a small but crucial mechanical part for the smooth functioning of any wheel and shaft. Founded in 1889 by Albert and Edward Rockwell in Bristol, New Departure took its name from the doorbell the Rockwells invented, which operated by twisting a permanent turnkey, giving "electrical results," a "new departure" from the conventional doorbell.

New Departure was the kind of manufacturing that had come to typify Connecticut, the home to tinkers and inventors. Connecticut never had rich farm land; most of its soil was rocky, thin and hard to till. The farmers who survived were those who had turned to specialty farming—tobacco, dairy, poultry and fruit. To prosper, Connecticut residents relied on inventiveness, design and manufacturing; thus the birth of Yankee ingenuity. Connecticut residents established and worked in factories to make clocks, pins, pencils and erasers, metal boxes, locks, metal tools, buttons, firearms, sewing machines, typewriters and even automobiles.

The Rockwell brothers' New Departure developed and manufactured the first conveyor belt ball bearing, the first double row dual-purpose ball bearing, the first sealed-for-life ball bearing (that would never need regreasing), the first fan and water pump bearing and the first bicycle coaster brake that enabled pedals to remain stationary while the bicycle coasted, and could brake the bicycle when rotated backward.

New Departure's fortunes were soon tied to those of Alfred P. Sloan, an investor from New Jersey, and later to General Motors. GM was formed in Detroit, Michigan, on September 16, 1908. Its nucleus was the Buick Motor Car Company, formed in 1902 by David Buick, who later merged his company with the Durant-Dort Carriage Company owned by William C. Durant. At the time of GM's formation, automobile companies were opening and closing regularly. Of the nearly 1,000 firms organized prior to the 1920s to build automobiles, only 200 stayed in business long enough to produce a car.

Yet with GM, Durant began to build a different kind of car

company, and along the way laid the foundations of the modern corporation, a method of organizing commercial and industrial activity that would eventually come to dominate the way Americans produced goods and services. By the end of 1909, Durant had purchased all or part of the stock of 22 different concerns and plants. Among the acquisitions that were part of GM by then, or soon would be, were Buick, Oldsmobile, Cadillac, Oakland (now Pontiac), Ewing, Marquette, Welch,

Robert Thomas Collins and Mary Close Savage, 1941.

Scripps-Booth, Sheridan, Emore, and Rapid and Reliance trucks. Chevrolet, formed in Detroit in 1911 by Durant and racing car driver Louis Chevrolet, merged with GM in 1918.

Also merged with GM that year was United Motors Company, a holding company for several firms, including Hyatt Roller Bearing Company of Harrison, New Jersey, and New Departure Company of Bristol, Connecticut, which by that time manufactured ball bearings. United Motors was dominated by Alfred P. Sloan, who began his manufacturing career with a $50,000 investment in Hyatt. By the time United Motors joined GM, Sloan's investment had grown in value to $13.5 million.

Under Durant, GM grew tremendously. In 1908, its first year of operation, GM's various car divisions sold one of every five cars purchased in the U.S. By 1916, however, Ford and other competitors had cut into GM's share of the market, so that only one car in 10 sold was a GM product. By 1920, GM was on the verge of collapse. Durant resigned that year and was succeeded by GM's largest shareholder, Pierre S. du Pont, who made Sloan of United Motors heir apparent. Soon automotive inventor Charles F. Kettering, the Dayton, Ohio automotive research pioneer, moved to Detroit when his Dayton Research Laboratories merged with GM. Eight years earlier, Kettering's Dayton Engineering

Laboratories Company (DELCO) had developed the first electric self-starter for automobiles. The electric self-starter, which first appeared in Cadillac cars in 1912, eliminated the need for the sometimes dangerous and unpredictable hand crank. More than any other device, the self-starter popularized motor cars.

As Sloan took over GM's operations, he organized the first modern corporation, which in effect held that corporate officers and a general staff existed at headquarters to assist and direct the manufacturing in GM's operating divisions. The divisions, in turn, gave corporate headquarters financial control, enabling corporate officers to allocate corporate resources and approve divisional capital investments. The divisions were in charge of the operational work associated with the manufacturing necessary to meet their financial goals. The idea, revolutionary in its time, was the model for corporations to come. On the individual level, Sloan said his method was "to give a man a clear cut job and get out of his way and let him do it."

Sloan's genius at organization worked at GM, enabling the car manufacturing organization to grow to dominate all of American industry. By 1936, automaking was America's No. 1 industry, and GM was America's No. 1 automaker. Indeed, GM was the largest manufacturing company in the world, and the most profitable. The 1.5 million automobiles sold by GM's auto divisions in 1936 represented 43% of all cars sold in the United States, and brought in $1.5 billion in revenues and $284 million in profits.

The GM system worked well for New Departure Division, which manufactured the ball bearings on the wheels of every GM car, indeed, the wheels of most of GM's competitors as well. Part of the success of GM was not so much that it was a car company, but a car parts company as well. Each of GM's divisions that manufactured parts and accessories such as batteries, generators, starter motors, lamps, and steering systems was encouraged to sell to anyone who wanted to buy, including competing car companies. By the late 1930s, when Robert Collins had joined New Departure, the GM Division has grown to the point that it had two manufacturing plants in Meriden and Bristol, employed 10,000 workers and was the largest manufacturer of ball bearings in the world, with sales exceeding $90 million a year.

General Motors and its divisions had grown to this position of economic prominence because of the immense impact of the automobile on American life. Americans' desire for the automobile and the changes it brought were reshaping the nation. At first, the use of cars was limited by the lack of adequate roads. In 1900, there were only 150,000 miles of surfaced roads in the entire country. Of the 2.2 million miles of roads in the U.S. in 1909, only 190,000 were surfaced. The problems caused by this lack of roadways was demonstrated during World War I, when dozens of divisions of soldiers, more than 2.5 million men and all their associated support goods of food, clothing, medicine and the like had to move across the country to the eastern ports for transport to Europe. Because of poor roads, entire army divisions raised in the Midwest and California never made it to the east coast by the time the war ended. If the United States was to play a role in world affairs, the nation would need a good road system.

After the First World War, General John J. Pershing sketched out a road network that would be useful in transporting military troops and materiel overland in the event of a national emergency. Pershing assigned a young West Point graduate and native of Kansas, Lt. Colonel Dwight D. Eisenhower, to cross the country in a military convoy and survey the route. The trip took 62 days, with the average distance covered 52 miles a day. When Eisenhower became president nearly three decades later, he would be instrumental in persuading Congress in 1956 to pass a federal highway bill. The legislation enabled the development over 13 years of a 41,000-mile network of roads that would link 42 state capitals and 90% of the nation's cities with a population over 50,000.

Meanwhile, the number of car owners and their political weight was increasing. Farm organizations, trucking companies, automobile clubs and civic groups, as well as automakers, were all pushing for improved roads. Huge sums were spent by local, state and federal governments to build roads: $995 million in 1921, with the annual rate of spending increasing to $1.6 billion a year by 1930, $1.7 billion by 1940, and $2.9 billion a year by 1950. The result was marked improvement in the quality and quantity of roadways. By 1920, 387,000 miles were surfaced, with that number doubling by 1930 and redoubling in 1940. By 1950, some 1.6 million miles of roadway had been surfaced.

At the time Robert entered New Departure's employment, the second war in Europe was widening. The United States soon began the Lend Lease program, and the construction of ships and other vehicles needed for the war against Nazi Germany was expanding. The ball bearings manufactured by New Departure were needed in bombsights for aerial bombers, as well as in every engine and on every wheel and shaft.

After war was declared on Japan and Germany, Robert's job was declared essential to the war effort and he was promoted to director of personnel and industrial relations at New Departure, with the prime responsibility for maintaining labor peace during war production. In 1944, Connecticut Governor Raymond Baldwin gave citations to Robert and to the head to the state's Congress of Industrial Organizations (CIO) for their work in keeping New Departure's ball bearings plants turning out the "tremendous trifle" necessary for the modern mechanized war.

After the war ended, Robert continued with New Departure; in 1947 he was promoted to general manager of production, in 1951 to manager of the Meriden plant, which was the work place for 6,000 employees and sold $65 million worth of bearings a year, and in 1953 to general sales manager. In the four years Robert had the sales position, New Departure's share of the market increased from 38% to 48%, and sales increased from $98 million to $150 million. In 1957, Robert was assigned to be New Departure's director of quality control and reliability, and the following year was transferred to GM's Delco Products Division in Dayton, Ohio, as director of production, material control and purchasing.

Robert and Mary (Savage) Collins' family, which included Tara Susanne, born November 24, 1945, Robert Thomas Jr., born December 26, 1947, and William Savage, born November 3, 1950, moved to Dayton in 1959, 40 miles from Middletown, Ohio, the birthplace of Robert's mother, Alice (O'Connell) Collins.

Robert was retired from GM in 1965 and he and Mary returned to West Hartford, where they lived at 151 Stoner Drive. They were divorced in 1969. Mary returned to work for the State of Connecticut, in administrative assignments, first in the Tax Department, than the Treasury Department. Mary retired in 1979 with 20 years-accumulated state service. She later worked as an editor in West Hartford on a magazine published by a weavers guild. Robert, who in retirement was a financial adviser and business consultant in Hartford, died October 31, 1988. He was buried in Wilcox Cemetery, East Berlin. The three children of Robert Thomas and Mary (Savage) Collins include:

Tara, the oldest, was graduated from Emma Willard School, Troy, N.Y., from The New School for Social Research, New York City, and from Queens College (CUNY), with a masters degree in art history. Tara worked as a graphics designer in Manhattan for 25 years. She and husband, David Gordon, adopted Samantha Collins Gordon in 1989. They reside in San Diego.

Bill, the youngest, was graduated from Western Reserve Academy, Hudson, Ohio, and from New York University with a major in theology. Bill and his first wife, Sally Townsend, met in Manhattan and later moved to Knoxville, Tennessee, where their son, Townsend Savage, and daughter, Caroline Sanders, were born in 1985 and 1989 respectively. They later divorced. Bill, a photographer, and active in the Episcopal Church, married Angela Livesay in 1998 and lives in Knoxville.

The middle child is your writer, Robert Thomas Jr. [#119]

[118] YUNG JA LEE was born September 15, 1928, in Kyoto, Japan, daughter of KOON WU and WUL KUK (LEE) LEE, Koreans who had moved to Kyoto a few years before to find work.

Yung Ja's father, Koon Wu, was born in 1882 in Soon Chun City, Chun Nam Province, on the southern end of the Korean peninsula. Koon Wu's family originated from the city of Chon Jo in the province of Cholla Pukdo, and were of the landed Yang Ban class. Yet Koon Wu grew up in a land locked in the vice of Imperial Japan.

Korea was established by a Chinese exile named Kija and his 5,000 followers in 1122 B.C. The kingdom Kija called Chosun, or "Morning Calm," became caught between the desires and fears of Russia, China and Japan for centuries. China's Mongol conquerors, Genghis Khan and Kublai Khan, overran Korea in the 13th century, using the peninsular nation as a staging point for invasions of Japan. The Mongol invasions of Japan were repelled, the second time in 1281 by a typhoon the Japanese later called Kamikaze, or "Divine Wind."

Korea was attacked by Japan in the 16th century, when Japanese warrior Hideoyoshi Toyotomi, known today as the "Napoleon of Japan," attempted to invade Korea to realize his dreams of an Imperial Japan, whose rule would spread from China to India. Though Hideoyoshi's invasion failed, it had a profound effect on Korea. For three centuries, Korea refused to let in any foreigners, earning the country the nickname "the Hermit Kingdom."

After Hideoyoshi's rule, Japan also remained closed until the visit in 1853 of Commodore Matthew C. Perry of the U.S. Navy, who wished to open trade with Japan. Treaties were signed. A group of daimios, or feudal lords, overthrew the ailing shogun and installed an emperor as the head of state. In 1867, Emperor Mutsuhito moved the capital of Japan to Edo, which was renamed Tokyo, and issued the Charter Oath, which urged Japanese people to seek knowledge from the outside world and make Japan strong enough to compete in world affairs. Japan modernized itself, quickly adopting the military, governmental, and industrial techniques of Western nations. Within a generation, Japan emerged from self-imposed isolation and entered the world community, a move that would cost its neighbor, Korea, dearly.

In 1876, Japanese envoys, cunning in the ways of the modern world after a decade of exposure to European methods, persuaded Korean leaders to sign a treaty opening Korean ports to Japanese merchants. Eight years later, the United States signed a commercial treaty with Korea, and other countries followed. Japanese influence in Korea grew. Japan's expansionist designs in Korea and elsewhere led to war with China in 1894 and 1895, and with Russia in 1905. Japanese victories in these wars brought to Japan Imperialist domination over Formosa, the Liaotung Peninsula on the southern most tip of Manchuria, the southern half of Sakhalin Island and, in effect, Chinese and Russian permission to dominate Korea. Japan was on its way to world power.

In 1910, through court trickery and brute force, Japan formally annexed Korea, making the Korean emperor a prince. For 35 years, Japan ruled Korea as a virtual slave colony, in a way that recalls the domination of Ireland by England in the 17th century. Korean language was forbidden to be taught in the schools. Korean children were to be given Japanese names. No Korean was allowed to have a position of authority in the municipal or national government bureaucracy, and the court system was controlled by Japanese. Koreans were excluded from international trade and shipping and transportation enterprises. Korean mountains and hills were stripped of their forests; the lumber was shipped to Japan for processing into building materials for use in Japan.

This was the Korea in which Koon Wu Lee grew up in Soon Chun. By the time Koon Wu was a teenager, Japan had an iron grip on the peninsula's economy. Koon Wu, as a younger son of his father's third wife, had no chance for a large inheritance. He possessed a 50-acre farm, but had little interest in farm work. He leased his inherited farm land and began a modest enterprise selling salt. Koon Wu would walk through the forests along the ancient trading trails over the mountains to the beach on the southern shore, where he purchased salt processed by local tradesmen. Packing the salt on his back, he returned to Soon Chun to sell it to farmers.

On one of these trips through the mountains in 1903, Koon Wu, then age 21, overcame a threat to his life that secured his reputation as a village leader. Koon Wu encountered one of the feared tigers that inhabited the Korean countryside before Japanese guns all but eliminated them from the peninsula. These ominous tigers, still the subject of great myths and legends, often were blamed for the disappearance of children and other loved ones who wandered away from the valley villages and never returned. Koon Wu had only a knife to protect himself on his overland journeys. How he defended himself is not known. Yet when he came back to Soon Chun with the tiger's body across his shoulders, his reputation as a fighter and leader was established.

At age 25, Koon Wu's family arranged his marriage to 20-year-old Wul Kuk Lee, a distant relative. Their first child, a son, was born five years later. When the boy took fever and died, the spirit left Koon Wu. Depressed and broken-hearted, Koon Wu lost interest in living. He became a gambler and a wanderer. His salt business failed. He had to sell his property to pay debts. The Lee family was destitute. By that time, the end of 1925, the Japanese grip on Korea was complete. Opportunity was limited in the extreme for Koreans in a society and economy dominated by Japanese.

The Japanese had expanded their influence into Manchuria to the north, obtaining control of the South Manchuria Railway. Japan, now a member of the League of Nations and part of the international community, had signed treaties with the United States, England and France that limited the size of its army and navy. Yet Japan was beginning to build what it called the "Greater East Asia Co-Prosperity Sphere," and it ignored the military limitation treaties. In this world, any native Korean who wanted a decent job or education had to immigrate to Japan.

Now recovered from his son's death, Koon Wu left Korea in 1925 and went to Kyoto, Japan, where he found work as a laborer on construction jobs and in restaurants. He saved his earnings and in January 1928 Wul Kuk and their two children joined him in Kyoto. They made their home in an old house in a poor section of town where other Korean immigrants lived. There was prejudice. Koreans banded together as best they could to protect themselves and their neighborhood. Koon Wu, whose reputation had been established by the tiger incident, was among the neighborhood leaders. This position of leadership would protect the entire Korean community in Kyoto later that year, when an earthquake struck Tokyo and Yokohama. Though not as severe as the 1923 earthquake in Tokyo, in which 143,000 lives were lost in collapsed buildings, fires, rioting and panic, the earthquake in 1928 set off a rash of looting and rioting. For some reason, the townspeople of Tokyo and other cities blamed the Koreans living in their midst for the earthquake and fires that followed. To be sure, some Koreans had looted some buildings in Tokyo, but those living in the other cities were innocent of any wrongdoing. Their crime was in belonging to a vulnerable minority in a country in panic. The Korean sections in Tokyo, Kobe and Osaka were overrun by Japanese mobs who indiscriminately burned Korean residences and murdered men, women and children. The carnage claimed thousands of lives.

Word of the mass rioting came to Kyoto, where Koreans feared for their lives. There was a neighborhood meeting. Koon Wu was selected to go to the Japanese police station to talk with the authorities. Somehow the message was conveyed to the Japanese police that there was to be no rioting by the Japanese mobs in the Korean section of Kyoto, and there would be no rioting by the Korean immigrants. The details of this agreement are unknown. Did Koon Wu threaten retaliation by Koreans against Japanese if there were riots? Were the Japanese sympathetic to the Koreans in their midst? How was word spread in Kyoto to leave the Koreans alone? The questions have no answers, but the result of the meeting was that there was no massacre in Kyoto and no riots against Koreans, as there had been in the other cities.

Koon Woo Lee (left) and Wul Kuk Lee at home in Soon Chun, South Korea, 1959

Later that year, a daughter, Yung Ja, was born to Koon Wu and Wul Kuk. Yung Ja and her older brother and sister, and later a younger brother, attended Japanese schools. Koon Wu found work in a silk-dyeing factory and the Lee family lived a modest life in Kyoto. Koon Wu was anxious to have his children educated. Koon Wu had never attended school and lamented his inability to read and write. "I have eyes but cannot see," he would say. Yung Ja and her brothers and sister did well in school, but prejudice prevented them from becoming friends with Japanese classmates.

By that time, Japanese attempts to dominate Asia were in full swing. By 1931, the Japanese army had overrun Manchuria, seized the province and set up a puppet regime, renaming the province Manchukuo. Japanese occupation forces imported thousands of Koreans and other Asian workers to Manchuria to build and work in iron and coal mines, steel mills, railways, refineries, power stations, and on roads and in other public works. Slowly, the Japanese government fell into hands of militarists whose visions of conquest and empire embodied in the concept of the "Greater East Asia Co-Prosperity Sphere" contaminated all of Japanese society, infecting what was printed, taught and worshipped in Japan. Japan extended its influence over other parts of Northern China and by July 1937 the conflict spread to open war between the two countries. By early August, Japanese troops occupied Tietsen and Peking, and by December, Nanking. In the months ahead, Japanese troops won control of northern and central China and by the end of 1938 had taken over Canton. By 1936 and 1937, the Japanese military government had signed treaties with Nazi Germany and Fascist Italy. In 1940, a year after Nazi Germany signed a mutual non-aggression treaty with Communist Russia, Japan followed suit. Despite its treaty with Russia, Japan kept a large army along the Manchurian border.

Throughout this period, Japanese schools and factories were fed a constant stream of propaganda about the war, victories of Japanese troops and the destiny of the Japanese people. The United States soon became a target of this propaganda. The war in Europe, which began in 1939, had led to the fall of France in 1940. With the defeat of the French, their colonial rule in Indochina collapsed, and Japan invaded and occupied what is now Vietnam. The U.S. reacted by reducing the sale of oil and scrap iron to Japan. With Japan strengthening ties to Germany and Italy, tension between the U.S. and Japan was high. By 1941, Japan was on a full-time war basis. On October 17, when General Hideko Tojo became prime minister after the fall of the civil government, Japanese militarists took full control.

On December 7, the Japanese bombed Pearl Harbor, the U.S. base in Hawaii. Within days, the U.S. was at war with Japan in the Pacific and Germany and its allies in Europe. The war would become the most massive conflict in history. In the Pacific, after months of defeat, the United States overcame Japanese forces at Midway and in the Coral Sea, and in island-to-island battles. Slowly and at great cost, Japan's empire was eroding. On July 18, 1944, General Tojo's war cabinet fell. Within months two other

Yung Ja Lee, Seoul

cabinets would fall.

Koon Wu, sensing the inevitable, worried that his family might be caught in the American bombing raids that would inevitably come. Yung Ja's sister, Chung Kok, had moved earlier to Manchuria with her husband, who worked on a Korean road construction crew. Chung Kok's husband worked with a Korean, **CHUNG KUK KIM,** who was born March 4, 1923, in the town of Keumneung, in the Kyungsang-Pukdo province in southern Korea, a son of **KIM SUNG HWA** and **SOON-YI,** whose family originated from the town of Kimhae, north of Pusan. Chung Kuk was working as a supervisor for a Japanese road building company in Manchuria. In Korean, Chung Kuk's first name meant Man from China Country, or China Man.

Koon Wu Lee knew Chung Kuk Kim's family, who had ties to Soon Chun City, and was able through friends to arrange the marriage of his daughter, Yung Ja, to Chung Kuk. In early 1944, Koon Wu and his family left Kyoto permanently, sailing back to Korea to escape the inevitable war in Japan. Their pretense for leaving was the marriage of 17-year-old Yung Ja to Chung Kuk Kim, the 21-year old road-builder working in China. The ceremony was held in Soon Chun March 10, 1944.

While Koon Wu, Wul Kuk and others in the Lee family settled again in Soon Chun City, newlyweds Yung Ja and Chung Kuk Kim went to Manchuria, where the young husband resumed his post in the road building company. Early in 1945, the battle over the Japanese islands began. American airplanes bombed industrial targets and coastal cities. American submarines cut off all shipping to Japan. Japanese troops throughout the Pacific and in China were increasingly isolated. By July, under the pressure of the Chinese nationalist and communist armies, Japanese rule in Manchuria eroded to the point where civil order was breaking down. Word spread that Chinese were slaughtering stranded Japanese troops and murdering Japanese and Korean civilians.

On July 27, 1945, Yung Ja gave birth to a daughter, Sun Soon. With the baby but five days old, Yung Ja and her husband fled for their lives ahead of the conquering Chinese armies. Chung Kuk had obtained passage August 2 on one of the last trains out of Manchuria leading to Korea. Japanese and Korean refugees mobbed the train. Passengers were crammed into the rail cars like cattle. Leaving behind all their belongings, money and property, Yung Ja, her husband and their week-old daughter traveled for a week on the train south. There was no food, no water, no privies. Often the train would be put onto a siding to make way for troop transports, and the refugees were forced to sleep on the concrete platforms of train stations.

Finally on August 9, the Kim family arrived in Soon Chun safely. The world around them had turned into chaos. Three days before, an American warplane had dropped a nuclear bomb on Hiroshima. On August 8, the Soviet Union declared war on Japan and sent an invading army into Manchuria. On August 9, the U.S. dropped a second nuclear bomb, this time on Nagasaki. Japanese nationals in Korea were in panic. The Russian army would eventually invade Korea and travel south to the 38th degree of latitude. Refugees fled south.

On September 2, the United States accepted the unconditional surrender of Japan. Under an agreement worked out earlier with the Soviet Union, the Soviets took control of Korea north of the 38th parallel, and the U.S. took responsibility for administering Korea to the south. Within months, the 38th parallel, the boundary between Soviet and American administrative districts, solidified, dividing Korea into two countries.

Korea was in ruin. For more than 35 years the Japanese had run everything: all public services, the utilities, the economy, the government. Now, abruptly the Japanese were gone and the war-weary Americans assigned to the Korean occupation were ill-equipped to deal with the people and their blighted country.

The months and immediate years ahead were hard. At first, Yung Ja and Chung Kuk lived with Yung Ja's sister, but the dwelling was too crowded and food scarce. In time, Yung Ja and her husband settled in a home abandoned by a Japanese businessman. Yung Ja gave birth to a second daughter, Sun Oak, December 18, 1947. Yung Ja became ill. There was little food. Often the only food Yung Ja and her children had was the powdered milk distributed free by the United States. As a liquid, the milk made them sick, so they fashioned the milk powder into a meal to bake into a nutritious biscuit. It saved their lives.

Beggars roamed the countryside. Neighbors were starving to death. The wandering living collapsed into the dead at roadsides in the night hours. Bodies of strangers were found in the morning light. Chung Kuk tried to find work with the railroad. He failed. For a time, he traveled to Seoul, purchased rubber shoes and brought them to Soon Chun to sell, using the meager profits to support his family. Finally, he applied for work as a member of the Soon Chun Police Department. He passed the test and in time was promoted to sergeant, then lieutenant.

Korea was in political ferment. Communist revolutionaries were among the tens of thousands of refugees who came south of the 38th parallel. They preached a political theology that had some attraction to some of the starving in the south. But among the communists' techniques were terror and sabotage. The government of the south, the Republic of Korea, created after the United Nations election May 10, 1948, ordered local police to jail anyone known to be a communist or who was sympathetic to the communists. Many arrested were hardened revolutionaries. Others, however, were simply caught up in events they knew little about.

Lt. Kim did his duty and arrested those neighbors known to sympathize with the North. Unlike other police, however, he allowed some of the prisoners' families to visit their jailed husbands and sons to deliver food, clothing and other personal effects. He was fair.

Following the creation of the Republic of Korea in 1948 there was turmoil. An ROK Army Division, while en route in the Korean Strait to Chey Judo Island, rebelled. Communists in the ranks mutinied. By the time the vessel reached Chey Judo all the officers had been murdered. The rebel division turned the vessel around and sailed back to Yosu, 30 miles south of Soon Chun, where the rebel army seized the town and rounded up local officials. After a cursory review before a rebel tribunal, judges, police officers, teachers and Yosu town elders were executed. The countryside around Yosu was in anarchy. Shortly, units of the rebel division arrived in Soon Chun, where town officials and elders again were and brought before a rebel tribunal for judgment. Lt. Kim was in communist custody.

When he was brought before the tribunal, one of its members recognized him as the police officer who had let his family visit him in jail. The local communist operative argued that Lt. Kim was one of the "good" residents and that his life should be spared. The other communist agreed on condition that Lt. Kim sit on the panel to judge his neighbors. Stunned and fearing for his life and that of his wife and daughters, Lt. Kim sat on the panel. Later he said he believed he had no choice and took small comfort in his efforts, sometimes successful, to argue that some of the townspeople brought before the panel be spared.

Days later, Soon Chun and Yosu were liberated by ROK forces. The communist rebels fled to the mountains. Lt. Kim, fearing that the ROK would execute him for sitting on the panel, joined the flight to the mountains, leaving behind his wife and daughters. For a year, Chung Kuk Kim stayed in the hills. Yung Ja and her daughters stayed with her parents.

While her husband was in hiding, Yung Ja worked as a sewing teacher, and at night sewed for her neighbors to earn a living. Chung Kuk was able to get word back to his family that he was miserable, that he hated the communists and that he wanted to come home. He didn't dare. Finally, the ROK government dropped leaflets throughout the countryside stating that a general amnesty was in effect, and all suspect communists should turn themselves in. Chung Kuk risked it. He returned home to his wife and children, but the reunion was to be short-lived.

After months of skirmishes along the 38th parallel, the North Korean army invaded South Korea in June 1950 to unify the country by force. Despite the desperate attempts by ROK and American forces to delay the Communists' advance, by August troops under the United Nations command were forced to withdraw to a 75-mile area around the southern port city of Pusan.

War had returned to Soon Chun. Chung Kuk was anxious. He was convinced the invading North Korean army would execute him because he had returned to South Korean authority. On the other hand, South Korean authorities might execute him as a suspected spy. He chose to flee. One evening, Chung Kuk slipped away from his family, found a fishing boat on the southern coast and fled to Japan. He was lost to his family forever.

During the siege of Soon Chun, Lt. Kim was in flight; control of the countryside was in doubt. Sun Oak came down with diphtheria, and Wul Kuk urged her daughter to get the baby to a doctor. Sun Oak had a high fever, and her throat was swollen. Wul Kuk feared if she didn't get medical attention soon, Sun Oak would die. Yung Ja took her daughter and walked two hours to the other side of Soon Chun, which was now deserted. She found a North Korean Army medical tent. A doctor with the enemy army saw this mother and baby as civilian innocents and gave Sun Oak a shot of antibiotics. Yung Ja walked back to the family hiding place; in a short time the fever broke and Sun Oak recovered.

Soon American soldiers and their South Korean allies were battling North Korean regulars around Soon Chun. Artillery shells exploded in the town and machine-gun fire filled the air. Yung Ja and her two daughters and parents huddled in the Lee home as the fighting took place nearby. Suddenly an artillery shell exploded in the front yard. Shrapnel ripped through Koon Wu's thigh. With her husband writhing in pain, Wul Kuk tore off his white muslin shirt and wrapped the flesh back into place, securing the wound. Neighbors ran through the village streets. Several were cut down by machine-gun fire, others were killed when shells exploded near them. Rumors abounded. It was time to flee. Wul Kuk urged her daughter to leave. Yung Ja, carrying young Sun Oak piggyback and Sun Soon by the hand, ran across a rice field at the back of the house toward the South Korean army line, where she had heard they would be safe.

Suddenly, the rice field was ablaze with explosions and machine-gun fire. The bullets whistled through the air around Yung Ja and her children as they continued to run. Neighbors a few feet away were hit, falling dead in the shallow water of the rice field. A man who was running ahead turned around and waved for Yung Ja to go back. He was hit and fell dead. Yung Ja continued running, stepping over his body as she continued, ignoring everything except her belief that she was running toward safety. In a few minutes, she was behind South Korean lines, away from the firefight and protected. Later she learned her parents also had escaped without further injury.

In time Soon Chun again was securely in the hands of United Nations' forces. After the landing of American forces at Inchon on September 15, 1950, the North Korean armies in the south were routed. But the war was long and life continued to be hard. There was little food, little work and little fuel for warmth in the winter. Refugees were everywhere. Neighbors froze to death. Yung Ja earned enough from her sewing to get by. In 1952, a friend told her that jobs were available at the American Post Exchange in Pusan. Yung Ja left her two daughters in the care of her parents and walked to Pusan, where she was hired as a cashier at the PX. She earned a decent wage and sent her earnings home. When the American headquarters moved to Seoul, Yung Ja followed.

On July 27, 1953, a truce was signed. The North Korean attempt to rule the South by force was defeated. The cost was high. There were more than two million North Korean and Chinese casualties. Some 54,200 Americans were killed, another 103,000 were wounded. The South Koreans suffered 1.3 million casualties, with some 415,000 killed, 428,000 wounded, and 469,000 missing. Among the missing was Chung Kuk Kim.

In Seoul, Yung Ja learned more about America and enrolled in night school to learn to read and write English. In these classes, she became aware of American ideas and way of life. In time she realized that her future was there. With her language improved, she got a job as a purchasing agent for the American Army Officers Service Club in Seoul. She prospered and was able to support her children, parents and several brothers and sisters and their families in Soon Chun. Once a month she traveled by train to visit her family. During the summer her daughters lived with her in Seoul.

When an American soldier proposed marriage in 1960, Yung Ja accepted. She agreed to leave Korea on the condition that she could send for her daughters as soon as she saved the money for their transportation. Yung Ja was married in Soon Chun and flew to the United States to start a new life. Her older daughter, Sun Soon, died. When word reached Yung Ja of Sun Soon's death, she immediately arranged for Sun Oak's transportation to the United States.

In March 1962, Sun Oak, aged 14, went by train to Seoul with a slip of paper giving—in English—her name, flight departure time and destination pinned to her overcoat. Thirty hours later, with little sleep, Sun Oak arrived at Logan Airport in Boston to meet her mother and start her life as an American.

Yung Ja and Sun Oak lived first in Salem, then Lynn, and finally South Lynnfield. Yung Ja worked as an accountant with the New England Telephone Company in Salem, and then Boston. The marriage to the American soldier failed. Yung Ja and Sun Oak took catechism and citizenship classes together. Sun Oak soon learned English. They were baptized in Salem and sworn in as citizens November 22, 1963. Yung Ja later married Edward Murdock. They lived in Tewksbury, Massachusetts, and Derry, New Hampshire, until their retirement to Florida, where Yung Ja is an authorized bridge master and Edward a golf pro. Yung Ja's surviving daughter is Sun Oak [#119].

Epilogue

[119] SUN OAK KIM, born about December 18, 1947, in Soon Chun City, South Korea, a daughter of Yung Ja Lee and Chung Kuk Kim [#118], and your writer, **ROBERT THOMAS COLLINS, JR.**, born December 26, 1947, in Hartford, a son of Robert Thomas and Mary Close (Savage) Collins [#117], met at a Halloween Party October 31, 1969, in Boston.

I was completing my senior year at Boston University's College of Liberal Arts, and Sun Oak was attending flight attendants' school with Northeast Airlines. Sun Oak had graduated from Ste. Cretienne's Academy in Salem, Massachusetts, and had attended Stonehill College, a Jesuit school in nearby North Easton, before joining the airline. I had graduated from Western Reserve Academy in Hudson, Ohio, and was majoring in government at Boston University.

The fact that we should both be at a party was happenstance. We met and that was that. We danced, we talked, we laughed. She explained and I listened, and I explained and she listened. We dated. We went to restaurants, to movies. We drove to the beach. We walked in the winter's snow. We were cautious, tentative. In time, we knew our lives would never be the same; better, and better still.

Between the time we met and April 24, 1971, when we were married, I was graduated from Boston University, began to work as a reporter with the New Haven *Register*, and moved to Guilford, on the Connecticut shoreline. Sun Oak had left Northeast Airlines and joined Trans World Airlines as a flight attendant, moved to New York City and was working as an international hostess on TWA flights to Europe. Sun Oak and I were married at St. George's Catholic Church on the Green in Guilford. We lived in Guilford for more than two years, saving our money. In the fall of 1973, we used our savings on housing and my tuition at Columbia University's Graduate School of Journalism.

Our daughter, **LEE KATHLEEN**, was born January 26, 1974, at St. Luke's Women's Hospital in Manhattan. I was graduated that spring and became a reporter with the New York *Daily News*. On December 3, 1975, our son, **MICAH THOMAS**, was born, also at St. Luke's Women's Hospital in Manhattan. I began writing on my own, had a book published and, growing out of daily newspapering, went into the oil business and later publishing. Over the years, we have called home dwellings in New York, Illinois, Connecticut and Virginia. The will to write continues, this chronicle being the result of perhaps some brehon's itch that I continue to scratch. May it help our children and theirs to come to know that the *American Union* still sails in waters charted by dreams.

Appendix & References

Events and Cultural Observations
by Ancestor

Winthrop's Fleet & Puritan Migration
To Massachusetts 1630-40

Edmund Lockwood [#1]	Watertown
Nicholas Knapp	
and Elinor Lockwood [#2]	Watertown
William Potter [#25]	Watertown
John/Sarah Reynolds [#27]	Watertown
Jeffrey/Mary Ferris [#13]	Watertown
John White/Mary Levit [#3]	Cambridge (Newtowne)
Rebecca Olmsted	
and Thomas Newell [#5]	Cambridge
Timothy/Elizabeth Stanley [#11]	Cambridge
Edward Shepard	
and Violet Stanley [#18]	Cambridge
Elizabeth Shepard	
and Thwait Srickland [#31]	Cambridge, Dedham
John Waterbury [#69]	Boston
Paul Peck/Martha Hale [#14]	Boston
Mary/William Cornwell Jr. [#7]	Roxbury
John Lothrop [#10]	Barnstable
Simon Hoyt/Deborah Stower [#51]	Salem
Robert/Joan Hibbard [#23]	Salem
John Coit/Mary Jenners [#6]	Salem, Glouchester
Thomas/Alice Kimberly [#16]	Dorchester
Samuel Boreman/Mary Betts [#30]	Ipswich

English Civil War
Banbury—Mary/John Betts [#4]
East Anglia—William Mead [#9]
Samuel Boreman/Mary Betts [#30]

Wethersfield Settlers 1635
Nathaniel Foote/Elizabeth Deming [#8]
William Mead [#9]
Elizabeth Foote/Josiah Churchill [#17]
John/Sarah Reynolds [#27]

Rev. Hooker's Company
John White/Mary Levit [#3]

Hartford Settlers 1636
John White/Mary Levit [#3]
Mary/John Betts [#4]
Rebecca Olmsted/Thomas Newell [#5]
Elizabeth/Timothy Stanley [#11]
Paul Peck/Martha Hale [#14]
Elizabeth/Richard Watts [#19]
George Hubbard/Elizabeth Watts [#20]
Hannah/John Cowle [#33]
Nicholas Disbrough [#80]

Hartford Schism
John White/Mary Levit [#3]

First Schoolteacher in Hartford
Mary Betts [#4] 1636-47

New Haven Settlers 1638-1639
William/Elizabeth Peck [#15]
Thomas/Alice Kimberly [#16]
John Moss [#21]
Peter Brown [#24]
Robert Johnson [#26]
John/Ann Wakefield [#42]

First Colonial Woman to Give Birth in New Haven
Alice Kimberly [#16] 1639

Windsor Settlers 1639
Edward/Margaret Griswold [#32]
Simon Hoyt/Deborah Stower [#51]

Guilford Settlers 1639
John/Hannah Parmalee [#29]

Greenwich Settlers 1640
Jeffrey Ferris [#13]
Robert Husted & Angell Husted [#89]

Farmington Settlers 1640
Rebecca Olmsted/Thomas Newell [#5]
Hannah/John Cowle [#33]
Rebecca Newell/Joseph Woodford [#38)
Abigail Stanley/Samuel Cowles [#49)

Stamford Settlers 1641
William Mead [#9]
Jeffrey Ferris [#13]
John Mead/Hannah Potter [#40]
John/Sarah Reynolds [#27]

Middletown Settlers 1650
Mary/William Cornwell Jr. [#7]
Elizabeth Watts/George Hubbard Jr. [#20]
John Savage/Elizabeth Dubbin [#35]
Thomas Ranney/Mary Hubbard [#37]
Nathaniel/Elizabeth White [#44]
Baltazar De Wolff/Alice Peck [#39]

Lyme Settlers (East Saybrook & New London) 1651
Samuel Lathrop/Elizabeth Scudder [#12]
Baltazar De Wolff & Alice Peck [#39]
    and son, Edward [#59]
Matthew & Mary Beckwith [#28]
    and son, Matthew Jr. [#62]
Martha Coit/Hugh Mould [#56]

Norwich Setters 1660
Francis Griswold [#58]

Killingworth (Clinton) Settlers 1663
Edward/Margaret Griswold [#32]

Proprietors of Greenwich 1664
Jeffrey Ferris [#13]
Joseph Ferris/Ruth Knapp [#45]
John Mead/Hannah Potter [#40]
Joshua Knapp/Hannah Close [#48]

Wallingford Settlers 1667
John Moss [#21]

Puritan Crimes & Courts
False Advertising—Nicholas Knapp/Elinor Lockwood [#2]

Witch Trial—Baltazar De Wolff/Alice Peck [#39]
Witch Trial—Mary/John Cole [#53]
Dress Code—Hannah Wakefield/Edward Grannis [#57]

Pequot War
William Mead [#9]

King Philip's War—Bloody Creek Massacre
Hannah/John Cowle [#33]
Elizabeth/Nathaniel White [#44]
Hannah Wakefield/Edward Grannis [#57]
Edward De Wolff/Rebeckah Masuer [#59]

Teutonic Knights/Hanse League/Livonia
Baltazar De Wolff/Alice Peck [#39]

Halfway Covenent
Jeremiah Peck/Johanna Kitchell [#41]

Union of Connecticut and New Haven Colonies
John Johnson Jr./Hannah Parmalee [#36]

Pirate Capture
Francis Griswold [#58]

Tavern Keepers

Baltazar De Wolff [#39]	Lyme
Ebenezer Mead [#68]	Mead's Tavern—Greenwich
Joshua Knapp III [#101]	Knapp's Tavern—Greenwich

Revolutionary War: Siege of Boston,
Battles of New York, Greenwich Terror Raids
Elisha Savage/Thankful Johnson [#96]
Seth Savage/Esther Prudence DeWolf [#99]
Benjamin Mead III/Mary Reynolds [#100]
Joshua Knapp III/Eunice Peck [#101]

New England Missionaries to Hawaii
Obadiah Mead/Ruth Hibbard [#106]

Pennsylvania: Yankee-Pennamite War,
Settlement of Meadville, War of 1812
Obadiah Mead/Ruth Hibbard [#106]

Civil War—Antietam, Fredericksburg, Andersonville
Henry Elliot Savage/Theodosia Caroline Knapp [#109]

Deputies to Connnecticut General Court (Legislature)

John Moss [#21]	New Haven, Wallingford
Samuel Boreman [#30]	Hartford
Edward Griswold [#32]	Killingworth (Clinton)
John Cowle [#33]	Farmington
John Mead [#40]	Greenwich
Robert Royce [#43]	New London
Nathaniel White [#44]	Middletown
Samuel Royce [#50]	Wallingford
Francis Griswold [#58]	Norwich
William Savage [#65]	Middletown
Ebenezer Mead[#68]	Greenwich

Militia & Military Service

Sgt. William Cornwell Jr. [#7]	Hartford
Sgt. John Savage [#35]	Middletown
Sgt. Nicholas Disbrough [#80]	Hartford
Edward De Wolff [#59]	Lyme
	King Philip's War 1675
Captain Nathaniel White [#44]	Middletown
Sgt. John Cornwell [#52]	Middletown
Captain John Savage Jr [#64]	Middletown
William Savage [#65]	Middletown
Ensign Samuel Royce [#50]	Wallingford
Sgt. Nathaniel Hibbard [#82]	Windham
	1712 British Expedition against French in Canada
Ebenezer Mead Jr. [#85]	Greenwich
Benjamin Mead Jr. [#86]	Greenwich
Lt. Benjamin Moss [#88]	Cheshire
Captain Thomas Johnson [#95]	Middletown
Lt. Elisha Savage [#96]	Middletown
	French & Indian War 1754
	Revolutionary War 1777
Cpl. Seth Savage [#99]	Middletown
	Revolutionary War 1776,1777-80
Benjamin Mead III [#100]	Greenwich Committee of Safety 1776-80
Sgt. Henry Elliot Savage [#109]	East Berlin, Civil War 1862-65

Deacons & Church Leaders

Elder John White [#3]	Elder, Second Congregational Church, Hartford

Paul Peck [#14]	Deacon, First Congregation Church, Hartford
Rev. John Lothrop [#10]	Barnstable
Edward Griswold [#32]	Deacon of Killingworth
John Savage [#35]	Founder, First Congregational Church, Middletown
Rev. Jeremiah Peck [#41]	Preacher, Saybrook, Newark, Greenwich & Waterbury
William Savage Jr [#84]	Deacon, First Congregational Church, Middletown
Nathaniel Boardman [#98]	Deacon, Westfield Congregational Church
Henry Elliot Savage [#109]	Deacon, Berlin Congregational Church
Willis Isaac Savage [#115]	Deacon, Berlin Congregational Church

Ireland: History, Culture, Kilrush & the Collapse of '63
Sinon Collins/Mary Langan [#110]

Irish Famine
Thomas O'Connell/Catherine Sheedy [#112]

Scots-Irish History & Culture
James Reynolds Howard/Mary Ann MaGee [#114]

Canal Building
Thomas O'Connell/Catherine Sheedy [#112]

**Railroads—Erie RR; Atlantic & Great Western RR;
and New York, New Haven & Hartford RR**
James Collins/Mary Kearney [#113]
James Michael Collins/Alice O'Connell [#116]

World War I
James Michael Collins/Alice O'Connell [#116]

Auto Industry—New Departure, General Motors
Robert Thomas Collins/Mary Savage Collins [#117]

Korea: History, Occupation by Japan, War
Yung Ja Lee/Chung Kuk Kim [#118]

Bibliography

Iused the normal sources for a genealogy: personal knowledge or family tradition, public records, and printed sources,
including academic publications, privately published narratives as
well as family typescripts and letters. I was also guided by many
in the community of genealogists on the internet. To the best of
my ability, I balanced the evidence. To my knowledge, everything
described in this chronicle is accurate and cross-checked with
sources that are commonly believed to be reliable. If a link
appears true but cannot be established, I say so. In addition to
general reference works and the letters, diaries, Bible records,
notes and newspaper clippings saved by family members over
the years, the following books and manuscripts were used to
complete this chronicle:

Adams, Charles Collard; *Middletown Upper Houses* (1908 The
　　Grafton Press, Genealogical Publishers, N.Y.)

Barbour, Lucius Barnes; *Families of Early Hartford, Connecticut*
　　(1977 Genealogical Publishing Company, Baltimore)

Barder, John Warner; *Connecticut Historical Collections*, contain-
　　ing...interesting facts, traditions, biographical sketches, anec-
　　dotes &c. relating to the History and Antiquities of Every
　　Town in Connecticut (1836 John W. Barber, New Haven &
　　A. Willard, Hartford; printed by B.L. Hamlen, New Haven)

Beckwith, Frederick H.; *Additional Beckwith Notes* (1956 Private Publication, Stamford, Ct.) to supplement: *Marvin Beckwith & His Wife Abigail Clark—Their Colonial Ancestors & Descendants* (1899 Private Publication, Elkhorn Wi.)

Blakeslee, Lt. Col. B.F.; *History of the Sixteenth Regiment C.V. Infantry* (1889 Record of Service of Connecticut Men in the Army & Navy of the U.S. During the War of the Rebellion compiled by Authority of the General Assembly, under the direction of Adjutants-General Smith, Camp, Barbour, White; Published The Case, Lockwood & Brainard Company, Hartford, Ct.); 2 (*1889 Record of Service of Connecticut Men in the War of the Revolution etc.*, compiled under same conditions above...); 3 (*Service Records of CT Men and Women in the Armed Forces of the U.S. During World War 1917-1920*, Office of the Adjutant General, State Armory, Hartford, Ct.; printed United Printing Services, New Haven)

Boulton, Richard N., and Clemow, Bice; *The West Hartford Story* (1954 West Hartford Publishing Co., West Hartford)

Brandegee, Emily S.; *Historical Papers—Berlin, Connecticut* (1928 Historical Papers Published by Emma Hart Willard Chapter NSDAR Berlin)

Camp, David N.; *History of New Britain* (1889 William B. Thomson & Company, New Britain)

Chapman, F.W.; *The Coit Family* (1874 Case, Lockwood & Brainard Co., Hartford)

Clark, William H.; *Farms & Farmers: The Story of American Agriculture* (1945 L.C. Page & Company)

Close, Lewis Giles; *Ancestors & Descendants* (1955 Author Typescript, DAR Library, Washington D.C.)

Coogan, Tim Pat; *The Man Who Made Ireland—The Life & Death of Michael Collins* (1992 Robert Rinehard Publishers, Niwot, Col.)

Crossley, Alan; editor *Banbury—A History* (1972 Abstract of The Victoria History of the County of Oxfordshire, Vol. X, University of London Institute of Historical Research)

Davis, Charles Henry Stanley; *History of Wallingford, Connecticut, from 1670—1870* (1870 C. H. S. Davis, Meriden)

Dexter, Franklin Bowditch; *Historical Catalogue of the Members of the First Church of Christ in New Haven, Connecticut 1639–1914* (1914 F. B. Dexter, New Haven)

Durant, Will and Ariel; *The Lessons of History* (1968 Simon & Schuster, N.Y.)

Feltus, Louise Celestia Mead; *Our Two Centuries in North Greenwich, Connecticut 1728-1924* (1948 Ray H. Prout Company, Troy, N.Y.)

Fischer, David Hackett; *Albion's Seed—Four British Folkways in America* (1989 Oxford University Press, N.Y.)

Grant, Ellsworth Strong, and Grant, Marion Hepburn; *The City of Hartford 1784-1984—An Illustrated History* (1986 The Connecticut Historical Society, Hartford)

Goldthwaite, Charlotte; *Boardman Genealogy 1525-1895* (1895 Case, Lockwood & Brainard Co., Hartford)

Hibbard, Augustine George; *A Genealogy of the Hibbard Family* (1901 Case, Lockwood & Brainard Co., Hartford)

Historical Section, Army War College; *Order of Battle of the United States Land Forces in the World War—American Expeditionary Forces* (1931 U.S. War Office, U.S. Government Printing Office, Washington, D.C.)

Hungerford, Edward; *Men of Erie—A Story of Human Effort* (1946 Random House, Inc., N.Y.)

Judd, Bernice, et al; *Missionary Album, Sesquicentennial Edition, 1820–1970* (1969 Hawaiian Mission Children's Society, Honolulu, Hi.)

Kellogg, Allyn S.; *Memorials of Elder John White, One of the First Settlers of Hartford, Conn. and of his Descendants* (1860 Hartford)

Knapp, Alfred Averill; *Nicholas Knapp Genealogy* (1953 A.A. Knapp, Winter Park, Fla.)

Locklin, D.P.; *Economics of Transportation* (1954 Richard D. Irwin, Inc., Homewood, Ill.)

McElroy, John; *This Was Andersonville*, edited with an introduction by Roy Meredith (1957 McDowell, Obolensky, Inc., N.Y.)

McGuane, James T.; *Kilrush From Olden Times* (1985 Clodoiri Lurgan, Inverin, Co. Galway, Ireland)

Maginnis, Carol S.; *Dolphs & DeWolfs* (1992, published by Richard Dolph of Kentucky, by Gateway Press)

Marvel, William; *Andersonville, The Last Depot* (1994 University of North Carolina Press, Chapel Hill, N.C.)

Mead, Spencer P.; *History and Genealogy of the Mead Family of Fairfield County, CT, Eastern New York, Western Vermont and Western Pennsylvania from A.D. 1180 to 1900* (1901 The Knickerbocker Press, N.Y.)

Meade, David M.; *A History of Greenwich* (1857 Baker & Godwin)

Melvoin, Richard I.; *New England Outpost—War & Society in Colonial Deerfield* (1989 W. W. Norton & Company, N.Y.)

Moody, John; *The Railroad Builders—A Chronicle of the Welding of the States* (1974 Yale University Press, New Haven)

North, Catherine M.; *History of Berlin, Connecticut* (1916 Tuttle, Morehouse & Taylor Co., New Haven)

Parker, Edwin Pond; *History of the Second Church of Hartford* (1892 Belknap & Warfield, Hartford)

Peck, Darius; *General Account of William Peck, one of the Founders of New Haven, Connecticut* (1877 Bryan & Goeltz, Steam Book Printers)

Perry, Charles E.; *Founders and Leaders of Connecticut 1633-1783* (1934 D.C. Heath and Co., Boston, et al)

Perry, Calbraith B.; *Charles D'Wolf of Guadaloupe, His Ancestors and Descendants*—A genealogy of "Rhode Island D'Wolfs", the descendants of of Simon DeWolf, with their common descent from Balthasar De Wolf, of Lyme, Ct. 1668 (1902 T.A. Wright, N.Y.)

Potter, Charles Edward; *Genealogies of the Potter Families and Their Descendants in America* (1888 Alfred Mudge & Son., Boston)

Potts, William; *A History of Banbury* (1958 The Banbury Guardian Ltd., Banbury, Oxford) revised by Edward T. Clark (1978 Gulliver Press, White Lion Walk, Banbury, printed by The Abbey Press, Abingdon, Oxfordshire)

Prebble, John; *The Lion In The North—One Thousand Years of Scotland's History* (1971 Penguin Books, London)

Rigler, Mrs. Robert G. and Greenwood, Mrs. Glenn R.; *Hawaii: Descendants of New England Protestant Missionaries to the Sandwich Islands 1820-1900* (1984 Records of Hawaiian Mission Children's Society Library, Privately Published by authors, Hawaii state and Aloha Chapter regents, respectively, NSDAR)

Reynolds, John E.; *In French Creek Valley* (1938 Crawford County Historical Society, Meadville, Pa.)

Rasmussen, Wayne D.; *Readings in the History of American Agriculture* (1960 University of Illinois Press, Urbana, Ill.)

Roth, David M.; *Connecticut—A Bicentennial History* (1979 American Association for State & Local History, Nashville, TN, published by W.W. Norton & Company, Inc., N.Y.)

Salisbury, Edward Elbridge; *Griswold Family of Connecticut* (1884)

Savage, Albert Wilcox, Jr.; *The New England Ancestry of Albert Wilcox Savage, Jr.—Volume I, Savage—Wilcox Lines* (1988 Gateway Press, Inc., Baltimore, Md.)

Savage, James Francis; *Family of John Savage of Middletown, 1652* (1894 David Clapp & Son Printers, Boston)

Savage, John; *Picturesque Ireland*, a literary and artistic delineation of the natural scenery, remarkable places, historical antiquities, public buildings, ancient abbeys, towers, castles, and other romantic and attractive features of Ireland (mid-19th Century Thomas Kelly, N.Y. & Philip Ryan, Worcester, Mass.)

Sawers, Mary Beeler; *Lineage of Jeremiah Mead, Jr. of Greenwich Connecticut—Soldier of the American Revolution* (1958 Typescript Middletown, Connecticut in NSDAR Library Washington D.C.)

Sears, Stephen W.; *Landscape Turned Red* (1983 Warner Books, Inc., N.Y.)

Shepard, James; *The New Haven and Wallingford (CT) Johnsons* (1902 David Clapp & Son, Boston)

Trumbull, Chaplain H. Clay; *A Good Record—A Sermon Preached before Petersbury, VA on Sabbath, September 25, 1864 to the Tenth Connecticut Regiment, at the Close of Three Years Service* (1864 Press of Case, Lockwood & Company, Hartford)

Trumbull, J. Hammond; *Memorial History of Hartford County Connecticut* (1886 Connecticut Historical Society, Hartford) an annotated version reprinted in 1986 by the Society of the Descendants of the Founders of Hartford; Trumbull's work being an annotated version of the volume *Original Proprietors* written by Mary K. Talcott.

Turner, Gregg M. & Jacobus, Melancthon W.; *Connecticut Railroads—An Illustrated History* (1986 Connecticut Historical Society, Hartford)

Williamson, James R.; *A Connecticut Settlement in Northeastern Pennsylvania: The Yankee-Pennamite Wars* (1980 Connecticut Historical Society Bulletin Vol. 45, No. 1), and *Westmoreland County, Connecticut: Bloodiest Battle of the Revolution* (1981 Connecticut Historical Society Bulletin Vol. 46, No. 3)

Wood, Joseph S.; *The New England Village* (1997 Johns Hopkins University Press, Baltimore)